Memes, Communities and Continuous Change

Chinese Internet Vernacular Explained

HUA NIE

Bridge 21 Publications | Alhambra, CA

Memes, Communities and Continuous Change: Chinese Internet Vernacular Explained

by Hua Nie

Published by Bridge21 Publications, LLC

Distributed by Casemate Group
Casemate Academic: USA and North America
Oxbow Books: UK, Europe and the Rest of the World

Published in the United States of America

ISBN 978-1-62643-018-1 Paperback
ISBN 978-1-62643-077-8 ePub | ebook pdf | Kindle

Contents

Preface

This book literally retrieves the trajectory of my PhD studies. Motivated by a most prominent consequence of the internet's integration with our everyday life – the novel ways we speak and communicate, my PhD journey was started with the focus on the various words and phrases once virally spread on social media, or linguistic memes, which are constituents of a supposedly unique language phenomenon, constantly discussed by ordinary people and scholars alike yet somewhat under-theorized. The conspicuous novelty then prompted me, following up on many previous studies, to proceed from the aspect of meaning change, and the memes were initially studied in terms of their unique yet largely ineffable functions that couldn't be achieved otherwise. It took me quite some time to approach the various linguistic aspects that could have been 'changed', which led me to all sorts of meaning indeterminacy and complexity. Only when I broke loose from such fixation, did I begin to rethink the objects of my study as precipitates from interaction and processes of meaning-making, at which point I was able to understand the actual flows where the changes were happening and follow them for in-depth investigation. With such an expanded scope, I started to locate the memes that involved remarkable meaning change, followed the digital flows that were generated in the process, and identified relevant questions based on my following practice, all of which informed me of the necessary theoretical focuses and analytical instruments for inquiring into the different dimensions of the holistic phenomenon.

This move can be considered the theoretical shift from the linguistic to the sociolinguistic system, which reveals a larger picture of the language practice on Chinese social media: what we experience as noticeable meaning change throughout a meme's diffusion may reflect and invoke, under different circumstances, interpersonal communicative effects, collective identities and community affiliations, as well as larger sociocultural values and ideologies. More importantly, such an ethnographic and exploratory journey, i.e. fully grounded research by following the actual flows within and beyond the digital medium, offers great theoretical and methodological purchase for arriving at meaningful accounts of using memes in interaction, and promises to be a useful approach for understanding social media communication in general. Therefore, I cordially invite the readers of this book to experience such a journey of following various memes with me, whereby the complex and dynamic sociolinguistic phenomenon which I call 'Chinese Internet Vernacular' will be elucidated to you as a deepening exploration.

This journey, which was full of angst, confusion and excitement, could never have been completed without the help and support of many people. I would first like to thank Professor Jan Blommaert, Professor Ad Backus, and Dr. Piia Varis, my dearest supervisors and mentors, who have always been there for me, and provided unconditional and unfailing care, guidance and encouragement. They have helped me develop, consolidate and refine each and every milestone along this intellectual journey. I'm also greatly indebted to Professor Sjaak Kroon, who never stops inspiring me with his trenchant wisdom, and Professor Odile Heynders, whose kindness and advice lend great strength to me. Besides, I'm deeply grateful to all the colleagues and peers of the Department of Culture Studies – Caixia, Kunming, Mingyi, Ying, Di, Gosia, Sandra, Suzanne, Janieke, Paul, Tom, and many others, with whom I've had so many fun and productive moments that greatly enriched my PhD life here in the Netherlands. Especially, a heartfelt 'thank you' should be extended to Karin, Carine and Erna, who have helped me with all kinds of daily matters as well as the making of this book! Moreover, I want to thank three people that are of special significance to me, Cong Peng, Yuxia Li, and Professor Gao Yihong, who have played vital roles, in one way or another, during this important stage of my life. Lastly, this book is dedicated to my parents, who never stop believing in me.

In Tilburg
April, 2018

Chapter 1
Introduction

Vignette 1

In the summer of 2015, before my fieldwork in China, I took a small break and visited my parents back home. When I told my father that I was going to interview some participants concerning their experiences with new internet buzzwords, he immediately asked, "So do you know what the latest buzzword is?" Just when I was about to give him some serious thoughts, he proclaimed, "It's duang!", with a hearty grin. "Seriously? How did you know it?", I was indeed surprised by my father's remarks, not because that I was exactly researching 'duang' but because my father – a middle-aged, old-fashioned bookworm – should hardly have known it!

"Why, it's all over my Wechat friends' updates!" he said.

Vignette 2

One day, my friend Yuxia came to me with great excitement, "Can you imagine what my mother just texted to me?" Her mother, a Chinese-Bengali woman in her seventies with only limited literacy in written Chinese, had just recently learned to type in Chinese on cellphones. "She said 'muyou'in her message!"

"Really? Does your mother know the word 'muyou'[1] already? How did she pick it up?" I was also utterly amazed, and begged Yuxia to ask her mother for more details of use. It later turned out that when she entered the initials of meiyou (a common shortcut method in Chinese typing), the typing application on her cellphone suggested muyou as the first candidate, and so she simply opted for it. She explained, "I gathered it must be some kind of novel way of saying it."

Moments like these are happening all the time in China. One of the ways most people experience the fast pace of the changing society, minuscule yet significant, is the language they're supposed to use every day. It is universally acknowledged that linguistic change is in a dialectical relationship with societal change, where the two processes reflect and reinforce each other in different (either explicit or implicit) ways. For the Chinese people (and possibly people all over the globe), it has never been so explicit and certain that they're actually and collectively experiencing it, and consciously talking about it. This grand, shared experience is without question afforded by the advancement of internet technologies, and most important of all, the popularization of social media. As the majority of the country's population (53.2%, per CNNIC 2017) become internet users, which is still fast growing, fewer and fewer people are exempted from this language change: many of whom become active creators in this movement, and more are helplessly involved in, usually through the weird and magic thing called 'trend', like my father, or by means of the everyday communication technology that they can no longer live without, just like Yuxia's mother. People don't need to think much before realizing that such language is trendy or novel – something to be opted for whenever they have chance to.

This book is all about this 'omnipresent' experience, which makes up a profound part of ordinary Chinese people's everyday language practice. For the past decade or so, this complex of language varieties has always been qualified with simplistic, and more often than not negative, features[2], which consequently

1. Muyou is a partial homophone, and also an internet neologism, of the word meiyou, meaning 'no/not'.

2. Such simplistic features include vulgar, deficient, sarcastic, etc., which will be discussed in detail in

reduces them to the marginal phenomenon, often labeled as slangs or jargons. However, I intend to treat it as a full-fledged and intrinsic dimension of the Chinese language today, in China and beyond, which constitutes the most important sociolinguistic environment for virtually all walks of Chinese life, as my two opening vignettes suggest. That's because ordinary users not only carry out hyper productive and dynamic activities with them, but also invest great efforts and attention in the continuous development of these varieties. This complex of language varieties, given their online character, is obviously literate/visual and multimodal, challenging some previous understandings and analytical frameworks focused on 'language as primarily a spoken phenomenon' which leads to the dominant view of interaction only as a spoken phenomenon as well. When we consider the online varieties of language, those views are no longer valid; we therefore need more complex forms of analysis. This book, I propose such a form of analysis, one that approaches these new online language varieties from multiple dimensions: I will examine their linguistic features, strictly speaking, but also the socio-cultural dimensions and the ways in which these varieties assist people in what Garfinkel (1967: vii) calls the "the organized activities of everyday life." It is the combination of these dimensions that gives us access to what Garfinkel saw as social reality: the inextricable and undeniable presence of these varieties in the sociolinguistic universe of Chinese people.

This choice for multi-dimensional analysis means that I will take the reader on a journey in which we start from language as a linguistic system to language as a sociolinguistic system, something Hymes (1974; 1996) always considered to be the essence of the study of language in society. The varieties that I will examine bear challenging linguistic features, forcing us to reflect on themes such as language change. Simultaneously, they cannot be comprehensively understood without understanding their social and cultural embeddedness, and their interactional deployment. Even more, defining the very object of my study requires a combination of all these dimensions, and in what follows I will attempt to elucidate this. Here is how I outline the object of my study.

Chapter 6.

1.1 Chinese internet vernacular

Since the initial popularization of the internet in China in mid-1990s (Hu et al. 2014), the language varieties associated with this new technology have stood out with its distinctive characteristics. Unlike the long-lasting contentions as to their denomination in the English-language context, in Chinese, a rather uncontroversial and explicit term is assigned to such varieties – Wangluo Yuyan (lit. 'internet language'). While many Chinese language scholars have subscribed to this term (e.g. 'CIL' in Gao 2012), I propose to call them 'Chinese Internet Vernacular' instead (henceforth CIV throughout the book), chiefly for the following three reasons (which will be discussed in Chapter 6): 1) they always assume an apparent opposition to the national standard language (in the internet context, the standard written form); 2) their 'authentic' users are by default a sub-stratum (or sub-strata) of the entire internet population (usership) in China; and 3) they constantly evade codification – i.e., there isn't a 'standard' variety and it may have various 'accents', 'dialects', 'registers', etc.

Over more than two decades, this complex of vernacular has notably developed and changed, in accordance with the growth of the very population that count as 'internet users' – or more often 'netizens' in the Chinese context. Most apparently, the major users have expanded from the tight cohort of technological elites and academics to the majority of the entire population, and so has CIV – no longer confined to a small group of people or certain domains of use. For ordinary Chinese people, especially urban dwellers (72.6% of all netizens are urban residents, per CNNIC 2017), CIV becomes an inseparable part of their everyday language resources.

This noticeable development accelerated around 2008, when that extremely eventful year spawned numerous novel words and expressions that got spread online and quickly picked up by keen netizens. These spreadable items can also be regarded as textual memes that transmit from user to user in a rapidly contagious way. Consequently, Baidu.com, the largest search engine and web services provider in China, began to publish its annual ranking on the popular phrases and buzzwords of the previous year (Figure 1.1). From then on, people started to have a clearer grasp of the notion 'CIV' as a collection of textual memes, and CIV has arguably become an integral part of the contemporary Chinese social life ever since.

The significance of CIV's increase and expansion in 2008 can also be corroborated with the attention from both the authorities and the academia, with new governmental reports on CIV released (e.g. LSC Team 2009) and the number of academic papers nearly doubled from the previous year (Hu et al. 2014).

十大流行语

排名	关键词	统计数据
1	很黄很暴力	
2	做人不要太cnn	
3	打酱油	
4	叉腰肌	
5	很傻很天真	
6	猪坚强	
7	三个俯卧撑	
8	很好很强大	
9	山寨	
10	正龙拍虎	

*以2008年百度网页搜索日志为依据

Translation:

Top 10 popular phrases[3]

RankKeywords

1 very erotic very violent
2 don't act like cnn
3 buying soy sauce
4 hands-on-waist muscle
5 very stupid very naïve
6 Pig Strong
7 three push-ups
8 very good very powerful
9 shanzhai (counterfeit goods)
10 Zhenglong photographs the tiger

* Based on the Baidu search logs in 2008

Figure 1.1 Baidu Annual Ranking 2008[4]

As an ordinary internet user with a long experience with CIV, I began to consciously collect the words and phrases that had become popular even before I started this project. Such textual memes impress me more than merely spreadable items online: they have naturally incorporated the various essential characteristics of the Internet Age and seeped seamlessly into our social life. In what follows, I will elaborate on each of these popular evaluations, based on both folk accounts and academic studies, which in fact serve as the starting points of my series of inquiries.

Interactive

What distinguishes the popular words and phrases of CIV from

3. See the glossary in Appendix I for the CIV words and phrases except for 'very erotic very violent', 'very stupid very naïve' and 'very good very powerful'.

4. Accessed from https://www.baidu.com/2008/#a04 on September 12, 2014.

previous (pre-digital) trends and buzzes may be the extensive participation of ordinary users, which is mostly afforded by the Web 2.0 technology that enables user-generated content and facilitates interaction. What's more, with the advent and rapid popularization of social media sites and applications in China, just around the year 2008 (CNNIC 2009), internet users got increasingly connected, and user-interactivity further encouraged. All of this has important bearings on the words and phrases netizens create and spread.

The outburst of CIV in 2008 has everything to do with the enhanced social net-working functionality and user-interactivity. As retrieved by Wu (2009), most of the buzzwords in 2008 originated from sensational news that became hot topics and targets of heated discussion on some major news platforms with interactive functions, such as NetEase News. NetEase News is most noted, and self-celebrated, for its gailou (lit. 'floor-building') feature as a crucial comment function, where a user's comment (or, a new floor) builds onto (instead of 'following below' as do most forum discussion threads) the previous user's comment (an old floor)[5]. The more comments are built on one another, in other words the more floors are stacked, the more grandiose the 'comments tower' is. In this way, the news was interactively and collectively processed by the users – evaluated, criticized, ridiculed, parodied, transformed, etc., the outcome of which is usually a catchy phrase that has great potential to spread much wider. No wonder that by the end of 2008, NetEase proudly staged a tribute to the impressive comments and all its users, titled 'No real news without comments: redefining the power of netizens'[6], to celebrate the users' authenticity, collective wisdom, great abilities of wittiness and humor, as well as their anxious concern with social issues.

Although NetEase was later overshadowed by other social media sites with more functions and attractions, its legacies in terms of interactive creativity, such as the emphasis on the uniformity and coherence between the wordplays, which the users call baochi duixing ('keeping the shape of the team') – a normative order with persistent regimenting powers – have also

5. See Appendix II for an example as illustration of such a comments-tower.

6. Retrieved from http://news.163.com/special/0001sp/2008ending.html on April 10, 2015.

been maintained as crucial mechanisms for users' interaction and CIV innovations in newer environments. One of such sites that dwindle NetEase is Baidu Tieba (lit. 'Baidu Posts Bar'), the largest online communication platform in China, which boasts millions of interest-based forums for users to interact in. This enhanced interactivity of Baidu Tieba has contributed to the majority of CIV innovations in the years that followed (Yu 2014), among which the most well-known phrase is perhaps diaosi ('loser') (Yang et al. 2015; Du 2016).

The launch of Sina Weibo (lit. 'microblog') in late 2009, an online news and social networking site, which is usually compared as Twitter's counterpart in China, further facilitated and enriched the interactions among internet users. By January 2017, Sina Weibo's active users amounted to 297 million[7], making it the largest public social media platform in China (cf. Twitter: 317 million users). As many researchers have argued (e.g. Gao et al. 2012), Weibo incorporates the undirected broadcasting function as in Twitter as well as the directed narrowcasting function (between mutually subscribed users) as in Facebook plus personalized profile, wall and timeline, making it especially suitable for transmitting information while forming weak-tie relationships among users. Moreover, its 'comment' function (which still keeps evolving currently), apart from 'mention' and 'forward', is the most crucial feature that constitutes the major part of the users' participation and interaction (Wang et al. 2016), arguably maintaining the 'glorious traditions' as demonstrated in NetEase comments. In recent years, Sina Weibo has become the most important source of CIV innovations and the major channel for their propagation.

There are, of course, other social media applications, which also play an important role in the practice and transmission of CIV, such as Tencent QQ (an instant-messaging client), Tencent Qzone (a blog-hosting and social-networking website), Wechat (an instant-messaging and social-networking mobile application), etc. As these applications are mostly private and only accessible between mutually approved users, who probably know each other in person, interactivity is supposed to be higher than on the public ones, such

7. Data provided by Statista.com, retrieved from https://goo.gl/Rq8SsI on February 14, 2017.

as Weibo. However, without the 'open space', users with these private applications behave more like 'end-consumers' of CIV, and less as participatory innovators than do Weibo users.

It is this interactive environment and form of practice that gives rise to CIV innovations. Any CIV words or phrases, from birth, are therefore imbued with this emblematic 'social media character' in the first place.

Changing

The prevalence of CIV in Chinese social life also attracts increasing observations and investigations – as even a quick glance at the mushrooming academic literature on the subject matter testifies. For many who are interested in the linguistic aspects, the most apparent characteristic of CIV is change (among the myriad studies, e.g. Xin 2010, also see Chapter 3 for a fuller review), a recurrent theme in the Chinese scholarship, as well as an impression shared by common netizens. However, change, or 'changingness' in a more processual sense, resides in multiple dimensions of CIV.

First off, the discourse journey of each CIV word or phrase has been more or less transformational, as each item has observably undergone changes of various sorts throughout its spread. This dynamic process can also be, perhaps for the first time in history, witnessed by users through online participation, recorded possibly in every detail, archived into databases, and retrieved at any later point. Interestingly, an innovated CIV neologisms usually manages to keep its 'linguistic' form[8] throughout its usually short-lived journey, largely thanks to the emerging normative codes of conduct on those most interactive platforms (such as NetEase), which may help maintain their high degree of formal uniformity, congruence, and recognizability. But on the other hand, the crowdsourced nature, egalitarian spirit, as well as the 'word-of-mouth' form of spread – features that are usually generalized as 'viral diffusion' (see Shifman 2014) – create entirely new conditions and contexts for the language use, inevitably affects the fundamental ways of how language is (collectively) mediated, and ultimately changes the way meaning is transmitted and constructed. In other words,

8. For instance, all of the 10 phrases in Figure 1.1 didn't develop otherwise in form till they mostly fell out of use online.

any CIV innovation is bound for fundamental variation and transformation in meaning immediately when it gets virally transmitted. Consequently, 'meaning change' has been generally maintained as the essential nature and automatic mechanism of CIV (Xin 2010) within the Chinese scholarship, which itself urges further exploration and theorization.

Besides, with the penetration of the internet into all walks of life and all sectors of society, CIV – formerly generalized as a somewhat single genre or sociolect – has also dramatically changed, or rather diversified. Correspondingly, the very style associated with CIV has undergone some noticeable transformation and ramification over the past two decades. As summarized by researchers (e.g. Chen 2016) and cordially recollected by 'senior' users[9], in the early days CIV was the exclusive vocabulary and style of the geeks on online bulletin boards[10] or the rebellious teenagers in chatrooms, with all its technical jargon and cheesy wordplays, such as the address term meimei (lit. 'pretty eyebrow') to refer to a girl and those mawkish lines and verses written in the so-called 'Martian' orthography (Dong et al. 2012), which we can't help laughing about or even cringing at in retrospect. Soon, when the enhanced participatory culture began to thrive and when internet journalism got to mediate netizens' vision of social issues, CIV became both the means and outcome of their participation in the fast-paced multitudes of social events and changes, reified as the inundating expressions imbued with overwhelmed sentiments – e.g., netizens use '70 km/h' to express anger and sarcasm, and they 'buy soy sauce' to be either concerned or cynical. Social media quickly altered, or expanded, the landscape of ordinary users' everyday online practice, by affording and fostering all kinds of niche formations, where consequently a variety of specialized, interest-based, and/or group-specific styles have emerged and hence largely enriched CIV. Moreover, with the accumulation of the above apparent changes, most people – language scholars, educators, policy-makers, and ordinary citizens alike – have generally regarded them as

9. For example, there would be posts and articles reminiscing Chinese netizens' previous online behaviors and practices every once in a while.

10. Chinese users usually call it BBS (Bulletin Board System), the most popular form of internet communication, especially in colleges and universities, before the domination of social media.

doubtlessly consequential, but differed as to how profoundly thesechangesimpact the Chinese language system[11]. Some, especially linguistic purists[12], regard CIV as items of external contamination that have intruded the standard language, propelled by whimsical fads, and can be disinfected if proper efforts are made. Whereas some others (e.g. Gao 2012), from the canonical perspective on language change basically as a mass and permanent phenomenon, envision that certain discrete linguistic features of CIV – the more common linguistic variety with the younger generations – would eventually lead to a tangible language change if practiced for long enough. However, as myriad observations and investigations have found, the ensemble of CIV may have realizations at all kinds of linguistic planes, practiced by netizens in all kinds of online/offline situations, talked about in terms of stylistic characteristics, and most essentially performed for social and communicative effects. The real changes can only be well examined with a broadened perspective – therefore, CIV as sociolinguistic change (Coupland 2016).

Affective

As a most noticeable corollary of the user-generated and enhanced interactive functions of social media, the current online space is saturated with heightened emotions, in terms of the abundance of overt emotional discourses as well as the general practice of 'personal' disclosure[13]. It's happening to social media all over the globe, therefore leaving media observers worldwide rather concerned over the 'predominance of emotion over reason'. Such observation is not incongruent with the 'demotic turn' (Turner 2010), postulated as the current cultural trend in the cyber space. When elevated emotional language and the voluntary revealing

11. As 'Chinese language' is a highly ambiguous notion, usually oriented to the centralist ideology, which may in reality subsume a wide range of regional varieties, functional registers, orthographic traditions, etc., I'm using 'system' as a lump category simply to avoid such sticky differentiations and specifications for now.

12. This is usually the point of view underlying most official internet policies and regulations, as well as some academic studies, where the use of CIV is considered at best nonstandard, and at worst harmful (see Chapter 6 for a fuller discussion).

13. The form and behavior of 'personal' disclosure, i.e. relating to the personal account and speaking from a personal perspective, doesn't necessarily mean the exposure of real personal content and privacy.

of personal specifics become the major mode of narratives online, would our common form of social interaction also be reconfigured? Such possibilities have in fact led media scholars (e.g. Papacharissi 2015) to discuss the gravitational force of affect in the formation and transformation of online publics at all levels – from the individual participation in online conversations to the crowd mobilization of a major social movement.

The Chinese social media is no exception, only except that such affective forces are viewed with more caution and potential hostility, especially from the top down, which has everything to do with the ways common netizens participate in discussions on various social issues online. All kinds of social incidents, trivial or consequential, are happening at an unprecedented pace and tremendous scale, when the country continues to transform under modernization and globalization. All kinds of personal reactions and voices, previously unable to be revealed, go rampant and infectious easily and rapidly on social media, a much less monitored and checked sphere than the traditional public one. During the past decade or so, there have been countless individual-level, 'trivial' and regional incidents, which, after spreading online and gaining wide emotional empathy, became influential nationwide issues. When individual emotions become public sentiments, they have proved to be especially effective and influential in demanding the open and fair treatment of many social problems, but many also fear that such formidable powers, if not supervised and curbed properly, may lead to mob violence and social instability.

In consequence, we have observed a continued mutual enhancement between the affective participation of netizens and CIV as the primary instrument to partici-pate affectively. Firstly, there's the affective need to keep up with the times and stay socially connected. A great number of CIV phrases are related to influential social incidents and issues, usually by metonymizing the very events and crystalizing the predominant emotions involved. For instance, the CIV phrase "My father is Li Gang!"[14] in 2010, meaning

14. In 2010, when a young man named Li Qiming was apprehended for hitting two college girls on a university campus while drunk driving, he was unruly and shouted "My father is Li Gang!", who turned out to be the deputy police chief of the very district. The remark soon became widely circulated and parodied on the Chinese internet, as a way to condemn the privileged transgressor who tried to pull

to shirk responsibility and exhibit one's privilege/impunity, was only supposed to be used sarcastically to express moral judgement (towards unfair social privilege and malpractice), a recognizable emotion and pragmatic usage that has been established during its wide spread and interactions among internet users.

Besides, there's also the individual desire to be intimate which demands and invites affectively driven interaction. The disinhibitory powers of the internet (with all its technological affordances) have allowed users to say whatever they wish, although various internet regulations and restrictions have been levied, making such practice a little bit tricky[15]. Because interactive online activities, say, forum discussions between users, mutual appreciation between Wechat group members, or collective idol-worshipping among fellow fans, usually generate rather passionate and intimate moments, internet users have to make the best of CIV in order to compensate for the absence of other expressive modalities (sounds, facial expressions, gestures, etc.). That's partly why there's a great deal of CIV phrases that have been developed to cater to such interpersonal and/or practice-based purposes, so that their heightened emotions and expressivity could be actualized when typed out and transmitted to other fellow users.

To recapitulate such mutual enhancement process, on the one hand, phrases with strong ambient sentiments and personal involvement abound in CIV, which has in fact been the focus of most Chinese academic discussion (e.g. Bian & Gao 2012), where the growing repository of CIV reflects important episodes in the changing social and cultural ecology. On the other hand, the affectively keyed communication also actively reshapes and transforms the discursive configurations of any CIV item along the way, at least from two perspectives. Firstly, a sort of 'affective clusters' have emerged, i.e. a paradigmatic relationship between certain CIV in terms of their comparable emotional effects and discursive

strings to escape punishment. The following stretch of conversion may illustrate how this phrase is used sarcastically:

A: Ugh, the line is so damn long! I wish I could just jump to be the first in line!

B: Forget it! Your father is not Li Gang!

15. For example, many forums have banned the use of certain swear words, and most social media applications have report functions where users can report offensive comments and messages.

functions. That is what we have observed new CIV phrases do, which usually converge with and eventually replace their older emotional and expressive equivalents. Secondly, this intense interactional practice has imbued CIV with great tendency to externalize the personal, connect with the interpersonal, and ultimately relate to the social. Interestingly, the multiple functions may be condensed in the use of any single CIV expression, an important momentum for the transformation of CIV's expressive and affective function in use. "I'm just using this phrase to willy-nilly express my intense feelings" is a remark we hear often as to the use of a certain CIV phrase. But what are the profound mechanisms that help embed the various subjective and intersubjective aspects in CIV, and what makes CIV so successful as an expressive instrument in our digitalized life? Questions like these haven't been well answered, and should thus be investigated with the rich empirical data of CIV.

Collective

The penetration of internet technologies, par excellence social media, has profoundly influenced our everyday sociality, bringing about new forms of collective existence and interactions. And these new forms are crucial, or even determinant, for the development, especially the spread, of CIV on the internet. In what follows, I will expand on the aspects where CIV (and information in general) is closely related to and dependent on these new forms.

It is a generally held assumption that any word or phrase, in order to be included in CIV, needs to have achieved a considerable degree of popularity, or in a trendy expression, gone viral. However, virality, though repeatedly talked about nowadays, is an under-theorized notion, especially in the humanities. Most accounts of viral spread, especially in the marketing literature (e.g. Mills 2012), examine its form as 'word-of-mouth' contagion, and highlight its large volume of dissemination among a huge population within a short period of time. Many endeavors have been made to understand how virality is achieved, and therefore effectively modeled and predicted (e.g. Weng et al. 2013; Goel et al. 2016), with the major focus fixated on how such a large volume of information diffusion (usually regardless of its actual content) is transmitted temporally and structurally, where voluminous empirical studies have focused on important influential users, active followership (which such literature usually calls 'community' in an information-structural sense), and the ability of a viral item to diffuse beyond (and between) such 'communities', as well as other algorithmic designs of the service interface or certain psychological-communicative mechanisms (such as the 'echo-chamber effect')[16] that facilitate the diffusion in certain directions. The important implications of such modelling of the viral diffusion inevitably accentuate the phenomenal 'social' structure (and therefore user-relations) that arises immediately out of any viral event, most of which are ephemeral and trivial compared with our offline social relations and 'real' communities.

In fact, such 'light' forms of collective practice and social relation that abound on social media have attracted attention of scholars in the humanities (e.g. Varis & Blommaert 2015; Blommaert 2018), and would bear significantly on the content and process of all our viral events. Here Malinowski's pioneering work on 'phatic communion' (1923) – which is the type of communication that doesn't convey any information but is mainly used to reaffirm social bonds, implying that a certain practice of speaking may be a crucial component of the interactional structure for a community – may help us understand the new forms with some insights. Varis and Blommaert (2015) propose that the phatic communication, or the sociolinguistic phenomenon of virality, achieves an important social and interpersonal effect – a feeling of conviviality, a sense of commonness among the users. Memes on social media, as "loose, temporal and elastic collectives" (2015: 31), on the one hand enable and sustain the users' participation and involvement of communication at "a socialstructuring level" (2015: 43), and on the other take shape as meaningful and sharable signs for the users. In other words, social media virality has become, for us ordinary users, our important form of everyday conviviality that hinges on, sustains and impacts any viral event or innovated meme, in this case, CIV words and phrases.

While this form of convivial viral participation arguably constitutes

16. An echo chamber is a metaphorical description of a situation in which information, ideas, or beliefs are amplified or reinforced by communication and repetition inside a defined system.

a major practice type on social media, it is also a gradable phenomenon, in terms of 1) the magnitude and vitality of the very collectivity, and 2) the users' engagement and identification with it. As well observed (e.g. Weng et al. 2013), the total diffusion of a viral event is always composed of multiple information cascades that traverse clusters of users of more condensed information flows. Such clusters may represent many different sorts of social collectivities, the most cohesive and enduring of which may be a cohort of users who mutually follow each other and are permanent friends offline, while the most loosely connected may be users who are totally unknown to each other and only happen to have stumbled upon the same internet content through a random click of sharing or liking. Between the two extremes, there're some other types of collectivity, which are well characterizable by means of an identifiable form and/or content of practice, relatively stable and endurable, yet considerably accessible and open-ended to ordinary social media users. They're usually called 'sub-communities' or 'niche communities' (Zhang 2016) on social media, as they're categorized in terms of stable loci of practice, similar interests, shared objectives, common discourse, etc., of the participants, which usually stand out and 'parallel' with sub-communities of other sorts.

Particularly visible and identifiable sub-communities on Chinese social media include the ACGN (animation, comics, games, and novels) scene, K-pop (Korean pop music) fandom, Chinese Gufeng (ancient culture) circle, military enthusiasts, and countless more, which themselves can be sub-divided into multiple communities of more specified themes and practices. It seems that the general social media public space is scattered with multiple 'subaltern publics', in the same logic as these sub-cultural groups occupy their niches within the cultural sphere of the entire society. However, the inter-connected nature of social media complicates such a neat geography, as the so-called 'sub-cultures' are less and less distinguishable from each other, or from the 'mainstream culture', especially on social media. These interest-based communities formed and operated largely through the internet are increasingly significant for the contemporary social life, especially among the young people – they're not only important sources of routine practices and everyday gratification, but are also indispensable components of identity. No wonder all social media platforms in China have generally adopted and benefited from the strategy to facilitate and strengthen such niche communities and practices (commonly called 'vertical' communities in Chinese terms, see CNNIC 2017).

Considering the fact that nearly all CIV words and phrases originate from various sub-communities, the dynamics and processes of their 'crossings' between different sub-communities of any types and viral diffusions over the larger space are crucial if we want to understand the real changes the phrases have undergone.

Summary

The above four features that have usually been attributed to CIV, each involving abundant folk perceptions and scholarly studies, help me see the language varieties from different angles and choose analytical frameworks to approach them as a researchable object. Over the years, CIV has shifted from a specific genre to a notably changed way of language practice on the internet, and the changing process is believed to continue especially for the younger generations.

Therefore, the first theoretical lens for examining CIV is how change happens at the linguistic level, where canonical studies of language change naturally come to the fore. However, as the above introduction shows, CIV is imbued with fundamental characteristics of social media, involving various novel and emerging communicative forms and norms that the classic theoretical models[17] do not focus on. Moreover, the internet has largely changed the diachronic/synchronic dichotomy, with online archives, the search function, automated suggestions and all kinds of algorithms that are offered for, or even imposed on, internet users, where the diachronic process seems rather 'accelerated' and 'cut short', while the synchronic process gets extremely diversified and easily messed up with the

17. For example, in Variational Sociolinguistics (see Sankoff 2006 for an overview), the 'apparent-time' and 'age-grading' models have been proposed to examine the regular progression and synchronic distribution of a certain linguistic variable across age groups within a specific population and help identify aspects of language change in progress.

polycentric and chaotic interplays of differentially ordered and multimodal resources. This urges us to shift from such traditional approaches, look beyond the linguistic system, and delve into the dynamic process where change happens.

In order to understand CIV as a changing and developing phenomenon, my study becomes largely exploratory in nature and remixed in methods, taking into consideration the various aspects and processes, as well as the multitude of semiotic resources, that have proved to play important roles in the social phenomenon distinctly perceived as 'language change' in contemporary times (Gao 2012). In this light, the focus of my exploration will be anchored in the actual behaviors and events that induce and produce change, extended to the various interactional dimensions involved in the processes, and then to the socio-cultural conditions that host and sustain the changes. Such a practice-based focus is certainly an increase in ethnographic and humanistic commitment, which will also require a shift of theoretical frameworks and methodology – i.e. by treating CIV as 1) 'sociolinguistic resources' (Blommaert & Backus 2013) that individual users actively appropriate for themselves, managed and regimented within the metapragmatic constructs that are available to them; and 2) an open-ended and unfinished system where the users continuously invest in and contribute to the changes through interaction.

Therefore, social media users (both as individuals and collectives) become the 'real subjects' of the investigation, while CIV, the object of this study, will be investigated as the precipitates, processes, and orders of indexicality from the users' interaction on social media. While my exploration of CIV shifts from the linguistic to the sociolinguistic systems, the research questions of each specific case study arise from the actual empirical data I've collected over a span of four years (2014-2017), where new questions were meaningfully prompted by previous observations and investigations as my research process deepened and expanded. With all the attempts, I hope to arrive at a comprehensive framework that does justice to the dynamics and complexities of CIV as a sociolinguistic phenomenon.

1.2 Structure of the book

Chapter 2 outlines the general methodology for the entire study that corresponds with the central theoretical rationales, i.e., exploratory, ethnographic and comprehensive, and explains in detail the rationale for specific methods in order to collect suitable data and address the changing, open-ended and interactional nature of CIV. Then I go on to explain how each constituent case study becomes necessary for the entire study, and how they relate to each other as the exploratory process unfolds. This is followed by a detailed summary of the entire procedure for all the case studies, including the respective rationales, methods used, participants (if any), collected datasets, etc.

Chapter 3 is my initial attempt to understand CIV as a changing language phenomenon, by starting from previous studies on CIV in relation to what we deem as 'standard Chinese', which looks directly into the linguistic form and features. Three CIV phrases of the same 'very X very XX' construction were selected out of the top 10 popular phrases in 2008 (Figure 1.1) and mixed methods were adopted for collecting and analyzing their occurrences, uses and functions for over 4 years (2009-2014) on Chinese social media. Intrigued by the phrases' noticeable changes in meaning and function on social media, I examine their pragmatic functions and communicative effects, and try to interpret such new features in terms of various linguistic dimensions. However, my findings posed challenges to both the ways that I collected the data and how I analyzed them, by highlighting the open-endedness of the phrases' development on social media and their considerable meaning indeterminacy when taken out of the interactional contexts. On the other hand, the limitations in the findings also redirected my focus onto more pertinent aspects and processes of meaning change in social media virality, and helped me revise research questions and data collection based on actual interactions, so as to better approach the changing process of a CIV item.

Informed by the first case study, I began to closely monitor the Chinese social media in hopes of capturing the dynamic and complex processes involved in a CIV neologism's virality. In early 2015, I was able to fully follow the viral spread of an innovated word duang, and practically recorded its entire viral spread on certain Chinese social media applications, which makes up the case study in Chapter 4. In order to see what more dimensions of analysis could enrich my understanding of CIV, this chapter then comprises of two main parts, inquiring into two important processes of duang's spread in virality. Firstly, a corpus-assisted study was conducted on the overall spread of duang in terms of its meaning/function change, trying to establish a connection between meaning variation and its viral diffusion. Moreover, focusing on meaning transformation, I also carried out a painstaking digital ethnography on the collected qualitative data throughout the viral diffusion, which uncovered the dynamic and complex processes of meaning construction and negotiation among the individual users, highlighting various ways they engaged with the meaning-making activities in virality. More importantly, both the statistical results and ethnographic analysis underscored the significance of collective practice and affinity when a certain meaning/function variant came about and got spread further, which then again prompted me further to concentrate my investigatory process in this important dimension in the spread of a CIV neologism – the more cohesive form of collective practice on social media.

With such more focused objective and research questions, I took special care in my daily monitoring work, during which I succeeded in locating the viral spread of an innovated phrase chesaika within the fandom of a Thai TV show on various Chinese social media platforms. Chapter 5 is then dedicated to the participatory digital ethnography on chesaika and is able to reveal sophisticated and complex language practices, rich and diversified meaning transformation, as well as dynamic interactions among the users underlying their seemingly uniform behaviors with the fandom-specific neologism. In light of the theory of 'enregisterment' (Agha 2007), I analyze how the viral word within a putative community is reinterpreted and reassigned with new meanings and effects that have important bearings on the members' individual and collective identities, and how such meaning transformation defies any linear prediction. This case study accentuates the central mechanism of the participants' (shared) metapragamtic constructs within the fandom for the spread and variation of the viral CIV item, which made me again wonder about the metapragmatic forces behind the ebbs and flows of virality on social media.

After examining the actual diffusion of CIV neologisms as meaning-changing and meaning-making processes, Chapter 6 returns to the various folk attributions of CIV, trying to investigate the metapragmatic norms and constructs that impact the viral spread of CIV. Specifically, I draw on the theoretical framework of register formations and regard ordinary people's daily CIV use as reflexive practices. Based on the ethnographic data collected from online observations as well as offline interviews over the years, four important reflexive processes have been found, underlying the various negative attributes attached to CIV, where ordinary users enact, perform and negotiate their social identities in online interaction, and in consequence collectively redefine what CIV actually means to them.

With all the above analyses and discussions, Chapter 7 concludes the whole book with hopefully comprehensive accounts of CIV as a dynamic, complex and ever-changing sociolinguistic phenomenon.

Chapter 2
Methodological preliminaries

In this chapter, I will explain the reasons why this book consists of four core studies of seemingly different methodological configurations, as well as the fundamental rationales underlying all the constituent inquiries that examine different aspects of the Chinese Internet Vernacular, i.e., CIV as semiotic resources, forms of performance, identity practice, ideological register, etc.

2.1 Rationale

In general, the case studies aim to form a comprehensive and holistic investigation of CIV, which have been conceptualized, prepared, implemented and organized with some general epistemological and methodological rationales, which I will elaborate on respectively.

Exploratory

As introduced in Chapter 1, the entire project is overall practice-based, i.e. investigating the various CIV practices in their naturally occurring situations, with their various characteristic aspects and dimensions as important points of entry to unfold and further my investigation in ways that are meaningful and relevant to the very practices. And such 'aspects' and 'dimensions', considering the under-theorized nature of CIV, all need to be located and approached in an exploratory manner, by the researcher as an immersed observer and engaged practitioner.

Therefore, besides getting sufficiently informed of existing theories and observations, as well as the local understandings of various practices involved in CIV use on Chinese social media, I began to form conceptions as to the patterns and variations of various CIV usages, based on which research questions were raised for more systematic and guided inquiries. Naturally, this process is largely inspired by the main rationales and guidelines of 'Grounded Theory' (cf. Bryant and Charmaz 2007 for an overview).

More importantly, such 'grounded' rationale is also exploratory in terms of how the main research questions (and objectives) were arrived at over the course of my research activities and the ways these questions related to each other. In fact, my initial focus was on certain linguistic forms that were particularly labelled and practiced as CIV, and my examination of them only raised more questions that gradually led me to each of the case studies with specific and distinct focuses.

Ethnographic

By fully grounding all my analysis on the actual empirical data throughout the studies, I'm taking the 'emic' (cf. Hymes 1974) perspective on any CIV phenomenon I study, which makes my project ethnographic in terms of methodology. Therefore, my overall research scheme, simplistically put, aims to theorize a local practice of a particular group of people based on detailed and thick description within a particular time and place (c.f. Blommaert and Dong 2010).

However, ethnographic research in electronic environments, or digital ethnography (cf. Varis 2016), takes new forms, particularly because of the changes we've had in nearly all aspects of communication on the internet as introduced in the previous chapter, and consequently requires adjusted operations from the researcher. Nevertheless, the core principles and commitments of ethnography, as a scientific paradigm, remain unchanged and become even more crucial when applied to the new medium. First, it is the ensemble of the local practice that concerns and challenges the ethnographer, with the very group of users always at the center of the practice while the actual focus of investigation may differ as per the specific research objectives. In other words, digital ethnography should never be reduced to any separate aspects (usually the texts) of the online practice or any single methods to approach it (Varis 2016), though the convenience or limitations of the internet usually tempt researchers to do so. For instance, the large quantity of accessible data on the web may provide us with more materials than we can possibly analyze and easily come up with certain patterns with quantitative significance, which, however, may only constitute a limited (or even biased) part of a whole set of online practices. Secondly, any ethnographically informed research online is also a 'learning process' (Blommaert and Dong 2010) for the researcher as both user and observer, where the experience of the researcher not only guides further inquiry, but also renders the seemingly monolithic internet as relevant cultural context(s) for the phenomena under investigation, only by means of such naturalistic approaches (Hine 2015).

Moreover, compared with traditional offline ethnographic fieldwork, the innovative and exploratory nature of digital ethnography also grants researchers with more opportunities, where s/he has the liberty (and technological facilities) to select and arrange specific research methods to interrogate and interpret the phenomena. This puts the ethnographer's discretion and accountability to the fore throughout the research procedures, including selecting participants/data, close reading, detailed analysis, inductive interpretation, etc. Most importantly, any decision-making should pivot on the crucial issue that is intrinsic to all ethnographic research – context. For digital ethnography, considering the formal convenience and physicality of 'sites', it is of vital importance that context per se is to be investigated rather than assumed (Blommaert 2007), which requires the ethnographer to resist any a priori categories or take-for-granted contexts for any practice to be examined. On social media in particular, it is usually different forms of contingent contextualization that reveal more about the practices of a certain group of users and have therefore become critical issues of investigation in extant digital ethnographic studies (cf. Varis 2016). I will constantly return to this issue and elaborate on it for the methods in each of the case studies.

Remixed

An especially important aspect of social media is 'remix' (Navas 2012), which underlies almost all that is understood as part of the internet, including the infrastructures, the products (most prominently, the memes), and the practices (online chatting, meme-making, trolling, etc.). In a narrow sense, 'remix' refers to the everyday practices of 'cut/copy and paste, the fragmentation of material' (Navas 2012) with computers, but in a broad sense, remix has become "the way we make sense of our world, by transforming the bombardment of stimuli into a seamless experience" (Markham 2013: 70). Therefore, any emic and ethnographic research on our digitally mediated contemporary life should also follow such a logic and perspective, both metaphorically and practically, in order to reflexively engage with the participants, practices, products, and purposes. Such engagement can be conceptualized as the 'Remix Methods' (Markham 2013, 2017) for social media studies.

Therefore, 'remix methods' should not be considered an independent methodology per se, but a highly responsive, ethically grounded and context-sensitive form of qualitative research. Centering on the two "critical aspects" (Markham 2013: 70-71) of remix and the 'Remix Culture', my entire project has also been conceptualized, designed, proceeded, and reflected accordingly. Firstly, remix relies on the appropriation, combination and complication of multiple methods and techniques to produce meaning. In order to engage with such practices and collect meaningful data, adaptive modes and methods of inquiry should be applied. Hence, my case studies may rely on various (combinations of) research methods that are considered necessary and appropriate according to the development and unfolding of the social media practices under investigation, including longitudinal participatory and/or non-participatory observations, online and/or offline interviews, web data mining and data crawling, various extents of statistic quantification, etc.

Secondly, remix always involves larger communities of collaborative 'remixers' along the continual flow and transformation of any remixed products, such as the so-called 'egalitarian memes' which I will focus on in later chapters. It is the interactions and negotiations in such temporary, ad hoc, yet active communities that help users derive meaning, contexts and structures of the very activities they participate in. Therefore, a digital ethnographer should constantly be aware and reflective of the continual, nonlinear and elusive flows of the target phenomena on the one hand, and the flows of his/her own research activities on the other, so as to grasp and make sense of the very ongoing socio-cultural processes where all of us are involved. Such a 'Flow Approach', as Markham and Gammelby (2017) call it, reflexively moves into and maps the data flows, both digital and non-digital, as learning processes to grapple with the complexity and entanglements of digital phenomena. It follows that question-raising and data generation, the usually pre-determined and well-defined procedures in many other paradigms, become key in a flow-oriented research process and may be constantly revised so that the research process stays relevant to the actual flows. In what follows, I'll elaborate on the entire research design and my own activities as user/researcher, in terms of reflexive flows. But first, I'll highlight and discuss several critical methodological issues for the whole project.

2.2 Critical issues

Web as/for corpus

Following from the above discussions, my research activity has been at once an inquiry into the remixed signs that get diffused and transformed on social media and a learning process to enter and map the digitally-contextualized practices centering on the products. In other words, I'm treating the various social media sites both as 'places' and 'texts' (Androutsopoulos 2013) of certain forms of digital practice, for which different data collection methods are employed, e.g. screen-based – "produced by participants and collected online by the researcher", user-based – "prompted by the researcher's activities and produced through their contact with CMC users" (2013: 240), or blended, in accordance with the specific questions that need investigating.

The main part of the 'screen-based' data produced by the participants were collected as various datasets for each of the case studies, in a way that is as systematic as possible and especially appropriate for my ethnographic focus. But I will firstly compare my data collection methods with the 'web as/for corpus' (cf. Gatto 2014) approaches that most linguistic studies on the internet work with. In a nutshell, 'web as corpus' treats the internet as a surrogate corpus, a naturally occurring and ongoing source of attested language use, and usually relies on search engines to interrogate the web and retrieve information. In contrast, the 'web for corpus' approach applies data-mining or data crawling tools to the creation of ad hoc corpora for specific research purposes. However, the very language phenomena I'm interested in are not independent practices per se, but an integral part of the social media activities of the participants. Therefore, while conveniently employing the methods and techniques of 'web as/for corpus' to compile sizeable (mainly linguistic, sometimes multimodal) corpora to inform myself about the 'system-oriented' aspects, I also use digital ethnographic methods to collect the related qualitative data concerning the 'speaker-oriented' (Androutsopoulos 2013) aspects into datasets.

Therefore, I'm relying extensively on the 'web for corpus' methods, e.g. the search engines hosted by various social media applications, to compile heuristic and provisional corpora as empirical basis for conceptualizing and analyzing particular research issues, which are determined by, and shall in return adjust, my research aims and desiderata (cf. Mair 2013) at different levels and points. Search activities, that is, querying the web and collecting the results under certain systematic criteria (Gatto 2014: 84-87), have not only proved to be a convenient and viable method in corpus linguistic studies (Buchstaller et al. 2010), but are also one of the core activities and types of social interaction that ordinary users engage with, both practically and epistemologically, on social media (Zappavigna 2015; White 2016). It is then arguable that my own search experiences are crucial for understanding, entering and mapping the digital flows of the participants' interaction and meaning-making processes on social media.

Quality and representativeness

As basically an inductive science, the issue of representativeness that validates deductive reasoning doesn't necessarily figure crucially in ethnography (Blommaert and Dong 2010) which aims at theorizing from empirical evidence, rather than validating hypotheses and generalizations. In contrast, one of the strengths of ethnography lies in its hypothesis-constructive quality, that is, ethnographic research yields plausible hypotheses – i.e. ecologically validated hypotheses that can be used as heuristic devices in follow-up and more general(izable) research (Blommaert and Dong 2010). However, as the description and the theoretical generalization should be grounded on the empirical data with a reasonable (in accordance with the researcher's objectives and designs of the ethnographic investigations) scope and scale, the decision-making in data selection should be correspondingly accountable, so that a certain level of quality and credibility is maintained.

As for digital ethnography in particular, quality and credibility is not necessarily predetermined by the way the data are collected and organized, but "[e]mbedded in the extent to which the production demonstrates resonance with the context, and also has resonance with the intended audience" (Markham 2013: 72). In other words, the ethnographic quality and credibility consists in the reflexive retrieving, mapping and sense-making of the very digital contexts in question as well as the participants' practices therein.

Sites and techniques

My entire project can be regarded as remixed and multi-sited research, including both online and offline venues as research sites, which of course requires differentiated techniques for data collection and interrogation. As for the online sites, my main focus is on the Sina Microblogging Service (Weibo henceforth), one of the largest social media applications in China, which is also the primary source of news diffusion and social innovation (Hu et al. 2017). I mainly rely on Weibo's own search engine (s.weibo.com) for information query and retrieval, which helps me 1) form a general grasp of the target language uses and related practices within a specified period, 2) form a rough account of their situations, such as estimated frequencies, ranking as hot topics, etc., and 3) reconstruct the (important) ways that ordinary users get to know them. All of these aspects are essential for making decisions at various points of my research activities, which will be elaborated on in each case study in detail.

Besides singly searching certain phraseological strings and examining the results (like most ordinary users do), there were circumstances where I needed to compile sizeable datasets in order to investigate the phenomena in certain quantities and over certain timespans. Accordingly, I conducted multiple queries and collected the top results in a random manner[18] in order to scatter the data as widely as possible, so that the data can be both feasibly quantifiable and qualitatively rich and diversified. On a side note, such 'scattered search' method is also intended to work around the search restriction imposed by Weibo, which only makes available a limited proportion of its entire search archive (so 'representativeness' is always compromised whatever method is applied) both via the Application Programming Interface (API)[19] and the manual search interface (Zeng et al. 2015). Detailed criteria for and procedures of dataset compilation will be elaborated on in each case chapter.

Interactive and contextual data, including observational notes, participants' profile data, related logs, participants' comments and replies, etc. were all collected into datasets of various sizes, organized in terms of types, themes and topics, in the effort to 'naturalistically' move into and map the flows of practice. More importantly, following the flows also took me to other online/offline sites that were rendered as relevant for the very digital practice that I was

18. This method of improving query data collection is also discussed in Gatto (2014: 84-94).

19. Most studies on social media applications rely on their API services that grant access to certain data from the servers in large quantities. For the detailed API implementation on Weibo, see Hu et al. (2017) for an overview.

observing, including Baidu Tieba forums, Douban communities, the Wechat application, mobile text messages, etc., which makes my studies practically multi-sited. It should be emphasized that the 'multi-sitedness' was not an intended methodological choice, but a necessary component of my research that followed from the digital flows investigated.

Research ethics

One of the central tenets of ethnography is to protect the participants, especially vulnerable or marginalized groups, from any harms and fully respect their personal rights throughout the research activities (cf. Murphy and Dingwall 2007). This usually comes in the form of guidelines and principles, instead of specific measures, as ethnographic research always addresses situated practices that require specific ethical decision-making accordingly. Specialized guidelines have also been proposed and adopted within the scholarship of digital ethnography (e.g. Markham and Buchanan 2012), but more chances of having to deal with 'ethically ambiguous data' (Sandler 2013) – mainly due to the 'public' nature of most social media applications and the easy access to myriad individual data online – urge the researcher to take a more reflexive and responsible stance towards any data s/he obtains and to illuminate the very ethical decisions being made at each point with regard to the guidelines and principles.

In principle, for the whole project, all data containing individual information, such as IDs, usernames, IP addresses, profile content, personal or institutional references, etc., were anonymized to the uttermost extent. However, contents from public institutions, public figures and celebrities were maintained in their original forms and provided with the sources[20]. As for the sticky issue of 'searchability' or 'googlability' (Varis 2016) where materials, especially sensitive ones, used in the research can be digitally retrievable and therefore put the participants' identity at the risk of exposure, only individual data that cannot be retrieved (e.g. not included in the searchable archive, or not provided by the website as retrievable data) were used with anonymization. I will account for how the data were

20. In such cases, the public nature of the content is uncontroversial, which has also been a common practice in Sociolinguistics and Linguistic Anthropology, as explained in Squires (2014).

selected and obtained in each of the case studies.

2.3 Summary of data

This section will briefly summarize the research designs of the four case studies that constitute the bulk of this book, and which also represent my entire research journey of entering and exploring the very digital flows that the participants engage with, centering on the various target CIV terms.

When observing the growing body of CIV on various Chinese social media platforms, in the early stage I focused mainly on 1) neologistic formations and 2) novel usages as entry points to investigate the phenomena. From a qualitative perspective, I compiled a sizeable yet manageable corpus (Message Dataset 1, henceforth DM1) of ca. 1000 messages containing the target phrases through scattered search in the Weibo archive over a timespan of nearly four years, in order to conduct a qualitative parsing on especially their meanings and functions. At approximately the same time, I organized offline focus groups and individual interviews (compiled into Focus-group Dataset 1, henceforth DF1) in order to elicit the participants' understandings and interpretations of the phrases' usage. As the preliminary findings with the data on the three phrases raised more questions as to the processual aspects of their meaning/function variations and the interactional dimension of the processes, I was then redirected to the ongoing flows of CIV neologisms where the changes were simultaneously happening.

After several attempts to locate the diffusion of a suitable CIV neologism, I was able to monitor the viral flow of 'duang', an innovated word that swept the entire Chinese social media in early 2015. From the very beginning of its spread, I managed to collect a large quantity of instances of 'duang' on Sina Weibo and other social media applications on a day-by-day basis for the first two weeks, and compiled them into two datasets. The small message corpus (DM2) of 1,392 original Weibo messages containing the target word 'duang' was mainly created to investigate the ongoing variation in meaning and function, while all of the messages' interactional content, including users' comments, reposts, replies, likes, etc. were compiled into another corpus (DC2) as important online ethnographic data to help conceptualize and characterize the very digital flow. In order to make the qualitative analysis of the data as reliable as possible, I invited another researcher, Dr. Yuxia Li to work with me on the parsing and interpretation of the messages. I also organized offline interviews and focus groups (DF2) to elicit the participants' experiences and attitudes with CIV, and one of the topics we discussed was the remarkable flow of 'duang' on Chinese social media. As important findings emerged in this case study concerning the users' digital practices with viral CIV neologisms, I was then drawn to the various forms of community practices that needed zooming in and further examining. When monitoring the Chinese ACGN community where 'duang' was first innovated, I took notice of several flows of neologisms generated in various sub-communities, among which I selected the innovated phrase 'chesaika' from the online fandom of a Thai TV show. As I approached nearer to the digital flows of the participants, I was able to move in and practice as a community member as well as the ethnographer, for which detailed observational notes and research memos were produced and organized into the Observation Dataset 3 (DO3). Besides, I also continually collected interactional data wherever I found the phrase was used, with all the necessary contextual information kept, into a sizeable corpus (DC3) for detailed qualitative analysis. As there were two seasons of the TV show, my data collection then comprised of three main timespans, i.e. the airing of Season 1, the hiatus between the seasons, and the airing of Season 2.

After moving into the viral flows brought about by the various neologisms, with focus on their meaning variation and the participants' community practice, I tried to integrate all my online and offline 'flow-following' experiences with CIV over the past few years, and examined the metapragmatic and ideological underpinnings of the use and spread of CIV. As my research focus was on the participants' perception and evaluation of CIV, I selected social media discussions on topics that emerged as especially informative and significant over a period of more than two years from the various digital flows I followed. I organized them into an ad-hoc corpus DC4, mainly containing four subsets of metapragmatic data. As for the offline data, I mainly relied on the interviews and focus groups that I had organized for the previous case studies (i.e. DF1 and DF2), which contained a large amount of participants' metapragmatic discussion of specific CIV items and CIV in general.

The following table sums up all the datasets compiled and used in the studies. It should be noted that the data in different datasets were labelled in different ways, reflecting the venues, temporal character, and participant types of the very data collected. I will explain the labels in each of the case study chapters.

Table 2.1 Summary of datasets

	Online Dataset	Type/description	Offline Dataset	Type/description
Case 1 Ch. 3	DM1	Message corpus Scattered search in Weibo archive (2009-2014), 1,002 posts	DF1	4 Focus group/ Individual interviews, 6 participants (March-May, 2014)
Case 2 Ch. 4	DM2	Message corpus Scattered search in Weibo archive (February 20-March 8, 2015), 1,392 original posts		
	DC2	Interactional corpus Comments and replies (contextual), 215 Weibo interactions	DF2	9 Focus group/ Individual interviews, 22 participants (June-August, 2015)
Case 3 Ch. 5	DO3	Observational notes and memos (March-December, 2015) on 3 main sites (Weibo, Bilibili, Baidu Tieba)		
	DC3	Interactional corpus Comments and replies (contextual), 187 Weibo interactions		
Case 4 Ch. 6	DC4	5 major comments datasets Crawling of comments and replies 6,455 entries in total	DF2+DF1	DF2 served as the main data, while DF1 was also consulted

Chapter 3
Meaning change in CIV neologisms: The case of three 'very X very XX' phrases

3.1 It all starts with...

A very early effort to chronicle and catalogue the growing spate of innovated words and phrases on Chinese internet was the Dictionary of China's Internet Language (Yu 2001) with obviously a lexical focus, which in fact promoted the increasing academic trend and significance of studying internet buzzwords (see Wang 2008 for an overview). The 'watershed' between the two largely distinctive types of internet neologisms around the year 2008, as introduced previously, also influenced the ways Chinese scholarship has approached the internet phenomenon, i.e. from a mainly domain-/ medium- specific lexical variety to certain styles of language use among ordinary internet users. Accordingly, these language studies have shifted from their early focus on word formation (Wu 2003; Liu 2010), semantic features and variation (Miao 2009), pragmatic functions (Wang 2011), and cognitive underpinnings (Ji 2012), etc., to a larger analytical scope that enquires into the neologisms as both precipitates and constituents of the changing and emerging social discourse and online culture in contemporary China (Cang et al. 2012; Luo and He 2015).

Three themes are especially prominent and recurring in these predominantly language-centered studies, namely

1) There is the constant concern and curiosity as to the relationship between the so-called internet language, represented by the buzzwords and catchphrases, and the 'common Chinese language', and how the internet language may, apart from mere lexical addition, if ever, penetrate and influence it, considering the many noticeable and distinctive linguistic features originated from internet use. A large pool of such studies have especially focused on certain influential and productive constructions (Yu and Qiu 2009) and phrases that have somewhat functioned as discourse or stance markers (Wang 2011). It is usually argued (Gao 2012) that only through continued spread and adoption would the neologisms eventually strengthen and sediment into such linguistic features in general use.
2) Considering that a large amount of internet neologisms quickly fade out of use, the 'aberrant' linguistic features that are intrinsic to such innovations are usually thought to fulfill functions and effects in themselves, even if they cannot persist in use for long, as long as they serve to spread the news, to create amusement, or to subvert the normal, among the younger generations. 'Carnivalesque', in the Bakhtinian terms, is usually the notion that many studies (e.g. Yang 2016) use to characterize the functions underlying and motivating the deviated and diversified usages, against the larger backdrop of inter-generational and inter-group differences in the contemporary Chinese society.
3) The similar short-lived cycles that most neologisms undergo have been repeatedly highlighted, arguably the consequence of the predominant 'attention economy' (Weng et al. 2012) that governs our daily life. Therefore, the vitality of any linguistic innovations depends on its creativity and originality, which itself is, however, doomed to eventual oblivion under the limited collective attention of internet users. Such a (pessimistic) view usually attempts to account for the 'unconventional' aspects of the catchy words and phrases and argues that 'popularity' (Xin

2010), in terms of both temporality and uniqueness, is the most essential component of any internet neologisms.

The above themes have indeed illuminated and characterized important aspects of CIV neologisms as one of the main phenomena and consequences of our accelerated integration with the internet, including 1) their diversified and changing linguistic nature, especially the ways their meanings are constituted and communicated, 2) the putative functions and motivations of their wide use by young people, and 3) the general mechanisms for their adoption and desuetude. These characterizations have blazed trails for further attempts at accounting for the apparent dynamics and complexities of CIV neologisms. First, the very 'conspicuous' linguistic changes that the neologisms have brought about to our common language, especially in colloquial use, need further theoretical investigation, which we could naturally and meaningfully compare with the growing studies of change and development in the Chinese language in light of the 'Subjectification Model' (Traugott 1989, 1995, 2010).

The gist of subjectification is that meanings tend to "become increasingly based in the speaker's subjective belief state/attitude toward the proposition" (Traugott 1989: 35), which is not just the main type of semantic change in grammaticalization, but can also be found in all types of semantic change. For a certain lexical item, an increase in subjectification means that it becomes interactive to the extent that it provides ways for the speaker to guide the hearer in interpretation, a mechanism that has been argued to underlie the diachronic formations of many discourse and pragmatic markers, such as 'well' (Jucker 1997), 'I mean' (Brinton 2002), and 'you know' (Fitzmaurice 2004) in that the gradual development of the phrases' abilities to express speaker-involvement and regulate interaction follows such an increasingly subjective path. Many Chinese scholars have also argued that subjectification serves as one of the driving forces in grammaticalization (Wu 2011; Dong 2016), and it sheds special light on understanding how lexical phrases, especially colloquial idioms, have integrated the subjective and communicative features from the dyadic interaction and become discourse markers (Yue 2011).

Secondly, what most studies on CIV have accentuated is its 'non-conventional' and 'internet-specific' features, where the neologisms are dislodged from their contexts, thus possibly missing an essential part of the functions and effects that the neologisms fulfill in actual communication. Based on my own experience, CIV neologisms appeal to internet users not only in their trendiness or popularity, but also in their great flexibility and serviceability in various contexts. In most cases, it is not the denotational meaning but the contextual construal that is invoked in an instance of the neologisms, which are usually used with intentional manipulations. Such 'meaning-manipulation' and 'function-management' is almost always carried out in a tacit way – i.e. nobody has to articulate or explain how the neologisms are used or construed in interaction. But it is by no means the case that the users are not aware of the 'proper' usage or function of the neologisms, as they are usually employed to smoothen and vivify, rather than impede or confuse, communication on- and offline.

Starting from these two reflections, I aim to further the investigation of Chinese internet neologisms as the artefacts, products, and means of practice in the users' everyday communication on and outside of social media. For this purpose, I'll focus on a group of neologisms that were 1) at least at one point virally spread and used, and 2) notable for an extended period of time on Chinese social media, so that there may be more opportunity to observe the trends, patterns, and processes of variation and sedimentation, all of which are relevant points informed by the extant studies and hence the starting points of my own investigation.

3.2 The three phrases

The group of three neologistic phrases investigated in this chapter were selected for their 1) similar linguistic forms of 'very X very XX'[21], 2) comparable virality and duration of spread on Chinese social media since 2008, and 3) observable changes in their usage

21. X standards for one Chinese character. Generally speaking, the X and XX are replaced with adjectives, but in certain cases, nouns and verbs can also fit in (Zhang and Zhao 2008).

and meanings. Table 3.1 summarizes basic information about the phrases and their spread on social media.

Previous studies have usually approached these phrases from a constructional perspective, and showed more interest in the formal properties, i.e. how the three phrases help consolidate the 'very X very XX' construction. For instance, Fan (2009) characterizes the prosodic patterns of the structure, together with its variability and constraints, and notes that the prosody fulfills a viable '2-syllable +3-syllable' pattern, which guarantees its general acceptance, and shows a new continuous, unstopped segment of two-phrase construction, which sounds novel and attractive in online communication. In terms of syntactic functions, which most extant studies focus on, many have noted their high flexibility (Zhang and Zhao 2008; Li 2009), in that the phrases not only fulfill adjectival and predicative functions in a sentence, but most of the cases serve as stand-alone clauses that express a somewhat independent tone and meaning.

Table 3.1 The three phrases

***'henhao henqiangda'* ('very good very powerful') (VGVP)**
According to Baidu Baike[22] (the most popular collaborative Web-based encyclopedia in China), 'very good very powerful' probably originated from the online community MOP.com before 2006. Back then, the forum site banned the use of vulgar language such as shabi ('stupid ass'), and the users then turned to niubi ('fricking awesome')[23] instead to replace Shabi, and used the expression 'very good very powerful' as a substitute to mean something really awesome. This immediately triggered the subsequent boom of its use throughout the Chinese internet.
***'henhuang henbaoli'* ('very erotic very violent') (VEVV)**
In a state TV news report about the necessity for Internet regulations on Dec. 27, 2007, a schoolgirl said in the interview, "The other day when I was browsing for some information online, a webpage suddenly popped out, 'henhuang henbaoli' ('very erotic very violent'). And I closed it in no time." The phrase 'very erotic very violent' was immediately ridiculed by the public as obviously pre-rehearsed (pre-coached), and soon became a popular mocking expression among Internet users in China.

22. http://baike.baidu.com/view/1120070.html

23. Both 'shabi' and 'niubi' are common colloquial words, with a tinge of vulgarity.

'*hensha hentianzhen*' ('very stupid very naïve') (VSVN)

In early 2008, the sex pictures of Gillian Chung, a Hong Kong pop singer, became widely circulated on the Internet. In a press conference later, Gillian regretted such indiscreet behavior and pled for forgiveness. The original remark, in Cantonese, goes, "This incident has caused great harm to me and people around me. I admit that I used to be quite ('hao', a degree adverb similar to 'hen') naïve as well as quite stupid." When reporting on the incident, the media unanimously modified Gillian's remarks to 'hensha hentianzhen' ('very stupid very naïve'), making this phrase extremely prevalent on the internet within several days.

In terms of semantics and pragmatics, however, not much has been said about the three phrases, except that many scholars have noted their playfulness or coolness in use by young people (Zhang and Zhao 2008) and their obvious association with the social events (Fan 2009). These studies have pointed out important characteristics of the phrases, but the following example of the use of the VEVV phrase still strikes us, as discussing the image of a historical figure wearing stockings may be marginally 'erotic' but by no means 'violent'. Yet we shouldn't dismiss it too quickly as a random individual 'deviation', because on Chinese social media there're thousands of instances like this that demand the reader to form a much expanded construal.

(1) Juran zai Lishi ke taolun Yalishanda Wangzi chuande shibushi siwa, wenkeban de nvsheng, *henhuang henbaoli*. '(They're) even discussing in the history class if Prince Alexander (Alexander I of Russia) is wearing stockings, girls in the arts classes, *very erotic very violent*.'

3.3 Research questions

To make sense of the myriad variations of the phrases on Chinese social media, this study focuses on the use of the three phrases (i.e. VGVB, VEVV, and VSVN) on Sina Weibo, investigates the meaning and function changes therein, and attempts to account for the communicative mechanisms. Specifically, I will examine the following questions:

I. During their spread on Chinese social media, what meanings and functions have arisen for the three phrases, and what characteristics has each phrase developed?

II. How do social media users account for the meaning and function variations of the phrases in social media use? What are the mechanisms and motivations underlying their daily use?

III. What implications do the variations have for the phrases per se, and for Chinese internet neologisms in general?

IV. What implications does this case study have for my further investigations?

3.4 Description of the collected data

First of all, it was necessary to determine if the three phrases were still used and circulated on Chinese social media and if there were enough instances from which a reasonable dataset could be built. However, it is extremely difficult to accurately pin down the trend of the phrases during their spread, as Sina Weibo does not make publicly available the total number of messages in its archives for each year. The following statistics contain the number of occurrences returned from its search engine as results on an every-half-year basis.

As suggested by Buchstaller et al. (2010), who encountered a similar situation with no available corpus size to arrive at accurate, reliable statistics, it may also be possible to show an approximate trend by normalizing the number of tokens of the target item from different periods with the tokens of the most common functional elements in a language. In this light, the three most frequent Chinese characters[24], de/ wo/ shi (DE-possessive/ I /be) were searched in the archive, and the mean values of their number of tokens were calculated for each period (see Table 3.2). Each number of tokens of the phrases was divided by the respective mean as a rough method of normalization. As a result, impressions of their trends are shown in Figure 3.1. Since such statistics are not the major concern of the present study, they will not be further discussed in what follows.

24. These three are among the most frequently used characters across most contemporary Chinese corpora, as summarized in Sze et al. (2014).

Table 3.2 Occurrences of the three expressions in Weibo Search Archive

	Periods (every half year)	VGVP	VSVN	VEVV	Mean
1	2009-08-16—2009-12-31	2918	551	671	5544200
2	2010-01-01—2010-06-30	13131	7295	3321	38927093
3	2010-07-01—2010-12-31	21885	17508	17508	166724793
4	2011-01-01—2011-06-30	58360	24803	24803	506454889
5	2011-07-01—2011-12-31	52524	93376	78786	831329932
6	2012-01-01—2012-06-30	78786	140064	71491	824485763
7	2012-07-01—2012-12-31	100671	214473	90458	1039654220
8	2013-01-01—2013-06-30	180916	202801	124015	1326119143
9	2013-07-01—2013-12-31	218850	183834	144441	1961009802
10	2014-01-01—2014-06-30	224686	150277	122556	3064886427

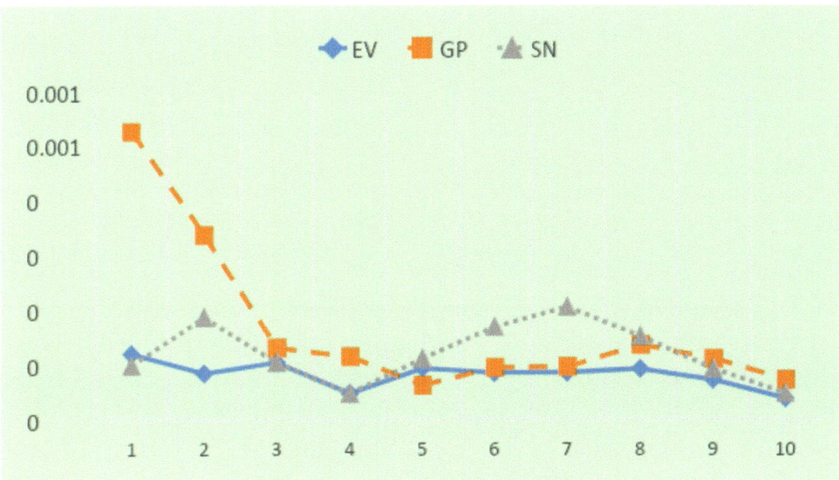

Figure 3.1 Trends of the 3 phrases

All of the textual data were collected from the Sina Weibo search archive. Queries with the three phrases as a whole (with quotation marks) were performed in the search archive with time restrictions for every half year since the beginning to the day of collection[25], which contains 10 collections for each phrases. Each period contains 20 random posts from the search results, which constitutes the dataset DM1 of 200 posts in total for each phrase. All the collected messages in DM1, together with their immediate contexts, were

25. Every collected period spans six months, except the first one that can only retrieve as early as the inception of Weibo service (see also Table 3.2).

parsed thoroughly. A qualitative analysis was conducted on the local meaning and function of the very phrases used in the posts. Different types of meaning and function variation were arrived at in the qualitative analysis.

As for the interactional data, I organized two focus groups and two individual interviews with six participants between March and May in 2014, in order to elicit their understanding of the phrases, as well as their use experience, attitudes, and preferences towards them. The following table summarizes the basic information about the participants.

Table 3.3 Interview participants (DF1)

Interview Type	Participants	Gender	Occupation
Focus group 1	CC[26]	Male	Graduate student
	FC	Male	Graduate student
Individual 1	PC	Male	Graduate student
Focus group 2	JX	Male	Graduate student
	GY	Female	Doctoral student
Individual 2	ZY	Male	College student

3.5 Analysis

All of the three phrases carried great meaning potential when they were first adopted by social media users in participating in discussions about social events. However, as the collected data dated behind the circulation of the events for over 1 year, the quotative or reportative uses, i.e. talking about or commenting on the events, of the phrases only make up a tiny proportion in the dataset. Instead, the majority of the phrases are used by the participants to refer to or comment on their daily issues or personal matters, where they have skewed, manipulated, or drastically changed the phrases from their original meanings. In what follows, I will present the major types and forms of variation of the phrases, in terms of both the extent of the variation and the motivations of the users.

26. With their consent, all participants were anonymized by their name initials.

3.5.1 Rhetorical use

On the whole, the users would usually employ some notable stylistic and rhetorical means, such as irony, sarcasm, punning, etc., so as to highlight their attitudes, beliefs or other aspects of their mental states in the very speech events, or what De Smet and Verstraete (2006) call 'pragmatic subjectivity'.

The large number of rhetorical instances of the phrases as found in the dataset may be motivated by at least two facts. Firstly, all of the three phrases are composed of intensified adjectives that are usually too strong or sharp for propositional use, such as 'very erotic or very powerful', and are therefore naturally employed to achieve various pragmatic purposes, e.g., VEVV for overstatement, VGVP for irony, etc. Moreover, such pragmatic effects and elevated emotions, such as humor, sarcasm, anger, etc., are also typical of the social media environment, as found by many internet scholars (e.g. Zappavigna 2012; Shifman 2014). The following illustrates how the three 'very-' phrases are usually employed rhetorically as found in the data.

Irony

Despite different conceptions and classifications of irony, it is generally understood that irony always involves some contrast between the very utterance's usual expectation and reality, which therefore includes rhetorical devices such as hyperboles and understatement (Gibbs 2000). In the collected data, irony is widely employed by the users, especially with the VGVP phrase, for instance,

(2) Henhao henqiangda, chu'er shangwu shoude shang, dao xianzai hai liuxie.
'Very good very powerful, got hurt on the second (New Year's Day) and still bleeding now.'

By uttering VGVP, the user in (2) is most likely to express his annoyance or frustration at the fact that his wound keeps oozing blood for days, rather than making a praise of any sort. Using VGVP in an ironic way highlights the contrast between the phrase's literal meaning and reality, therefore elevating the speaker's negative emotions. Such usage also alludes to the early hype on its original platform as an ironic substitute for the profane expression shabi ('stupid ass'), which again consolidates the effect of irony. Besides the type of oppositional irony, a good number of VGVP instances are used in a hyperbolic way to evaluate things, make judgments, and convey comments in conversations.

Parody

Parody is found to be a major form of humor on social media and one of the primary means by which internet memes spread (Shifman 2014). Through parodies of the latest memes, social media users not only participate in the 'ambient culture' (Zappavigna 2012) online, but also exhibit their own subjectivity and creativity by means of 'remixing' in various degrees. It is especially notable in the VSVN phrase that most of its instances in the collected data show various parodic elements that can be drawn from the original scandal, as illustrated by the following example.

(3) Wo xiang quanguo renmin rencuo juran zai zhe jiyi laodongrenmin yubeiqi younanxiangbei ben de zhongda shike hai zhuomo zhe xiang nongdao Shenzhen huo Guangzhou dao Wuhan de huochepiao feijipiao dou beng xiang! Hensha hentianzhen! Huogai wo zouhui Wuhan

'I apologize to all the people of the nation I even thought of getting a train ticket from Shenzhen or Guangzhou to Wuhan at such a major moment when several hundred million people traveling from South to North Even flight tickets are out of reach! Very stupid very naïve! I deserve to go back to Wuhan on foot'

All experienced social media users may readily recognize the association between the lines in (3) and the original VSVN incident (cf. Table 3.1). The user apparently parodies Gillian's public apology for her sexual imprudence to achieve a humorous effect, i.e., self-sarcasm for failing to buy a train ticket. (3) is rather a parody in full, mimicking both the structure and the apologetic tone of the original. But more often than not, users would simply employ the VEVV phrase alone to either jokingly regret over one's own mistakes or sarcastically criticize others' deeds. In such cases, VEVV parodically projects the 'apologetic scene' where a special relationship between the posting user and other user(s), be it a particular user in conversation or simply the general audience, is to be enacted – i.e., the speech roles of apologizer and criticizer.

Punning

Another form of humorous language use that deviates from the phrases' original meaning is punning, which is especially notable in VEVV. By playing on the homonym or sound approximant of one Chinese character in the phrases that can be relevant in a completely different or strange context, social media users have in so doing greatly extended the applicability of VEVV and achieved playful effects. For example,

(4)Jichang haizai xiayu, dengji shi dou chuanshang le yuyi, mouzong shi duyiwuer de liang huangse, dique henhuang henbaoli 😁 😁
'Still raining at the airport, everyone puts on raincoats when boarding the airplane, some boss is wearing a unique bright yellow one, indeed very erotic very violent😁 😁'

The character huang in henhuang hen baoli (VEVV) can also mean 'yellow', and the VEVV expression has been observed, rather frequently, to describe things that are yellow in a positive way, such as in (4), an amusing yellow raincoat. Besides such homophonic punning, the VEVV phrase has also been employed in terms of its semantic constituents, i.e. used on something that can be associated with either violent (e.g. a very erotic very violent hurricane) or erotic (e.g. a very erotic very violent flirtation). Punning happens much less frequently with the other two phrases, as there is less punning potential with the characters for 'powerful', 'naïve' or 'stupid'.

Generalized tropes

Besides the above rhetorical devices intentionally employed to heighten the users' specific emotions and attitudes (i.e. jocular, sarcastic, or playful), these popular internet phrases have further become common tropes, mainly through the conceptual mechanisms of metaphor and metonym, when they're increasingly recontextualized by social media users to represent their personal experiences and thoughts. The following examples illustrate how the meanings of the three phrases become further generalized and abstracted in such uses.

(5)Wan wow name jiu... jianguo wushu haoren... ye jianguo wushu jianren... buguo ci jianren... hen huizhuang 'hensha hentianzhen'... nvren xin juedui shi haidizhen ya... wo buxiang zaigen ciren you renhe jiechu le!
'Having played wow (World of Warcraft, an online game) for so long... seen numerous good guys... as well as assholes... but this very asshole... is very capable of acting 'very stupid very naïve'... a woman's heart is really deeper than the deepest sea... I don't want to have any dealings with her anymore!'

(6)[XMTH ceng jiaodao women] nimen bujiao ruzhi, jiao congzheng. nimen yao you jiangzi de yishi, nimen jijiang tashang de shi yitiao bojuyungui, henhuang henbaoli de buguilu, xianhua he zhangsheng, tiechuang he shoukao, yexu zhishi chaoxizhishi...
'[XMTH (another Weibo user) has once lectured us] it should not be called entering into career, but rather stepping into politics. You should have such awareness, that you are going to step on an unpredictable, very erotic very violent path where there's no turning back, flowers and applauds, as well as iron bars and shackles, may all be a matter of time...'

(7)Jintian he Lixiang wan de henhao henqiangda! Haiyou ni nabang gemen, henhao.
'With Lixiang today, (we) played very good very powerful! And there's also your bunch of dudes, very good.'

From the perspective of 'Conceptual Metaphor Theory' (Lakoff and Johnson 1980), the three examples above all involve conceptual procedures where the posting users activate mapping relationships, in terms of resemblance or affiliation, between the CIV phrases and the intended objects. In (5), the VSVN phrase is first conceived metonymically, that is, it stands for the qualities that are reflected in the scandalous case of Gillian, who appeared to be innocent and apologetic but was still voluntarily involved in something foolish and despicable. The metonymized phrase is then again projected metaphorically onto the situation at issue, that is, to qualify the girl in the WOW game as likewise deceitful and despicable, a set of characteristics ordinary users can relate to and imagine based on the very well-known incident. Slightly different, the VEVV expression in (6) metaphorically describes the 'career path' as 'erotic' and 'violent', comparing the dangers and struggles in choosing such a career to the sensations that are directly connected with unhealthy and graphic content that internet users may occasionally encounter. To understand (7), reading users have to map the sensation and consequence that are usually conveyed by VGVP onto a different conceptual domain, i.e. the state and intensity of an action. Such metaphorical extension here is converted into a positive tone and strong intensity that may be sensed and expressed with an activity (in this case, playing with someone).

In actual social media communication, such 'elaborated' conceptual trajectories may be quite direct and automatic, when these phrases become recognized metaphorical and metonymic tropes. The significant frequency and saliency, afforded by the phrases' online virality, keep consolidating their tropic potentials, during which process the metaphorical and metonymic effects get further generalized and abstracted, largely blocking the phrases' literal meanings. In consequence, the three phrases can be employed more freely, with each of them covering a range of tropic meanings that can be projected onto a wide variety of different contexts. For instance, based on the collected data, VSVN may generally refer to anything related to lack of maturity or sophistication, as well as complication or deception; while VEVV and VGVP can have such generalized ranges as to cover anything intense and of fierce involvement.

When the neologisms are so generalized and expanded, what

then is being intended and conveyed by the posting user with the phrases, and how do the audience figure it out as such? In order to find out how ordinary social media users infer pragmatic effects and meanings from these neologisms, I turned to the offline participants, and arrived at several major functions of the phrases in social media communication.

3.5.2 Expanded use as meta-utterance

Before proceeding, there is one very important syntactic aspect of the three phrases that is worth noting, i.e., their relative independence from the main sentence as a 'stand-alone clause' (Zhang and Zhao 2008), with an ambiguous, and therefore flexible, scope over the sentence. In other words, the logical subjects of such adjectival phrases, basically working as predicative or modifying clauses, are only to be implied (from the contexts) and not necessarily definite. This characteristic not only contributes to the (intended) ambiguity in using these phrases in many situations, but also facilitates a number of expanded functions that, in effect, invite re-interpretation of the very messages. Under such circumstances, the CIV phrases themselves are sufficient indicators for the users to purposefully retrieve the real intentions of the messages, instead of construing them at face value – or rather, the use of the phrases immediately warrants a 'pragmatic orientation' (Mertz 1996) towards the messages. The specific ways that theses phrases function as 'pragmatic indicators', or 'meta-utterances' (Hübler and Bublitz 2007), may vary in actual social media communication, where a variety of pragmatic effects of the phrases can be activated – e.g. it's irony, it's supposed to be critical, it works to maintain interpersonal harmony, etc.

In order to pin down the effects and functions of the meta-utterances, I consulted all the focus group participants on identifying and classifying the functional variation, with typical examples selected from the corpus, and asked them to freely comment on such uses, based on which I was able to arrive at some major meta-functions for the phrases.

"Like an emotional final particle" (DF1/CC)[27]

One prominent form of such highly generalized and abstracted usage is when these phrases are used mainly to highlight the posting user's emotional state and inner feelings. In such cases, the stand-alone phrases deliver an even more abstracted meaning and indicate a less explicit modifying relation. Moreover, such uses are usually situated in heightened emotions, expressed in various combinations of semiotic signs (e.g. texts, emoticons, punctuation marks, etc.). In consequence, readers would have to retrieve and infer the 'most relevant purpose' of such use from the surrounding texts, and thus regard the phrases per se as emotional components of and additions to the message, as illustrated in the following examples.

(8)Jianzhi xiang xia diyu, henhuang henbaoli, dan you fa buqi qingxu, zhenshi jian jiujie de shi. 😫😫😫
Almost want to go to hell, very erotic very violent, but can't throw a tantrum, really an upsetting thing.

(9)Nandao yijia ka aiqing dou xi gan ka??? Wo tai Out la, hensha hentianzhen... 😫😫😫
Are all relationships now just like this??? I'm so Out, very stupid very naïve...

The VEVV in (8) can only be understood as an emotional outburst, emphasizing the user's frustration with sulky undertone, which could be functionally replaced with 'damn!' or 'ugh!'. In (9), while it is not impossible to read the VSVN as self-confession for the user's own ignorance, only in a highly abstracted sense, it also makes sense to understand it simply as an emotional marker of dismay or disappointment. The more conceptual meaning represented by VSVN, i.e. judging something or someone as unsophisticated, is somewhat blocked when reading the message, while the more pragmatic understanding, i.e. to express personal frustration and disbelief, is inferred as more likely and relevant in this situation. Moreover, both examples exhibit heightened emotions. Note the

27. All offline data cited in this chapter are labelled in the format (DF1/participant).

emojis in (8) and the excessive use of punctuation marks in (9), which provide cues to understand the emotionality of the messages. Although each of the 'very-'phrases may be ambiguous per se, the emotions implied in each message are however quite self-evident.

Furthermore, such interpretations were also confirmed by the offline participants, who provided their accounts as to why these phrases could be construed as such. All the participants said they had no problem understanding such uses as expressive of the posting users' emotional states, although one participant, ZY, found such use intentionally outlandish. Interestingly, another participant, CC, compared it to the typical emotional final particle in Chinese, which are particles carrying important affective and epistemic meanings and having a scope over the entire utterance (Jiang 2016). CC even reflected on his own experience of using VEVV in such a way.

> I just happened to use [VEVV] myself the other day, when I was chatting with my friend online. I just thought of (using) it... because um... the way I used "very erotic very violent" is not to express something as very erotic or very violent, but it's just um, a way to strengthen my tone, so that I can deliver something in a more impressive manner. (DF1/CC)

It is apparent that in practice CC consciously attributed to the use of EV an emotive speech act, and expected his audience to simply retrieve his emphatic or expressive purpose when construing such use. Similarly, other participants would also naturally deter a literal reading whenever they encounter such 'exaggerated' (DF1/ZY) and 'wuxiaxian' (without limitations, beyond moral bounds) (DF1/GY) use of these phrases online, and they agreed that such emotionally excessive phrases, such as VSVN or VEVV, were one of the 'typical practices on Chinese internet' (DF1/GY) to show personal feelings and engage readers.

Therefore, this use serves an important meta-function for the audience to momentarily suspend the literal construal, and go for the posting user's emotional and psychological state – hence a meta-utterance. Such a pragmatic inference points to an emotive purpose, instead of contributing a conceptual meaning to the message, which would be increasingly strengthened when common users keep on with the practice.

"It's just dismissing something in teasing" (DF1/PC)

When certain rhetorical effects, such as sarcasm, irony, or overstatement, are increasingly associated with the phrases in their spread, they begin to bear such stance-taking and evaluative functions that help the posting user present ideas and convey judgments. An important consequence is the emerging meta-function, with continued practice of such usages, of signaling or activating a shift in stance or perspective. Previous analysis has shown the metaphorical or ironic usages of VSVN to predicate something as wrong or stupid, often with a regretful overtone that is metonymically derived from its original apologetic scenario. With one step forward, this pragmatic force of signaling the posting user's stance of negation or ridicule may be generalized and highlighted as the major purpose in the sentence. When VSVN becomes increasingly attached to the preceding statement or description, such adversative or shifting stance is especially obvious, accentuating the negative truthfulness or likelihood of the content in the message.

For instance, the following example illustrates how the mocking and/or dismissive effect that is usually expressed by VSVN is projected onto the whole chunk of discourse. In (10), VSVN is used in a stand-alone way, i.e. it doesn't have a definite modifying relation with its linguistic surround and its logical subject is ambiguous. Consequently, the VSVN phrase here is more likely to be understood as revealing the posting user's attitude towards the previous content – moral measures without the rule of law are simply absurd or unacceptable, which in effect serves a somewhat adversative discourse function, i.e. marking the posting user's contrastive judgment of the likelihood or existence of the preceding information.

(10)Dangnian gaokao de shihou zhengzhi zhongdian shi fazhi, shiduonian guoqu le turan gaicheng hexie le. Hexie muqian yuedengyu huoxini... lian fazhi dou muyou gaolisuo, jiu xiang zhuyao kao daode yueshu, hensha hentianzhen, kai shenme wanxiao

'The key point for the politics test in the college entrance exam

I had was the rule of law, and it has been suddenly changed to harmony after a decade. Harmony approximately equals muffling things down... Even before the rule of law has been handled properly, moral measures are called for, very stupid very naïve, what a joke'

Many of the offline participants (CC, FC, PC, GY) concurred that the key to understanding such adversative function of VEVV is the common knowledge of the "typical grassroots[28] culture on Chinese internet" (DF1/GY) that is replete with "mutual teasing and self-teasing to dismiss something or express some negative or oppositional opinions" (PC). Therefore, the use of VEVV under such circumstances invokes an opposing and dismissive stance and judgment, instead of a qualification or statement, of the very message at issue. In other words, such usage, as meta-utterances, not only engages the audience in an attitudinal way by shifting the perspective of modifying a statement to taking a stance, but also prompts them to reflect on the discourse relations being expressed between the components in the very sentence.

"Just for the sake of attention" (DF1/PC)

Somewhat similar to the emotive function of the phrases, when they're uttered to express the posting user's emotional state at the start of a message, they not only declare the affective ambience of the message, but also topicalize the following information and attach a special weight to it. This function has been found in all the three phrases, but most frequently in VGVP, for instance:

(11)Henhao henqiangda wo ban huijia le zongshi zuo sushi zuikuai xiaoshi de yige... xiwang zai huilai de shihou wo nenggou jiejue diao yixie dongxi biande zhengchang yixie houhou
'Very good very powerful, I just moved back home, always being the first to disappear from the dormitory... hope when I'm back again, I can solve some problems and (things) become a bit normal, hoho'

---

28. The notion of 'grassroots' in a cultural sense, in contemporary Chinese society, mainly refers to the populist and low culture that is in contrast with the official and high culture.

The VGVP phrase in (11) doesn't convey any real information, and an 'emotive' function of its use would be an over-interpretation, nor does the abstracted or rhetorical meanings of VGVP – i.e. something generally laudable or ridiculed – can apply here, as the following information can hardly said to be laden with feelings. However, the use of VGVP does, or intends to, attract the audience's attention to the following information as something of importance to the posting user, and thus topicalizes 'moving back home' as the central message. Such usage can be somewhat compared with the discourse marker "well" in English whose interactional functions have developed into different frames in discourse progression, one of which is to introduce new information (Jucker 1997).

Interestingly, the topicalizing use of the phrases was easily identified by the participants, but they seemed to entertain different ideas, and produce different attitudes too, as to why the phrases can work like a topic-marker. For instance, some participants (ZY, FS, GY) argued that the phrases' ability to attract attention and topicalize the message lay in the fact that they were already attention-catching neologisms per se. In particular, ZY voiced quite vociferously his displeasure at such usage as "childish and clichéd", which would seem more nonsensical as the phrases became less circulated. By contrast, PC acknowledged some communicative merits in the function:

> It's quite commonly used in response or when you want to announce something in your posts, especially when you can't describe them very well. For example, if you want to post something you saw, and you want to say, "Wow, awesome!" In fact, such a remark is really meaningless, and it's very plain, with not much meaning. But when you say "very good very powerful", people immediately get you, and it's that kind of feeling you want to express. (DF1/PC)

Apparently, for PC, the potential of neologistic phrases such as VGVP to attract attention and mark topics lies not only in their ineffable yet strong emotive and expressive effects (as discussed previously) as well as the interactional frame, described by him as a sort of staged introductory speech act, but also, even more importantly, in the common communicative knowledge so that everyone 'immediately gets it'.

Trendy yet replaceable

While the above usages as meta-utterances to invoke, shift and frame new functions in discourse can be well observable in the datasets and easily identified by the participants, another recurring and significant aspect of using the phrases in online communication in all the interviews was the participants' almost unanimous tendency to understand the phrases' meta-functions with other CIV neologisms and to compare their degrees of perceived popularity. Therefore, such constant concerns and considerations may work at a higher level and influence the ways the meta-functions are being inferred.

Quite notably, when the participants reflected on the three phrases, all of them relied on other CIV neologisms to recall, compare and interpret the usages, especially their functions as meta-utterances. For instance, the VSVN phrase is "simply equivalent to 'tu yang tu senpo[29] '" (DF1/FS) when it was to invoke an adversative stance-taking function, and VEVV can have more or less the same function as shang bu qi (lit. 'can't stand the hurtfulness') (DF1/PC) in order to playfully accentuate personal feelings. According to my own daily monitoring as well, many new neologisms over the years carry very similar emotive and emphatic functions just like the three target phrases, including yeshi zui le (lit. 'intoxicated as well'), buyao buyao de (lit. 'need not, need not-ly'), mei shei le (lit. 'without anyone'), and have virtually replaced them quite rapidly. The following three examples illustrate how the three different neologisms can express the same, generalized emphatic feeling of shock or bewilderment at one's outfit that may be too exaggerated or inappropriate.

(12) Ni chuan cheng zheyang chumen, henhuang henbaoli a!
You're going out dressed like that, very erotic very violent!'

(13) Ni chuan cheng zheyang chumen, wo yeshi zui le!
'You're going out dressed like that, I'm intoxicated as well!'

(14) Ni chuan cheng zheyang chumen, jianzhi meishei le!

29. See Appendix I for detailed explanations of the several CIV items here.

'You're going out dressed like that, indeed without anyone!' Replaceability is also related with the popularity of the phrases perceived by the participants, which is also the most apparent reason given by all the participants as to why the three phrases were "not useful anymore" (DF1/ZY). The participants seemed to be quite aware of the "fatality" of all the neologisms just like that of the three phrases. For instance, as FC remarked,

> It's just like a gush of fad. Back then, when the [VSVN] video was leaked, it went viral like crazy, and so did the phrase. Just look how long it persisted. Phrases like these, usually after a period of time, they just become more… they become replaceable. It doesn't mean that they're not good or interesting. They're simply replaced. (DF1/FC)

Therefore, there has always been the factor of online popularity that motivates and validates the use and construal of the various meta-functions. In other words, without sufficient perceived online virality, the meta-functions of the phrases, which largely depend on the audience's reflexive interpretations and invocation of certain interactional frames, would simply be replaced or cease to be functional or effective.

3.6 Discussion

Based on the retrieved data in Sina Weibo during the period from August 2009 to June 2014, the use of the three CIV phrases (very good very powerful, very erotic very violent, very stupid very naïve) shows a somewhat steady yet slightly declining trend (see Figure 3.1). The available Weibo archive may have missed the most viral spread of these expressions, yet the large quantity of their occurrences suggests that their use was still noticeable and the spread still continued. It offers us a special opportunity to examine their meaning/function variation in actual use during their spread on social media.

As shown in Section 3.4, during their spread and use on Weibo for more than four years, the three phrases have developed an array of variations in semantic components, linguistic behaviors, pragmatic effects, and most importantly, metapragmatic functions. These new changes are also found to be coupled with their heightened subjectivity and increased communicative potential on social media, which in fact highlight the following three important aspects concerning the spread and variation of internet neologisms.

3.6.1 Elevated subjectivity in CIV neologism

As illustrated by the majority of the instances in the dataset, these three CIV phrases are readily used with manipulations and distortions of their meanings in one way or another, and would be easily recognized as such by the audience. The pragmatic manipulations easily activate and deliver personal emotional states and inner feelings onto the digital interface – emotions that are clearly felt without being articulated as such. For instance, the previous analysis has shown how VGVP is used ironically to vent one's frustration, how VEVV is jokingly used to highlight one's delight, and how VSVN is sarcastically cast on others as rebuttal.

More importantly, when the various rhetorical manipulations become increasingly practiced with the CIV phrases, such 'pragmatic subjectivity' (De Smet and Verstraete 2006) is most likely to become intrinsic and natural to the phrases' meaning package. This process is comparable to what many linguists have called 'semanticization', i.e. the process where external, speaker-related aspects become internal to a word's ideational meaning (cf. Traugott and Dasher 2002), in that certain emotions and sentiments have been somewhat internalized, via mechanisms like metaphorization or metonymization, into the phrases. Therefore, we've amply noted instances where the three phrases are used as generalized tropes for describing certain qualities and expressing certain emotions. However, it should be noted that the uptake of such generalized meanings and functions varies among different users, which is why some participants would find certain usages weird or exaggerated. Even so, it is nevertheless an ongoing and emerging process of how inferences of such generalized meanings come about, especially when some participants tried to understand such instances as 'just typical neologism usage'.

3.6.2 Pragmatic orientation and expanded use

My analysis has highlighted another major and important function of the neologisms in social media communication, with the help of all my offline participants, i.e. their easy and ready tendency and orientation to retrieve the pragmatic undertone and hidden purpose of the phrases, while treating them as 'meta-utterances' (Hübler and Bublitz 2007). Whenever these phrases are used, they redirect, or even preempt in some cases, our literal construal of the utterances, and make us reflect on other aspects of the very message, e.g. the posting user, the local context, or even the larger society, which can in fact be considered as different kinds of 'reflexive activities' (Lucy 1993) highlighted and prompted by the phrases.

As summarized in Section 3.4, such meta-functions can again serve four sub-types. First, they can re-orient users' focus from the utterance to the posting users' emotions and inner feelings and accentuate the very speech act as emphatic, expletive and emotive. Another sub-function of the phrases is to highlight the posting-user's stance-taking activity in the utterance and (sometimes) alter the perspective of the utterance. For instance, the negating and teasing function of VSVN, while serving as a predicate, can work to impose the posting user's evaluation and attitude on the narration of a certain event, and in consequence possibly modify the power relations between the posting and viewing users. As for the third sub-function, these phrases may call for the audience's attention and cast the limelight on something in the posts, where they function as topicalizers. The fourth sub-function is how they offer a brief reflexive moment for the audience to relate to a larger 'cyber-social' context, that is, how these phrases work as substitutes for previous neologisms and how they relate to each other in terms of their meanings and functions.

In sum, such 'meta-functions' of the phrases are multifarious and multi-dimensional in social media communication. They may not only work at inter-textual level, but also inter-personal level, or even beyond. In other words, the users' metapragmatic engagement with the phrases produce indexical meanings at multiple layers and scales, or in Silverstein's terms, orders of indexicality (2003), which certainly warrant further investigations with an expanded theoretical scope.

It should also be noted that the functions as meta-utterances are not mutually exclusive with other meanings and functions, such as rhetorical and stylistic choices. That is why these phrases may encourage or dictate users to fish for the reflexive aspects within and outside of a message, while still maintaining their linguistic function as a modifier or predicate. However, this also leads to the issue of unequal and unstable inferences among different users, as they may end up invoking different pragmatic effects and functions when contextualizing the same message in different ways. And whether such discrepant inferencing would result in clashes in communication remains as another important question.

3.6.3 Possible subjectification and pragmatic change?

With the above-mentioned functions being added to the meaning potential of the phrases, it may raise the very big question – would such variations lead to further linguistic change in the phrases or even to the larger language system, as the changes are well comparable to the increased subjectivity and strengthened pragmatic meanings in the formation of pragmatic markers or further permanent change?

To briefly reflect on this question, let's revisit the studies on grammatical or pragmatic change in light of Traugott's semanticization model. For Traugott, the key mechanism for semantic change of any linguistic item is the process of subjectification. To keep this process going and make the change routinized in the language, a certain subjectified meaning variation needs to gather enough frequency and saliency to be generally recognized and finally encoded as viable pragmatic inference for the very item[30]. In comparison, the meaning and function variations of the three neologisms do resemble such a process to some extent, in that heighted subjective and inter-subjective aspects are expanded onto the phrases in their actual use. However, as we have already discussed, the social media culture, i.e. playful, ironic,

30. In fact, Traugott's IITSC (Invited Inferencing Theory of Semantic Change) model is far more sophisticated and complex in explicating the mechanisms and processes of pragmatic inferencing in semantic change. However, as it is not the central task of the present chapter, I will not expand on it.

novel, etc. promotes a rather 'liberal' inference of the neologisms and offers much reflexive freedom for the users, therefore defying a steady formation of a certain pragmatic inference that can easily be routinized. More importantly, the short-livedness of most viral neologisms, which nearly amounts to nothing compared with the historical formation of a pragmatic or syntactic item (cf. Diewald, 2002), may also defy any kind of remarkable language change. On the other hand, we have indeed observed strong inter-textual tendencies of many neologisms, and their meaning and function variations may build onto each other in the long run and finally result in some fundamental changes in the language. This may be one aspect that warrants further studies.

3.7 Concluding remarks

Informed by the previous studies on the language varieties used on Chinese internet, I started my tentative exploration of three neologisms, mainly in terms of linguistic change. With pilot observations, I focused on the changing trajectories of the phrases' meaning/function along their spread on Chinese social media. Through detailed qualitative analysis, it is found that these phrases do exhibit meaning/function variations, in that ordinary users have to resort to a 'pragmatic reading', to various extents, in order to arrive at reasonable and smooth understanding. Such pragmatic readings were found to show certain regularities for all of the three phrases, analyzed as different meta-functions added to the phrases' meaning potential, which can be actualized through users' reflexive invocation in their daily communication.

However, such primary findings, as well as my exploratory process per se, raise more questions about this language phenomenon. First, the issue of pragmatic inferencing, which is in fact very unstable and fairly discrepant among different users. This problem not only questions if the increased pragmatic effects are recognized enough, but also prompts me to consider the roles of context and interaction in the processes of pragmatic inferencing. Besides, as many of the offline participants regarded the popularity or virality of the phrases as an important factor when they tried to produce certain pragmatic readings, it therefore begs the question if aspects and processes of the virality itself would have important bearings on such meaning/function variation of a phrase. Moreover, to go down that path a bit further, besides the perceived virality, would there be other motivations and mechanisms for CIV neologisms to undergo further change in meaning/function?

All these questions direct me to the viral spread of the neologisms as a holistic phenomenon, and also urge me to expand both my theoretical and methodological scopes for further exploration. And that's what I will do in the next chapter.

Chapter 4
Meaning change in virality and viral diffusion as meaning-making: The case of 'duang'

4.1 Introduction

The word 'duang' made its debut as a meme on Chinese social media in late February 2015 in a fan-made remixed video that parodies a shampoo commercial featuring the Kung Fu movie star Jackie Chan. 'Duang', a spontaneous sound originally used by Chan when he describes the sudden formation of his exuberant and firm hair, was articulately transcribed as such (i.e. in Latin alphabet) and repeatedly highlighted in the doctored video. The video, typically funny and parodic with nothing particularly new (considering the ridiculed commercial is almost a decade old), together with the non-existent word 'duang', immediately swept the entire Chinese social media in a flash. Like numerous internet memes throughout the years, 'duang's' noticeable virality lasted a few weeks before plunging rapidly towards near-abandonment. I was able to observe this entire process and closely recorded data of the meme's actual use along the spread, so I decided to examine its usages at various points, especially in terms of meaning change, and hoped to arrive at findings that may answer the questions that emerged in the previous chapter.

4.1.1 Overview of 'duang's' virality

On February 20, 2015, the second day of the national holiday of Chinese New Year, one user uploaded a self-made Guichu[31] video onto the 'bilibili' online community, a popular platform for manga and anime lovers in China. The video, titled '[Jackie Chan] My shampoo', received immediate accolades from viewers on bilibili. Within the first week after its release (according to the bilibili ranking report[32]), that is, by February 27, the original video had been viewed 2,570,948 times, favorited 67,620 times, and gathered 18,549 comments. The video is a parody of a well-known shampoo commercial[33] by Jackie Chan in 2004. The re-made video utilizes the background music from the song 'My skateboard shoes', another viral meme on Chinese social media since 2014, where Chan's original lines are crosscutted and remixed to the music, and the main part of the edited lyrics are as follows:

> When I first learned that I was about to do a shampoo commercial, I actually, actually refused it
> I told the director, I refused because I have in fact no hair
> The director told me that after the shooting, he would apply special (visual) effects, and the hair would be like very black very smooth
> After applying the special (visual) effects for one month, and then the hair DUANG~
> Later I also found out that they were, were fake, were in fact chemical ingredients
> Now I'm still every day applying the special (visual) effects, and after applying the effects,
> My hair DUANG~ DUANG~ DUANG~

Considering that bilibili is an online community particularly created for manga/anime lovers and the jokingly-termed 'deadly

31. 'Guichu', a concept borrowed from Japanese cultural products, originally means brutal, barbaric, or evil. In the Chinese ACGN community, this concept has been increasingly used to describe those mash-up videos that have repetitive, ridiculous or mind-tormenting patterns, according to Baidu Encyclopedia (accessed from https://baike.baidu.com/item/ on May 20, 2016).

32. Weekly BiliBili Ranking Report # 245, accessed from http://www.bilibili.com/video/ av2067567 on April 20, 2015.

33. In the original commercial, Jackie Chan's line "I actually refused it when the director asked me to do the commercial" had been well known among Chinese internet users, as the shampoo product was later exposed as containing noxious ingredients, and Jackie Chan was also mocked for his false advertising in the commercial and lack of social responsibility as a celebrity.

Otaku' circle[34], the influential spread of this new word depended on the more popular social media platform, Sina Weibo. Since February 24, 'duang' began to be increasingly used by notable (in terms of follower base) Weibo bloggers and were continuously reposted. This was also corroborated with the data I collected on Weibo with an outburst of the instances of 'duang' on that day.

According to the statistics provided by Weibo Data Center,[35] 'duang' had been among the 'hot words' in Weibo for more than a month (February 20 – March 29), where we can observe a rocketing increase of its use since February 24 (48,040 posts) to the peak on February 27 (1,395,086 instances), a subsequent sharp decrease till March 8 (405,001 instances), and steady yet slightly declining trend till the end of the month.

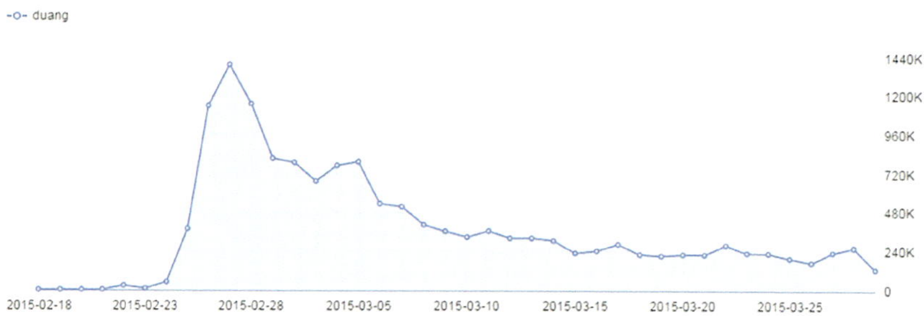

Figure 4.1 'Duang's' hotness over one month, generated by Weibo Data

Table 4.1 Day-by-day trend of 'duang' as 'hot word'

Date	Counts	Date	Counts	Date	Counts
02/20	32	02/27	1,395,086	03/06	535,250
02/21	647	02/28	1,152,376	03/07	516,416
02/22	25,464	03/01	814,173	03/08	405,001
02/23	7,549	03/02	789,022	03/09	365,135
02/24	48,040	03/03	674,029	–	–
02/25	379,131	03/04	771,068	03/28	260,195
02/26	1,140,755	03/05	793,670	03/29	126,540

34. Somewhat different from the word's Japanese origin that simply refers to the obsessive anime and manga fandom, or the ACGN community, the Chinese users have further derived meaning of this term, mainly based on the literal sense of the character in Otaku ('ta' in Japanese and 'zhai' in Chinese, literally meaning home or house) that especially highlights the social withdrawal and reclusiveness of the ACGN community.

35. Data generated by Weibo Index with the keyword 'duang', accessed from http:// data.weibo.com on April 20, 2015.

4.1.2 Preliminary observations

As a Chinese social media researcher/user, I was first intrigued by 'duang' in one introductory Weibo post on February 25, and watched the video on the 26th. At the same time, 'duang' became a phenomenal word, discussed on various media platforms[36] and entered in many online dictionaries, where this novel and idiosyncratic sound was said to simply denote 'adding/applying special effects' or 'representing the video My Shampoo'.[37] Besides, I was also attracted to the emerging derivations of the meme, most of which played with the novel word in various ways. Among others, the existing rage comic meme 'Jackie Chan WTF' (Figure 4.2a) was also appropriated to accommodate the new meme: where Jackie Chan shows a frustrated or confused look and utters 'duang~' (Figure 4.2b). With such vivid visual representation, this newly remixed meme must have given new meaning to the word 'duang' – probably 'mental confusion' or 'disorientedness'.

Figure 4.2a
The original Jackie Chan WTF meme[38]

Figure 4.2b
The re-made "duang" meme[39]

In the meantime, I also noticed the increasing use of 'duang' by ordinary Weibo users in their self-initiated posts (not sharing or

36. Several internationally renowned news agencies, including BBC (http://www.bbc.com/news/ blogs -trending-31689148), Foreign Policy (http://foreignpolicy.com/2015/02/27/the-word-that-broke-the-chinese-internet-duang), etc., have reported on the phenomenon of 'duang' and characterized it as a new character invented by the Chinese netizens.

37. Entry 'duang' on Baidu Baike, a Chinese online encyclopaedia, accessed from https://baike.baidu .com/item/duang on February 27, 2015.

38. Retrieved from http://knowyourmeme.com/photos/230191-wtf-is-this-shit on March 20, 2015.

39. Retrieved from https://baike.baidu.com/item/duang on March 10, 2015.

reposting) and comments, many of which exhibited a great variety of novel and interesting usages. I thus intend to investigate the question, which has also been asked by anyone who wants to analyze this new phenomenon[40], "Besides the 'stipulated' meaning of 'adding special effects' or reference to the viral remixed video, what is the actual meaning of 'duang' as used and understood in Chinese social media?"

With this general question in mind, I will keep following the digital flows of 'duang's' viral spread, making use of the opportunity and collected data to investigate the following four questions:

1) Has 'duang's' meaning changed in the diffusion? If so, how?
2) What are the relationships, if any, between (different stages of) virality and 'duang's' meaning variation?
3) What interpersonal and social processes are involved in 'duang's' viral spread and its meaning variation?
4) What are the meaning-making mechanisms and processes that sustain such virality on social media?

Therefore, to thoroughly examine each of the questions, the bulk of this chapter will be divided into four main parts.

4.1.3 The data

As the major venue for the viral spread of 'duang' is Sina Weibo, I mainly rely on its own search engine to elicit the target data. Based on the trend provided by Weibo's official statistics, I decided to especially focus on the first 17 days of the spread of 'duang' (February 20–March 8). I limited the searches to only 'original posts', excluding retweeted or shared posts, and confined the period of time to 21:00–22:59.[41] Table 4.2 summarizes the number of query results returned from the search engine, conducted on March 20, 2015. To make the analysis feasible, I randomly selected 50 posts from the total search results for each hour, except for the

40. For example, various news articles unanimously raise this question when reporting on the phenomenon.

41. Based on our observation of the query results on a 24-hour basis, the 21th and 22th hours of the day usually contain the most instances of 'duang'. And intuitively, it is also the time of a day when individual users are most active on Weibo.

first four days that had fewer than 50 instances within the two hours. In total, 1,392 Weibo original posts that contained instances of 'duang' were collected as the main dataset (DM2) for the meaning/function analysis. Besides, 215 messages that contained interactions, including comments, replies and retweets, were randomly selected from DM2 and compiled into the interactional dataset DC2 for detailed analysis.

Table 4.2 Original posts containing 'duang' during the two hours

Date	Total	21th hour	22th hour
2/20	7	1	1
2/21	47	6	1
2/22	615	22	29
2/23	438	19	13
2/24	655	86	109
2/25	16,804	1,561	2,417
2/26	18,080	5,417	5,892
2/27	19,266	9,569	10,497
2/28	20,286	8,455	9,307
3/01	21,552	6,625	7,174
3/02	23,044	5,339	6,107
3/03	24,912	5,142	5,967
3/04	27,091	4,706	5,033
3/05	29,911	5,155	5,357
3/06	32,812	4,307	4,849
3/07	36,475	4,222	4,578
3/08	40,807	3,668	4,379

4.2 'Duang's' meaning variation as a viral meme

4.2.1 Categorization and coding scheme

Besides the main dataset DM2, I have in fact closely recorded instances of 'duang' on February 26 and February 27 on a 24-hour basis and set up a pilot corpus in hopes of forming a general yet well-informed overview of different meanings and functions of 'duang'. The two researchers[42] then independently parsed through instances of the two days except for the ones that were selected into DM2 (21:00–22:59), and found that the meaning/function variations were distinct and dispersed enough to form separate categories. We then attempted a tentative taxonomy of the variations based on the detailed qualitative characterization of each category. In operation, we started from the beginning (0:00 AM) of February 26, and arrived at most of the meaningful variations within the first two hours on that day (which is why most of the illustrations below come from the first two hours). We continued such qualitative work on the rest of the instances, and made necessary complementation, adjustments and modifications on the categorization. A provisional list of categories was eventually arrived at, which was then tested by the two researchers separately on 100 instances (inter-rater reliability was above 0.85).

However, we did not regard this list as permanent criteria for distinguishing the meaning variations of later spread. Instead, this categorization was always open-ended and always open to modification when we conducted the analysis and coding on DM2 over a larger temporal span.

4.2.2 Tentative framework of meaning variation

In order to avoid essentializing meanings of 'duang', the framework of categorization is functionally based and fully grounded on data, which has three levels that reflect different aspects of using 'duang', thus capturing the necessary components and nuances of its contextual meanings and functions. In a nutshell, the examination of meaning variation is basically performed on each individual use of 'duang' in relation to the original viral artifact – the mash-up video.

Firstly, as a viral item that is complex and multimodal (visual, audio and textual), it is necessary to distinguish the practice that spreads the viral product in whole, which basically involves 'copying and imitation' (Shifman 2014) of the original viral product, from the practice that extracts '*duang*' and spreads it separately.

42. As explained in Chapter 2, I invited another researcher in the parsing and coding process in order to arrive at meaning/function categories that were as reliable as possible.

Such distinction has important bearings on how meanings and functions can be interpreted locally.

Therefore, as for the first level, which I call 'types of usage', an instance of '*duang*' is firstly identified as 1) *copying use*, entirely embedded in or in reference to the entire viral product, 2) *imitative use*, initiated by the individual user to imitate the usage in the original video, which may or may not be parodic, 3) *ideophonic use*, individually used, without reference to the original viral product, in a message as an ideophone of various effects, or 4) *transposed use*, with '*duang*' also being individually used, assuming other syntactic functions (such as adjective, verb, or noun) than an ideophone in a sentence, probably the most transformed usage type of all.

After being categorized as one of the four types of usage, an instance of '*duang*' is further specified in terms of its major communicative function realized by the very use. 'Function' here refers to the (different) characterizable act of communication that can be directly inferred by others, or in other words, the most possible function realized by a certain syntactic role of '*duang*'. Such functional categories can be regarded as the intermediate level of characterization, whereas the next level makes finer distinctions about the local meanings and functions of the specific use within a certain communicative act.

Table 4.3 Meaning/function categorization of 'duang'

Types of usage	Functional category	Meaning/function specifications
Copying use	1. Meme intro with video	1a. Single use 1b. With description
	2. Meme intro without video	2a. Single replica 2b. With description 2c. Metalinguistic use
	3. Hashtag	
Imitative use	4. Parodic use	
	5. Mimicking sounds	
Ideophonic use	6. Sound of fanfare	

Types of usage	Functional category	Meaning/function specifications	
Ideophonic use	7. Sound of effect	7a.	Special effect
		7b.	Action involvement
		7c.	Physical effect
		7d.	Mental effect
		7e.	Change
Transposed use	8.'Duang'-related state	8a.	Emotional
		8b.	Physical
	9. 'Duang'-related action	9a.	Effect-applying
		9b.	Sound-making
		9c.	Generic performative
	10. 'Duang'-related notion	10a.	Effect of any kind
		10b.	Special thing
	11. Substitutive use		

This three-level categorization especially suits the purpose of examining the diversity and range of 'duang's' meaning in use, avoiding a rigid assignment and classification of it. All the three levels are mostly concerned with the functional usages directly corresponding with different forms of 'duang' in a sentence, while leaving their specific meaning nuances undecided for now. The first two levels are comparatively more straightforward and apparent in their respective functions, on which the two researchers had few disagreements in data-coding, while the third level involves relatively more contextualized interpretation, thus leading to more negotiations between the two researchers to reach a shared understanding.

4.2.3 Illustration of the categories

I. Copying use

Copying is one of the two basic means of meme diffusion from person to person, as pointed out by Richard Dawkins (1976) when he first introduced the concept 'meme'. When 'duang' appeared on Weibo during the first days, it mostly spread through copying, inseparable from the mash-up video. It usually served the functions of introducing, passing along or sharing the viral product as a whole, and the word 'duang' would become the focus and the main piece of information in the entire post. As the following four examples illustrate, the copying function of 'duang' delivers the word as it is, usually embedded in the sharing of the mash-up video, as shown in (1) and (2), with (Category 1b) or without (Category 1a) the user's own (usually multimodal) remarks to describe the video, such as the direct copying of the lines that contain 'duang' in the video in (1), or the 'doge' emoticon[43] added to a simple copying of 'duang' in (2) to imply the user's somewhat bewildered amusement.

This copying use is more marked when the video is not attached in the post, where '*duang*' obviously stands out. Users can simply copy '*duang*', as in (3), or (chunks of) lines from the mash-up video, as in (4), while adding more personal remarks to the messages. Note that such simple copying can also fulfill the introductory function, which is what User B picks up in (3).

(1)Is the special effect on hair, is the chemical ingredient, is the hair with special effect, duang~~| [link to the video] (26.0.10)

(2) duang | [link to the video] (26.1.15)[44]

(3) A: duang~ (26.0.6)'

>[45] B: Is this again a new meme

> A: @B: haha yea

(4)duang~very black very shiny~special effects special effects (26.0.1)

The simple copying use of 'duang' may again work in another way, i.e. Category 2c – the 'metalinguistic use', as shown in (5). This use of 'duang' recognizes and acts on the virality of this meme, which can be regarded as a higher step than Category 2a. In such use, the posts would not only introduce and bring up the word 'duang', but refer to, elaborate on, and comment on the very virality. Such use is usually loaded with the users' perception, attitude and judgement of the meme as a phenomenon.

43. The 'doge' face, a dog staring with eyes rolled back, has become a tremendously popular emoticon on Chinese social media, whose function and meaning may defy a clear interpretation.

44. All the collected instances were labelled in the format (day. hour. assigned number).

45. The '>' symbol means that the message is a comment to the previous post or comment. Users can also reply to each other in the comments, which is indicated differently on different applications. For instance, on Weibo, replies within comments begin with the form '@ [the replied user]' (i.e. the replied user is tagged), while Baidu Tieba adds 'reply to [the replied user]' to the very comment.

(5)The entire Weibo is on the duang~duang, feels like my cellphone is shaking (26.1.37)

Besides the above-mentioned sub-types of ‘copying’, ‘duang’ has also amply occurred in hashtags. The various meta-functions of hashtags on social media, such as marking experiential topics, enacting interpersonal relationships, and organizing text (Zappavigna 2015), have been well noted, and the use of ‘duang’ is also in line with these previously identified functions.

(6)I’ve been waiting so long for today #duang# [46]
[attached with a photo with the caption ‘duang’ on it]

Although the use of hashtags may in some cases resemble that of a single use of ‘duang’, in other cases, such uses may involve much more complicating factors. Such as shown in (6), most of such hashtags are generated automatically by the use of the ‘duang’ photo sticker[47] that was released by Sina on February 26. Since such indirect use of hashtags and convenient application of the sticker may complicate, and not necessarily concern the meaning variation analysis, I have thus excluded such instances when building the dataset.

II. Imitative use

The other means of diffusion of memes is ‘imitation’, which has been elaborated on by Shifman (2014) in her treatment of the ‘meme group’. Among the various types of imitations, parody is especially prominent, showing the user’s personal stance and creativity. However, different from Shifman’s treatment of parodying the meme that is mainly audiovisual, ‘duang’ as a textual element can hardly be deconstructed in terms of Shifman’s triadic framework of memic imitation and deviation. The ‘parodic use’ (Category 4) in my categorization may refer to any imitations of the original lines in the video, to various extents, without limiting such imitation only

46. As ‘hashtagged’ is not counted as meaning/function variation, this post is not included in the dataset.

47. Sina Weibo and other social media providers have named such an overlay on pictures as ‘stickers’, usually captions, emojis, or animations that users can choose to place on their pictures, which may automatically generate hashtags, hyperlinks, etc. on the post.

to parody in the narrow sense, in which Shifman emphasizes the user's critical stance and mocking as key. For instance, as shown in (7), the user almost completely imitates the structure of the original lines but replaces the content with his own situation, i.e. finishing homework, thus a parodic use of this meme.

(7)When the homework was given, actually I refused it, let me tell you, I refused because I didn't know how to do it at all, and you told me, to add special effects to the homework, to copy others' answers duang~duang~duang~my homework, it's copied copied copied, it's the homework with special effects, and its special effects added on homework duang~ (26.0.20)

It should be reiterated that the 'parodic use' only involves the imitation of the mash-up video, and I distinguish such use from the imitation of the word 'duang' per se, which focuses on its onomatopoeic function to represent (a usually impactful) sound while describing things, as in the original video. Such use is categorized as 'mimicking sounds' (Category 5) under 'duang's' imitative usage.

(8)The big bell on the bronze gate~duang~~~(26.9.8)

Just as shown in the above example, such mimicry of 'duang' is observed to have covered a wide range of natural or artificial sounds, many of which don't necessarily echo the mimicked sounds, such as the sound of striking a bell, or any other similar sounds that have a striking or vociferous quality.

III. Ideophonic use

Besides mimicking real sounds, when the onomatopoeic meaning of 'duang' gets expanded and employed by the users to describe things, express feelings or even represent events, this memic word can be regarded as an ideophone, where uttering the word is not to make the sound, but is instead triggering a sensory imagery of various kinds (Dingemanse 2012). More importantly, when an onomatopoeic word performs in a specific linguistic context, or becomes 'ideophonic', it becomes highly iconic (Nuckolls 1996) and triggers cross-modal mappings of various sensory imageries onto the vocal imagery (Dingemanse 2012), a process involving complex mechanisms in cognition and pragmatics in its performance.

As said previously, the categorization doesn't wish to predetermine or fabricate meaning categories from the instances, but attempts to arrive at functional varieties from the ground up. With such efforts, the 'ideophonic use' can functionally fall into two major groups, i.e. 1) device of proclamation, and 2) representation of effects. The functional base of this division is 1) the respective frequencies of occurrence as well as 2) the saliency of functional differences of the two groups. In what follows, the two groups of 'ideophonic use' will be described in detail.

Category 6: Attention-grabbing

As an impactful sound, 'duang' is frequently observed to stand alone at the beginning or immediately follow the central message in a post, almost always in an emphatic manner. This usage may derive from the sound of fanfare, or in a more Chinese scenario, the sound of beating gongs[48] to attract attention, and thus indicating a sensory mapping of such vociferous quality onto the very Weibo message. Moreover, there is also a metonymic mapping at work, in that the fanfare would usually pertain to and thus trigger a conceptual association with the start of a ritual procedure by such a sound. For instance, in (9), the user yells 'duang' when he is announcing or exclaiming the imminent start of the new semester, and performs a metaphorical act of ceremonial announcement. In effect, this use functions as a topical marker, or topicalizer, to guide the audience's attention and highlights what should be the most relevant and central information in the message.

(9)New semester is coming, new semester is coming, new semester is coming duang~duang~duang~ (26.0.42)

This usage of 'duang' is readily comparable with 'ta-da' in English, a sound usually made before a dramatic entrance or

48. The gong is a traditional musical percussion instrument in China that is hit with a mallet, which is often used for ceremonial purposes.

announcement. However, it should be noted that there isn't such a fixed common ideophone in Mandarin Chinese for this usage[49], and the innovation of 'duang' may arguably complement such a functional hollow and is thus particularly appealing for the users.

Category 7: Showing effects

Apart from the 'attention-grabbing' function, the ideophonic qualities of 'duang' are also used to be metonymically associated with multimodal (audio, visual, kinetic, etc.) sensory scenarios that may possibly[50] have such a sound as an effect, and in so doing vivify such representation or narration of the very events in the messages. For conceptual and operational convenience, this group of ideophonic functions can be further divided into different themes, or experiential domains.

7a. Special effect. Firstly, such an effect may most directly derive from the imitative use of 'duang' in reference to the original mash-up video, which also has a parodic function. 'Duang' in this case works as the spontaneous sound from the special effect of any kind taking place. Although users would usually spell out 'special effect' in their messages, it is rather metaphorical and can refer to many different effects or transformations, either positive or negative. The following example is just one typical usage where 'special effect' refers to photo-editing techniques, one of the most common visual effects that ordinary users can master:

(10) This photo is added with special effect DUANG [attached with a photo] (26.0.39)

When 'duang' is further generalized, and used on more effects in our everyday life, most of which are not naturally associated with the sound, we then need to invoke further metonymical and metaphorical mappings in order to make sense of such usages. For

49. As Liu (2012) notes, the fanfare, or attention-grabbing function in Mandarin Chinese is usually realized by repeating a content word with optional modal particles, such as 'Kaishi-la! Kaishi-la!' (lit. 'Begin-la! Begin-la!') which may translate as 'Tada! Here it begins!', just as the former part of example (9) shows.

50. As 'duang' is a rather 'artificial' sound, which is not naturally produced by any action or object around us, the association of 'duang' with any scenarios is intentionally manufactured and equally possible.

instance:

(11)Playing this damn game drives me crazy and I can't stop, DUANG! [attached with a snapshot of the smartphone game] (26.2.39)

(12)The reason I look thin is because I have very little clothing! on! me! When I take them off, I'm still like duang~duang~duang~ (26.0.50)

(13)Can't fall asleep, feeling angry, what rude behavior, duang duang duang (26.1.50)

The above three examples show how effects of different sensory domains are expressed by 'duang'. To metonymically retrieve the event that 'produces' the sound 'duang', be it however unlikely, one may arrive at an action that is intense and/or vociferous. We can see there is a further conceptual abstraction at work, in that 'duang' removes from the direct, spontaneous sound of the action but signifies the intensity or engagement with the performance of the action. As shown in (11), 'duang' is used when the user describes how he plays the game: what can be implied from such use is the emphasis on the intensity of being involved with the very action (i.e. continuation of the playing), and hence the subcategory *7b. Action involvement.*

The spontaneous sound of 'duang' may be easily associated with the physical action of bumping or swelling. When it comes to the human body (one of the most common topics on social media), a quite notable usage in the collected data is to apply 'duang' to describe the chubbiness of certain body parts or the physical state of being fat/gaining weight[51], such as in (12). Although this subcategory *7c. Physical effect* predominantly pertains to this specific bodily feature, uses on various other features, such as flashiness, firmness, or even

51. An early instance was sighted as one influential blogger, a cartoonist named Xiao Mao, used 'duang' in this way (After lots of food during the Spring Festival, my face duang~~~~) on February 25, with an animated illustration of the swollen and flabby fat on his face. This post had been reposted 10,900 times and replied with 1,900 comments (retrieved from https://www.weibo .com/1134233684/C5VFiz84v on May 26, 2015), probably enacting a considerable spread of this meaning/function variation.

adroitness can be found, showing a rather wide range of this 'effect'. 'Duang' can also be used to signal the effect of one's feelings and psychological state, hence the subcategory *7d. Mental effect.* This usage may originally come from the mental reaction of watching the mash-up video, which is later extended to a number of impacted feelings and emotions, and 'duang' is usually used in a repetitive way. When 'duang' fulfills such expressive and emotive function, it redirects the audience's construal to retrieve the speaker's emotions, usually elated, shocked, or irritated ones, as well as their attitudes in the message. Most of the observable 'duang' effects are related with negative mental states and emotions, i.e. anxiety, frustration, such as (13).

7e. Change. Another major association of 'duang' as a trigger of effect is the sudden change of state, which also involves a temporal dimension. 'Duang' in such use can be readily likened with other existent ideophones in Mandarin Chinese,[52] which people use to describe a quick, impactful or unexpected change. Interestingly, in such cases, 'duang' would be (momentarily) packaged into such fixed 'ideophonic constructions' (e.g. Liu 2012; Akita and Usuki 2016) as 'duang de yisheng' ('in a sound of duang') and 'duang de yixia' ('in a stroke of duang'), which are very common constructions formed with ideophones that work as an adverbial phrase in a sentence and highlight the qualities of such changing effect. The underlined phrase in (14) illustrates such usage that also accentuates the rapidity and suddenness of the change, which may be functionally equivalent to 'in a jiffy' or 'with a bam' in English.

(14) Some of the things are destined. When you have met him, you won't meet another one. Those two can't coexist. They can't have both appeared in a sound of duang. (26.1.43)

As for such ideophonic use, not only has 'duang' expanded its functions to trigger various sensory imageries by virtue of metonymical and metaphorical mappings, but, as a result of such conceptual processes, the word has also been generalized of several of its recurrent or prominent features, which we'll see more clearly

52. There're in fact plenty of such ideophones across languages, such as 'bam' and 'boom' in English.

below. Moreover, it should be noted that dividing such ideophonic use into various experiential sub-categories is a highly interpretive task and may not be uniformly agreed upon among different social media users. Therefore, the main purpose of such sub-categorization is to examine the range of its functional versatility and variation, and may not be utilized for rigorous quantification.

IV. Transposed use

As the above examples show, 'duang' as an 'ideophone' exhibits syntactic independence and tends to occur only at clause edges (Dingemanse 2012), but there are also plenty of instances in the collected data where 'duang' occupies a central place in a clause, i.e. it assumes a syntactic role in the sentence that is normally enacted by a content word, hence the 'transposed' use. The possibility of such 'transposition' lies in 1) the fact that Chinese shows a considerable flexibility in terms of word classes and there're no grammatical inflections to mark them (Schachter and Shopen 2007), the practice of which is a common rhetorical device and means of linguistic creativity (Zhang 2007), and 2) that the generalized or abstracted effects of 'duang' as discussed above make the very sound well conceivable as a mood, an act, or an object, and thus readily projectable.

Category 8. 'Duang'-related state

This category is in fact a metaphorical extension of the various 'duang'-related effects discussed above, projected onto a 'tangible' state of some sort, thus syntactically realized as a predicate or predicative clause, which can be mainly conceptualized as 8a. Emotional state and 8b. Physical state.

8a. Emotional or psychological state

(15)With no down jacket on me, I feel I'm like totally duang 
feeling explosively cold (26.11.25)

When 'duang' is used as a predicate, such as in (15), it's most likely to express the user's intense feelings that are caused by something. Although it's difficult to pin down the exact meaning of 'feeling totally duang' in the example, its surrounding information, as well as the crying emoticon, contributes to a probable inference of such a mental state as feeling sad, unpleasant and miserable from the coldness. Besides such negative state related with the frustrated and confused effects, the instances where 'duang' predicates a positive state are not infrequent. In either case, such mental states are usually expressed in the fixed construction as shown in (16).

(16)

Original	*zhengge*	*ren*	*dou duang le*
Gloss[53]	whole	person	all duang LE
Translation	be like totally duang		

8b. Physical state

With the potential to be associated with various vibrant and intense effects (as discussed above), 'duang' has been observed in more cases to predicate a physical state of comparable effects. For example, in (17), the phrase "duang! duang! duang!" is used to emphatically predicate the state of the hair after fixing, probably lush and beautiful.

(17)Looks like the hair in the pictures really needs some fixing, which makes me even less fond of taking pictures...... How I wish I can do the special effects of Uncle Jackie!! So that my hair can then be duang! duang! duang! (26.1.19)

The most frequently observed 'duang' of this usage would adopt the clause ii in (16) as shown above, and interestingly, such repetitive predicative clause would usually convey a sense of positive, solid and well-formed quality, quite unlike when 'duang' is used to predicate a mental state. This may be probably due to the convergence between the phrase "duang duang de" (cf. clause ii) with an established colloquial idiom 'gang gang de' which means 'in a good, solid way', and may thus be consolidated with its predication of positivity.

The generalized and abstracted qualities of 'duang' can then

53. Gloss is provided when necessary linguistic aspects are at issue.

again be actualized as, i.e. further metonymized onto, something concrete, such as Category 9 'Duang'-related action or Category 10 'Duang'-related notion. As this practice indeed involves complex conceptual work, it does require considerable cognitive efforts to process, which is also confirmed by the participants in the offline interviews. Therefore, such usages are much less sighted in the dataset, but there're still some noteworthy instances.

(18)Hair looks too thin, I also want to duang it. (26.1.3)

(19)Many friends recently began to watch Indian 50-cent-worth [low quality] Duang Duang films, I'm a little confused and overwhelmed... always feel that the Indian Duang makes me distracted... (27.1.20)

The whole idea of 'special effect', derived from the mash-up video and consolidated by way of various parodic and imitative practices, has become the most identifiable quality of the meme, and naturally the most 'ready' component to be freely and creatively applied. In implementation, 'duang' becomes the action of 9a Applying a special effect, or effects of any kind, usually in a positive way, just as shown in (18) where 'duanging' the hair could be understood as fixing the hair and making it look good. Similarly, when 'duang' is improvised by the users to refer to a specific object, other than the metalinguistic reference of the meme as discussed in Category 2c, it may either be 10a – the concept of special effects – or effect in any sense. For example, the instance of 'duang' in (19) simply refers to the visual effects or filming techniques.

(20)The alarm clock is duanging (26.5.49)

Action that makes a sound, i.e. Category 9b, such as hitting a drum, ringing a bell, knocking on something, etc., is the most natural instantiation of 'duang' as a verb, which is also quite transparent in meaning and less effortful for users to interpret, as illustrated by (20). There are also actions that are less typical of the 'duang' sound (or even seemingly quite irrelevant) but are still represented by 'duang'. For instance,

(21)My recording in PaPa [a voice remix app] sounds nice, but I feared I would duang~ so I didn't post it (26.0.18)

(22)I figure that I'm quite a nice person!  never quarrel nor suck up to anyone  even if I don't have much duang, why isn't anyone interested in me  (26.0.17)

In such rare cases, the use of 'duang' becomes so vague that it defies any characterization. Therefore, 'duang' simply works as <u>*9c Generic performative*</u> or <u>*10b Special object*</u> whose contextual meanings can only be figured out by users that are (potentially) involved in the interaction. For instance, in (21), based on the information surrounding 'duang', we may infer that the user is afraid to look stupid or be laughed at for his voice recording. In this case, 'duang' can be construed as a generic verb to mean 'fail' or 'snap'. In (22) the uptake of 'duang' is even more hampered by the meaning ambiguity, which we may only vaguely understand as something that may be special, remarkable, mind-blowing, etc. However, such vagueness still doesn't quite hinder the understanding of the entire message.

Category 11. Substitutive use of 'duang'

Substitution is an important means of linguistic creativity on the internet (Zhang 2007), and so is the case of 'duang'. For example, since the very early stage of the spread, some users already started to replace words in lines of songs with 'duang' as their own humorous way to participate in the virality (see the discussion in Section 4.5.1 for an example). Generally, this substitutive use has been employed in ways that common users are able to figure out without much difficulty, usually by replacing one character of a well-established idiom or expression. For example,

(23a) (26.6.2)

Original	*Yao*	*bei*	*ziji chun*	*Duang*	*le*	*2333*[54]
Gloss	Would	PASSIVE	self stupid	Duang	LE-particle	[laugh]

54. '2333' (with infinite repetition of 3) is a way to represent laughter on the Chinese internet, which is originated from the MOP.com community.

Translation My stupidity would make me Duang, lol

(23b)

Original	chun ku le	/	chun si le
Gloss	stupid cry LE	/	stupid die LE
Translation	extremely stupid		

As for (23a), the user works on a common resultative construction in Chinese: V + R, where V causes/brings about the result or effect of R. In colloquial Chinese, the R component of this compound construction is frequently realized with the word 'die' or 'cry' (23b), meaning the quality or action causes one nearly to die or cry. In this case, such substitutive use of 'duang' doesn't make sense per se but intends for the emphatic meaning afforded by the 'V+die/cry' expression.

4.2.4 Meaning variations

The results show the occurrences of each of the characterized categories of 'duang's' meaning and function in use over the initial 17 days (February 20–March 8) on Sina Weibo. All the data were then further normalized by representing the occurrences of a certain category as portions of the total instances on the same day, i.e. a certain category's ratio (No.Categoryn/No.Total). Such resultant data were used to compare the variability of 'duang' and the change of various categories over time. Note that there were fewer than 100 occurrences of 'duang' during the targeted hours in the first four days, therefore their ratios may not be statistically comparable with those from the fifth day on[55].

With regard to the trends and developments of the virality introduced in Section 4.1, the way 'duang' is actually used also shows comparable variations and fluctuations. On the whole, the viral increase of 'duang' is coupled with the expansion of the various meaning/function types, both in terms of diversity and volume. This indicates that 'duang's' viral spread is at the same time accompanied with its memic development (cf. Shifman 2014).

While the outburst and diffusion of internet memes usually

55. This fact, however, doesn't essentially hamper my later discussion of their distributional character at each stage, and the trends of variability mainly since the pre-viral peak (the fifth day onwards).

relies on mass copying and imitation (Weng et al. 2012), and appears so to the public impression, a closer look into a meme's actual functions and performances throughout its virality may reveal a vastly different picture. In the case of '*duang*', a great range of diversity has been found beneath the seemingly imitative and similarly interjectional uses. In a grounded manner, 11 major distinct categories of usage were gradually gathered and identified that share similar linguistic behaviors and functional types, which can of course be further differentiated for more specifications in meaning and function. These major meaning/function categories inform us of how a textual meme such as '*duang*' undergoes virality on Chinese social media.

The issue of parody and derivative

While all sorts of adoption of the meme during its virality are copying and imitation (cf. Dawkins 1976) in nature, parody is an important user-generated form that gives rise to mutation, deviation, and creativity, the power source for memic diffusion and variation. In the case of 'duang', parody-like practices also play a crucial role. Here I'd like to employ a broader view on parody, not just the imitation that conveys skeptical (Jenkins 2006) or critical (Shifman 2014) stance about the original product, but, as defined by Dentith (2000), a cultural practice of imitation that may serve "to attack, satirise, or just playfully to refer to elements of the contemporary world" (2000: 6).

'Duang' is a peculiar case. As the original mash-up video per se is a parody of the shampoo commercial, quite patent of irony, mockery and playfulness, the copying and imitation of such a complex and multimodal product takes various forms. The viral engagement with this meme has, to various extents, transformed, condensed, or reduced the video into textual representations on social media. I use 'parody' to refer to the posts that imitate the original video in terms of its form, including the structure of the lines and the interjection of 'duang!' as culmination. The 'duang' parodies are found to be more playful than critical or cynical as they're mostly self-referential expressions. On the other hand, I use "derivative" to refer to the isolated use of 'duang', extracted from the surrounding original lines, which in fact constitutes most of the meme's presence on social media. It should be noted that such differentiation is mostly instrumental for separating and discussing the different functional types with conceptual ease, while it should never be denied that parody is an essential element permeating all kinds of social media creativity and involvement (cf. Varis and Blommaert 2015).

Mechanisms

Besides the imitative parodies of the meme as one of the main viral practices and their influence as an important component in the meaning potential of 'duang', my focus is on the further meaning development of the neologism, usually used in an isolated form, i.e. the Categories 6-11. As shown in the detailed descriptions above, the categories (and sub-categories) differ from and relate to each other in conceptually characterizable ways. Compared with the subjectification process for a Chinese internet buzzword (or, a textual meme) in which it develops more meaning components and pragmatic potential discussed in the previous chapter, 'duang' shares such a changing path yet shows its uniqueness as an onomatopoeic word (or ideophone).

Apart from the meaning component derived directly from imitating the original meme, various ideophonic qualities have come about metonymically from a great variety of scenarios, which again conceptually embeds the effects from the respective scenarios into the instances of 'duang'. Such a process may be the primary mechanism of how the functions in Categories 6 (Sound of fanfare) and 7 (Sound of various effects) have come into shape. The meaning expansion also involves metaphorical transfer, which is in fact the more important mechanism here. As observed in the collected instances, the various onomatopoeic qualities of 'duang', involved in a wide range of related scenarios, have been extracted, distilled and generalized, and then metaphorically mapped from the audible domain to other domains in a rather diversified manner. Metonymy and metaphor also work collectively where a rather complex chain of conceptual mappings are needed in order to make sense of a certain instance of 'duang', such as most of the usages in Categories 9-10 as described above.

Moreover, as demonstrated in the previous chapter, the more subjectification a neologism undergoes, the more discourse functions it may develop. 'Duang' is also a telling example in this regard, partly due to its ideophonic nature. The representational use of 'duang' for various effects (e.g. Category 7) very easily emerge as a means to fulfill the expressive and emotive functions, prompting the audience to retrieve the speaker's emotional and psychological state as related to the very message. Also, 'duang' is used to guide the audience's attention to a topic or mark the speaker-user's emphasis or intention. Such discourse-marking function is most prominent in the usage of Category 6. A less tangible function of 'duang' is to implicitly shift between the narrative and expressive perspectives in discourse, which juxtaposes or confuses the speaker-user's stance with the text. Interestingly, such expansion and variation of functions may also correspond more or less with the diachronic evolvement of functions of ideophones in a language, the so-called 'implicational hierarchy' (Dingemanse 2012: 663).

sound < movement < visual patterns < other sensory perceptions < inner feelings and cognitive states

What differs is the rate of change, where the meme of 'duang' has undergone this development in a rather rapid and condensed manner – in other words, in virality.

Range of variation

Although the above categorization does indeed reflect extensive variation in use, it's intentionally function-based. This is partly due to the emerging and forming nature of 'duang's' various meaning components, and most importantly, my focus on the meaning potential instead of rigid or codified meaning categories. However, even without a formal estimation of its range of meaning variation, we can already see how diversely 'duang' is used, at least from the following aspects.

1) As demonstrated by 'duang's' versatility in Category 7 to describe things, the perceptual scenarios which 'duang' is related to and

metonymically represents vary to a great extent, ranging from everyday objects to social practice and to conceptual ideas. In a word, anything that makes an impact with sound has the potential to be associated with 'duang'.

2) The complex conceptual mapping of 'duang' has in effect abstracted and generalized a wide range of distinct yet related qualities and characteristics, which also become spreadable and effectual for further metaphorization. This is especially notable for usages in Categories 8-10 (i.e. 'duang'-related state, action and notion). Take the Subcategory 8b (Physical state) for instance. The so-named 'physical state' can refer to a solid state of movement, an intense state of action, an obese state of the body, a satisfactory state of behavior, a flashy state of effect, and many more, which are all distilled and actualized as qualities of 'duang'.
3) The categorization on the whole also reflects the considerable range of functional variation, covering many experiential and perceptual domains. In terms of formal features, 'duang' can assume various syntactic roles, either as an independent clause or as a clausal element.

To sum up, in this section, I have done a comprehensive analysis of what new forms of meaning/function have developed in 'duang's' viral spread. In what follows, I will expand the exploration by taking into consideration the diffusional and processual dimension of virality to see how the meaning/function variation proceeded in reality.

4.3 'Duang's' variations throughout virality

As all the collected instances of 'duang' are coded, the frequency of each functional category in the dataset is therefore available, and so are their respective ratios throughout the target period. Such simple and straightforward statistics may help us form a larger picture and see how different varieties perform differently, in relation to the temporal characteristics of virality.

In what follows, I will compare the meaning/function variations of the meme with the different stages of virality, trying to account for each viral stage with the features and characteristics of certain functional categories that are most prominent during that very stage, and to discuss the implications of such connections. With such efforts, I'll also attempt to discuss the differential distributions of the various categories, focusing especially on their features and aspects that are prone and sensitive to the virality, and how they would contribute to 'duang's' meaning and function in the long run, based on their exhibited trends.

4.3.1 Initial period (February 20-23)

During the first four days, which can also be regarded the pre-viral period, the majority of the retrieved Weibo posts engaged in sharing and introducing the original remixed video and the meme. Such functions were achieved mainly through Categories 1 and 2, i.e. making known or passing along the mash-up video with or without further comments. At this point, the video was the memic object to be spread, and had not fully developed what Shifman calls "egalitarian memes" which are the various individual derivatives of the "founding meme" (2014: 58), as the counts of Category 1 (passing along the video as it is) far outstrip those of Category 2 (abstracting certain elements from the video).

As shown in Figure 4.3, which displays the most-occurred categories (1-2, 6, 7) during the first stages of 'duang's' virality, the first two categories counted for the absolute majority of the posts even in the first five days, but rapidly declined as the meme increases its virality in a dramatic way, with only a small rise (less than 20% of the entire posts, and third in place in occurrence) during the viral peak, implying that the greater momentum for 'duang's' viral spread, at least partly, lies in the productive development of the 'egalitarian memes' instead of the sole passing-on of the founding one per se.

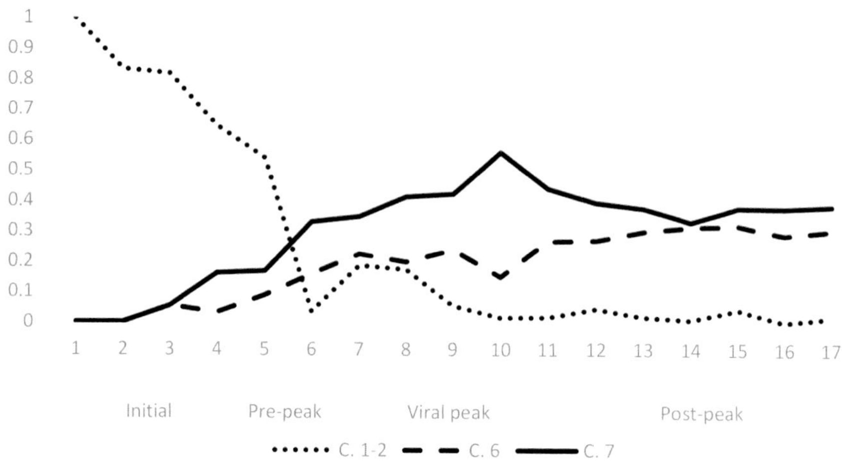

Figure 4.3 Trends of Categories 1-2, 6 and 7

4.3.2 Pre-peak period (February 24-25)

This stage was most marked with a dramatic surge of Category 3 Parodic imitations (Figure 4.4), ranking second in place in occurrence of all categories (only below Categories 1-2 on February 24 and slightly below Category 7 on February 25), implying that at this stage imitating and parodying the mash-up video became one of the most employed means for Weibo users to engage with the meme. After this point, although Category 3 was still repeatedly opted for by the users throughout the virality, it generally stayed at a rather limited ratio of occurrence overall. In fact, imitating and parodying the meme resembles a double-edged sword, which on the one hand highlights the creator's playfulness and ingeniousness as well as his/her community affiliation (which will be discussed in detail later), while on the other demands too much effort or threatens to turn into cliché as people's curiosity rapidly wears out.

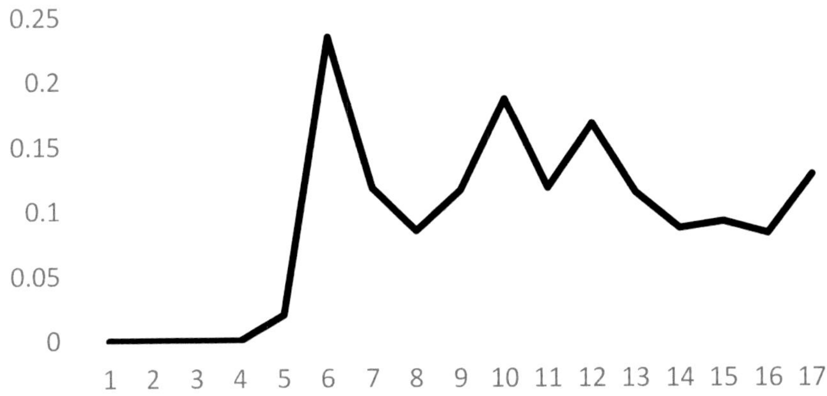

Figure 4.4 Trends of Category 3

Besides, this stage also witnessed the increase of all the other categories from non-existent to their fair shares. Take February 25 for instance. Each category seemed to display a relatively substantial number of occurrences on that day, as shown in Appendix III. It's also notable that some rather highly transformational categories (see Figure 4.5, and pay attention to the nodes 5-6 on the temporal axis), such as Category 8 'Duang' as representations of various states, show some considerable presence. On the surface, it may seem that even during such early period, the meaning variations have already been well developed and widely distributed on Weibo; however, a closer, ethnographic examination delving into such seemingly 'full-blown' distribution may reveal a different picture of this memic practice on Weibo.

4.3.3 Viral peak (February 26-March 1)

During this stage, the categories employed for introducing (Categories 1-2) and rehashing (Category 3) the meme dimmed down rapidly, giving way to the usages of 'duang' that were more isolated in form and expanded in meaning, inducing more active and interactive communication with the meme. It doesn't mean that 'duang' had been fully popularized or that few users engaged in introducing it at this stage, but overall, significantly more users began to make use of and play with the meme in their personalized ways, instead of merely treating it like a trendy artifact to pass along.

All categories are sighted during this stage, all with sizable distributions. Specifically, the sub-types of Category 7 (see Figure 4.3), that of uttering 'duang' with a variety of transformed meanings and functions, occupy approximately half of all the instances, with the highest proportion (0.56) on March 1. The absolute predominance of such functions continued, though with a slightly declining tendency, throughout the period when 'duang' remained the hottest meme on Chinese social media. One possible reason behind this preference for Category 7 may be that after the virality permeated the Weibo public, more and more users participated, actively or passively, into the virality, mostly in a casual and less original way to engage with the meme. Unlike categories that require considerable creative engagement and cognitive effort, the various functions developed in Category 7 help users be playful and expressive of their personalized feelings, attitudes, or opinions, while displaying their participation into the most recent internet trend, which apparently appeals more to the public at large.

4.3.4 Post-peak period (March 2 onwards)

During this stage, the various usages of 'duang' seemed to display a more 'normalized' proportion in terms of their distributions. Functional types of 'duang' that involve more cognitive or communicative transfers from the original usage tended to maintain a limited proportion. For instance, the uses of 'duang' to simulate one's physical or emotional state (Category 8) and to imply certain actions or activities (Category 9), which certainly require more interpretive and mapping efforts, stayed around 10% of all variations during this stage. As for the more transformational uses of 'duang' to substitute certain things or certain words in a phrase (Category 10 and 11), only a tiny proportion is sighted sporadically.

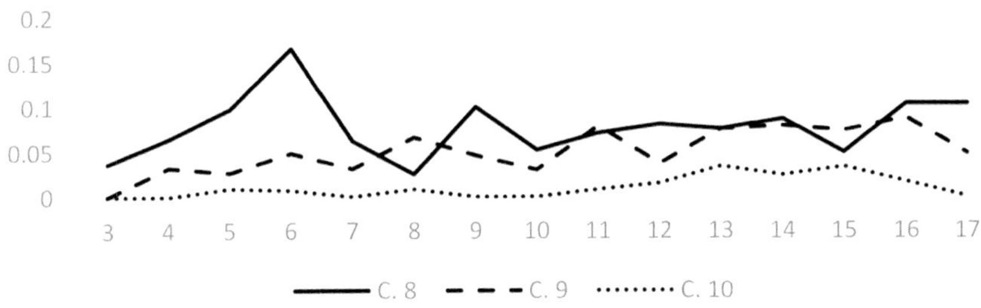

Figure 4.5 Trends of Categories 8, 9 and 10

It is noticeable that Category 6 (see Figure 4.3), the effect of fanfare for attention-grabbing, showed a somewhat steadily increasing trend throughout the virality and occurred as the most frequent usage from here onwards. This category stays close enough to the original meaning, and involve the direct and natural interpretation of 'duang', which may arguably withstand people's aversion to the meme's excessive spread better than the other categories.[56] More importantly, this usage is especially fit for online marketing or promotions, and has been observed frequently to be utilized with such purposes.

Category 5 Mimicking sounds, imitates the original use of 'duang', and the statistics (see Appendix III) show no patent increase of this particular use throughout the virality (on certain days, there are no occurrences at all), possibly implying that the viral spread relies more on 'sensational' and 'noteworthy' uses of the meme, and hence the more transformed usages. However, its noticeable peak on March 5 was apparently occasioned by the Lantern Festival, when most of the instances were used to describe the sound of explosion (of fireworks) – a common and natural sound of 'duang', which again demonstrates that such use, though prompted by the virality, can only take up a limited proportion.

4.3.5 Distributions and conventionalization

56. In offline interviews, many participants have pointed out that their perception of the 'excesses' of 'duang' lies in their observations that other users would seemingly aimlessly use 'duang' in many unnatural ways – or in my analysis the much transformational and expanded meaning/function variations, which the participants have evaluated rather negatively.

It is quite apparent that 'duang's' meaning variation and pragmatic strengthening already started taking place from the very early stage of the viral spread. This may pertain closely to the previous observation that the use of 'duang' would immediately form alliance with and draw heavily from the intertextuality of the ever-growing and ever-updating repository of internet vernacular items, which may have undergone similar patterns of propagation as the ones I have presented in the above analysis.

To recapitulate, 'duang's' initial stage was characterized by the predominance of Categories 1-2, to introduce and broadcast the newly invented meme, with all the other meaning/function variations only beginning to develop. Its pre-peak spread immediately witnessed a drastic plummet of Categories 1-2, and rather interestingly, all the functional types had their fair shares in the distribution, with the activities of parody being the most prominent (Category 3). Such an equilibrium of meaning/function varieties quickly shifted in the stage of the viral peak, with Categories 6 and 7 significantly outperforming the others, both in quantity and in their own variability, and the introductory functions of Categories 1-2 also took a noticeable comeback. After the viral peak, all the other categories began to give way to Categories 6 and 7, which absolutely dominated the usages of 'duang' in the spread.

Such distributional differences across different stages have revealed important features and aspects of the newly-developed meanings and functions, which emerged in considerable numbers and faded away rapidly as the perceived virality fluctuated. Simplistically put, the more virally 'duang' spreads, the more momentum and liberty there is for all its meaning/function variants. Yet some categories are more sensitive to, and reliant on, the perceived virality, such as the more expanded and transformed variants of Categorie 8-10 that especially flourished around the viral peak and quickly lost their luster and gave way to the less transformed and more resilient usages of Categories 5-7. However, these differences may also raise another important issue, that of the major (groups of) participants who actually practiced with certain functional types of the meme and whose collective activities helped constitute the distributional composition of 'duang's' meaning/

function variations at a certain viral stage. Of course, this issue urges an expansion of the data as well as a more ethnographically oriented perspective.

Although Category 6 & 7 turned out to be the most used categories, and can thus be considered the main meaning/function usages of 'duang' in actual, and overall, use, it is still hard to claim that they're in fact 'conventionalized', in the traditional sense. First of all, representativeness and statistical rigor are not the central concern of the present study, and to substantiate such a claim obviously requires data on a much larger scale. More importantly, as the general social media is composed of a plethora of niched 'subaltern publics' (Zhang 2016), a certain usage of 'duang' may bring about unequal 'joint saliences' and result in discrepant 'frequencies of use', which are both necessary conditions for the conventionalization of linguistic features over time (Croft 2000), across the different sub-publics. Therefore, the very notion of conventionalization of a viral item's usages needs to be reconceptualized as the sum total of various 'sub-conventionalizing' events and situations, which would require a much expanded analytical scope.

4.3.6 More observations about post-viral 'duang'

Beyond the target duration of virality and the collected data, 'duang' has been visible even till the end of 2015. I also carried out a somewhat casual longitudinal following of 10 popular Weibo accounts and an even more casual monitoring of random users in my own daily social media practice, in terms of their use of 'duang', from the viral period to the end of 2015. On a brief note, three interesting phenomena were noticed about the 'post-viral' use of 'duang'.

1) '*Duang*' is by far more used by public or institutional accounts than personal bloggers, mostly employed for promotion, advertising, fame-gathering, and other marketing purposes; and correspondingly
2) Category 6 (Attention-grabbing) becomes the single most utilized meaning variant, while the other expanded and transformed usages quickly decay away, and
3) Category *5* (Mimicking sounds) and Category *11* (Substitutive

use) seem to be among the variants that "die hard", which would sporadically reemerge to represent or replace a certain sound or quality in a playful or unexpected way.

There're also some unique cases where 'duang' has persisted with frequent presence in certain communities. For one thing, on bilibili, the 'duang' has been officially[57] enshrined in the Guichu[58] wall of fame (or, Guichu Quanmingxing, lit. 'Guichu all-stars'), and continuously re-appears in new mash-up videos. Also, one pet owner account that I've followed has used 'duang' to refer to her cat's belly fat, and in the blogger-follower interactions, many followers have continued to use 'duang' to tease and play.

On the whole, this section has attempted to map the wide range of meaning/function variations of 'duang' to the progression of its viral spread, and has revealed 1) the distributional patterns of the various functional types at different stages of the virality, and 2) the fluctuations and discrepancies among the variations. However, my tentative efforts to account for such differences have only led me to the more intricate nature of the social media space as composed of myriad sub-communities, which my 'post-viral' observations have shed special light on. Therefore, I'll continue the investigation with such a focus in what follows.

4.4 Communities in virality

The numbers and statistics, no matter how rigorously obtained and measured, may still inform us of only limited aspects and factors in the process of meaning variation. To move further into the viral flows of 'duang', I will shift my focus to the participants, especially on their collective activities and informational flows that contribute to the variations of the meme. Such viral flows in huge volumes have also been found to be structurally diversified, and social media statisticians have used the notion of 'community' (e.g., Papadopoulos et al. 2012; Quinn et al. 2016) to describe and analyze such structural diversity, which

57. Accessed from http://www.bilibili.com/ranking on December 10, 2015.

58. See footnote 31.

is technically defined as "groups of highly connected nodes[59] ... such that a node has a high number of edges within the group and few outside" (Quinn et al. 2016: 212).

This notion of 'community' to visualize and conceptualize the information flows can also be used to characterize the wide range of online formations where users discursively carry out community practices and construct their 'memberships' of various forms (Angouri 2015). In other words, the online flows are, from another perspective, actualized by the community practices of a group of social media users, formed around the transmission of a certain information artefact (say, an idea, a piece of news, a cultural product, a common hobby, etc.). And such online communities can be either extremely loose and light, such as the virality-induced collective participation in the spreading of a single meme on Weibo, or well-organized and closely-knit, such as the online rheumatoid arthritis forum (Sanderson and Angouri 2014) which can be analyzed as an online 'community of practice' (Wenger 1998).

On a side note, I regard Weibo as a general online public, as it encompasses the most publicly accessible resources on the internet and provides the most accessible venue for public engagement which are needed for the formation of a public space online. I also employ the notion of 'subaltern public' or 'subaltern community' (Zhang 2016) as opposed to the 'overall' or 'general' public, in order to study the multiple niched, interest-based, and relatively enclosed online communities, which Squires (2002) has called 'counterpublics' due to their variance with the general public and mainstream culture.

The diffusion of 'duang' has been characterized, simplistically though, as the outward spread from the ACGN community to the most general online public, according to various social media analyses (e.g. Zhang 2015; Huang 2016). The success of the virality, in terms of the meme's remarkable diffusion and influence over the entire social media, judging from the mechanism of 'structural diversity' of viral cascades (Shakarian et al. 2015; Goel et al. 2016), consists in the meme's tremendous diversity of participating nodes which further involve a large variety

59. Any online network of information diffusion can be visually depicted using a graph, which is made up of "a set of nodes connected by a set of edges" (Quinn et al. 2016: 211).

of qualitatively distinct sub-communities. It has in fact been corroborated in various analyses (e.g. Huang 2015) that influential Weibo bloggers from different circles and communities, many of whom are probably motivated by the profitable 'trendjacking'[60] opportunities in social media marketing, played pivotal roles. In what follows, I will locate such diverging nodes at various points of the virality, focusing especially on the participants' discursive activities pertaining to their community affiliations of various forms.

The ethnographic investigation will employ constant profile-checking so as to identify or approximate a user's community affiliations, usually by virtue of the user's own descriptions as well as his/her subscriptions, in the assumption that the more ACGN-related bloggers a user subscribes to, the more s/he identifies with the ACGN sub-community.

4.4.1 In-group diffusion

The original mash-up video was first uploaded to the Guichu section on Bilibili, which is usually nicknamed as B site by the users. This particular form of fan-made products appeals not only to Guichu practitioners and enthusiasts, but is appreciated by the general audience on Bilibili as well[61], and can thus be regarded a generally ACGN cultural artifact. The first days (the 'pre-viral' stage) witnessed the video's increasing, yet to a limited extent, dissemination not only on Bilibili, but also on Weibo, a more general social media platform, by linking to or embedding the original video hosted on Bilibili. Given the limited number of posts, which involved quite limited reposting, as well as the homogeneity in the users of all the posts (who were obvious ACGN members, judging from their profiles), the video and the meme were only being circulated within the ACGN fans, who had probably already been connected to each other on Weibo.

60. 'Trendjacking' (trend-hijacking) is coined to broadly refer to the strategy by institutions or individuals to mesh a product with an emerging trend, by inserting their branded messages into social media conversations around trending topics (Lambrecht et al. 2015).

61. Of the top 30 most viewed videos on bilibili by the end of 2015, nine of them were Guichu mash-up videos, and 'duang' ranked the highest in the Guichu section (Bilibili Tieba, accessed from http://tieba.baidu.com/p/4168533120 on December 20, 2015).

Although the posts are not many in number, they involve intense interactions among the users, which may function to be one of their routine practices as ACGN practitioners. While many of such interactions were enthusiastic mutual exchanges of appreciation and amusement of the new meme among the practitioners, a good number of the posts were the users' creative and playful transmission of the meme to other ACGN sub-communities than the Guichu circle. For instance, users who were also affiliated with the gaming circle, such as the sub-community of *League of Legends* (e.g. 23.21.01), shared the parodies of the meme they had created in their gaming activities on Weibo, to the amusement of their fellow members (based on the passionate and amused exchanges between them in their Weibo interactions). They were also aware of the meme's exclusive spread within the ACGN community at that very point, as one user wondered if other people would be able to understand the meme as a laughable gag in his Weibo post (23.22.01).

Interestingly, the posts sharing the video displayed a small peak (615 original posts in total) on February 22 while somewhat cooled down on the next day (438 posts). It's possible that such in-group spread within the ACGN community reached a sort of threshold or saturation on the third day. Without more users bringing the meme forward to the larger population, it would probably have ceased to be contagious. Further spread could only happen once the meme spills over to the wider social media through other 'heterogeneous' nodes.

4.4.2 'Boundary-crossing' nodes

A spate of interesting interactions happened on February 24, a crucial day for the meme's virality when it was apparently spread beyond the ACGN community on Weibo. Two types of interaction are especially helpful to the 'boundary-crossing' of the meme, and they both involve users of multiple 'memberships' on Weibo.

Meme-enhancers (big-Vs)

While the mash-up video per se had been successful on Bilibili, it did require some retouching and repackaging when it was introduced to a wider audience, and it did take some committed and laborious users[62] to achieve this task. One popular Bilibili uploader, Chongzhi Xiansen (Mr. Worm), who also has a considerable number of followers on Weibo (his Weibo page is connected with his page on Bilibili), made a successful promotion of this meme by turning the mash-up video into a parody, both introducing the meme and inventing a novel Chinese character to represent the sound 'duang'. It is said to be the first of its kind (Huang 2015), but actually not, based on my collected data where there had already been a number of parodies among Bilibili users before him. Then again, it may be one of the earliest influential parodies of 'duang' for the Weibo public.

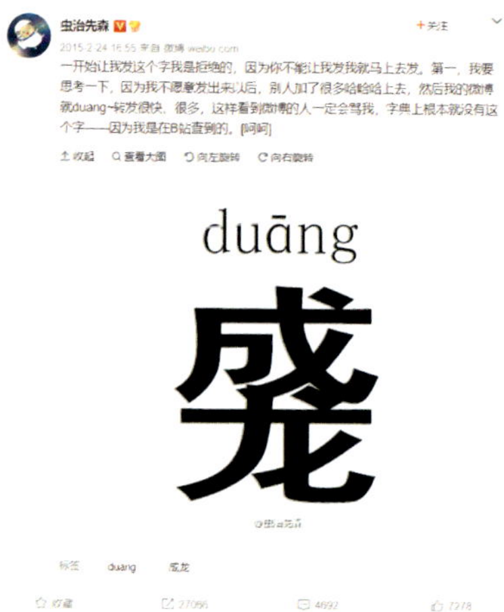

Figure4.6 Screenshot of the parodic post with the invented character

Translation:

I actually refused it when I was first asked to post this character, because I wouldn't simply post it immediately when you asked me to. First, I'll have to think about it, because I don't want it when others add a lot of hahaha to my post [and repost it], and then my Weibo would duang~ have very fast very many reposts, and then people who read my post would surely scold me, because there's no such character in the dictionary – that's because I saw it on the B site. 🙂

Tags: duang, Jackie Chan reposts: 27066; comments: 4692; likes: 7278

62. It should be pointed out that the 'Attention Economy' of social media has spawned myriad 'entrepreneurial' users, under the epithet of 'grassroots media practitioners', who grasp every opportunity to follow, utilize or even create viral trends in order to increase their presence, namely, to gain more clicks.

This parody by Mr. Worm was probably targeted at the general audience on Weibo, without providing or even referring to the mash-up video, and succeeded (judging from the number of reposts and comments) in informing of and popularizing the basic elements of the meme – i.e. the structure of the lines, the ironical tone, the uttering of 'duang', the entire novelty of the meme (represented by a weird and funny forged character), as well as the articulate association with the ACGN culture (the highlighting of Bilibili in the lines).

Besides this effortful re-invention by Mr. Worm, the sharing and highlighting of the original video by verified and influential Weibo bloggers (so-called big-Vs) also contributed greatly to the meme's 'cross-community' fame. On the same day, two reposts of the original video were considered critical for the diffusion surge, i.e. by Musi and Shituzi (Huang 2015). These two bloggers were both famous online manga artists by profession, i.e. their popularity lies in the center of the ACGN community, and are both visible personalities on Weibo with a huge fan base (1.3 million and 6.5 million followers respectively), i.e. their influence may well extend to the general social media public.

Meme-spreaders (active users)

Besides the influential bloggers, who would usually initiate 'top-down' popularization of the meme, common users, who were affiliated with the ACGN community at this stage, also contributed significantly to 'duang's' viral success, which was most noticeable in their collective playful practices.

One of such contributive instances was in fact related to Jaycee Chan (son of Jackie Chan), who happened to post a 'hair-related' message on February 24 after a long absence,[63] and immediately attracted a huge amount of comments and reposting, many of which involved the meme of 'duang' and were mostly made by the ACGN fans.[64] Considering the early stage, the unexpected predominance

63. It was the first Weibo post since Jaycee was released from prison for using illegal drugs, which was sensational national news in 2014. Jaycee remarked in the post that the hair-cutting meant a 'new' (punned with 'sincere' in Chinese) start.

64. For instance, all the top 5 most liked comments with 'duang' to the post were made by Weibo users who were either affiliated with the ACGN industry or subscribers of various ACGN accounts.

of 'duang' in the comments excited vehement inquiries and discussions of the meme. Also, the 'pile-up' reposts (see Figure 4.7) they made, which are reposts that consist of a chain of previous reposters' comments, not only helped disseminate the meme, but could also be regarded as early memic play and exhibition to the wider audience on Weibo.

Figure 4.7 A pile-up repost (February 25, 25.12.04)

The above pile-up reposts consist of reposted comments by ten users: each one's comment was triggered by and piled on to the previous user's with bits and pieces from the mash-up video, forming a chain of collective play with, and a noteworthy showcase of, this 'unripe' meme, which was still in the initial stage of being spread to the public and only began to whet the curiosity of 'outsiders' and 'onlookers' outside of the ACGN community.

Diffusion in other communities

While the above two types of interaction by 'cross-boundary' users continued to flare up curiosity and enthusiasm about the meme, most of the original posts on February 25 were in fact qualitatively different from the previous day, in that the most reposted and commented posts[65] with the meme were in fact made by non-ACGN

65. Four most reposted posts have been identified by Huang (2015) on February 25, namely the ones by Jiaoshou Yixiaoxing (40k reposts), by Sidao (180k reposts), by Wode Pengyou Shige DaiB (30k reposts), and by Wangnima (10k reposts). All of these Weibo accounts can be considered duanzishou, i.e. 'professional joke writers', micro-marketing or promotional accounts.

members. Unlike the ACGN in-group members who would simply imitate and parody the meme in playful ways, these bloggers would usually engage with plenty of metalinguistic comments, among which were the bloggers' bewilderment with the meme as well as their great effort to obtain knowledge about the meme. In fact, this kind of anxiety and urge to stay in the know also exists among ordinary users, which has led to interesting interactions on Weibo.

I. In-group collaboration

On February 25, the account 'Jiangnan Jingge' (lit., 'Jiangnan Police Brother') who was verified as a police officer in the city of Xuancheng (who might also publish posts on behalf of the police bureau he worked in) and had 240,000 followers, posted a message at 21:47 (note the time of posting, apparently off-work time).

Excerpt 4.1

JJ: Duang是个什么鬼? 为什么我满屏都是duang~duang~duang	JJ: What the heck is duang? Why is my screen full of duang~duang~duang
>A: 其实第一次听说要给警哥解释我是拒绝的，因为你你不能让我解释，我就马上去解释，第一我要试一下，因为我不愿意解释完了以后再加一些特技上去了，解释"duang"的一下，很全很亮	>A: When I first heard that Jingge wanted us to explain to him, I actually refused it, because I can't just explain it to him immediately when he wants it, first, I have to try it myself, because I don't want special effects after I explain it, so my explanation becomes very comprehensive, very shiny, in a 'duang'
>B: 关注B站鬼畜区我是好人不谢	>B: Check out the Guichu section on B site, I'm a good person, you're welcome
>C: 哈哈哈哈哈一看你就不逛B站	>C: hahahahaha I bet you don't visit B site
>D: 比如拿警棍敲你的脑袋 duang	>D: Just like hitting your head with a baton, duang

>E: 不上B站不是好条子，duang~	>E: Those who don't visit B site are no good cops, duang~
>F: duang!!duang!!duang!!江南赤手空拳揍鳄鱼的声音	>F: duang!!duang!!duang!!The sound of Jiangnan beating a crocodile barehanded

This post attracted 225 comments and 345 likes (at the time of collection), nearly doubling the usual amount of interactions this account had before and after this post, implying that this post was indeed quite prominent. The six selected comments were among the most liked ones randomly displayed by Weibo.

As a police officer who is probably responsible for publicizing the official work of the police bureau, Jiangnan Jingge has constructed an easy-going and light-hearted persona on Weibo, and would employ various trendy topics to cater to his wide range of followers, who are certainly not only interested in police and administrative matters. So when he asks about the newest meme on Weibo, his followers react quickly and passionately, and of course, playfully. The majority of the comments introduce and play with the meme in question, and this stretch of interaction can be considered a paragon example of the diversified forms of memic participation and engagement that has been repeatedly observed on Chinese social media.

On the whole, such a small community, or rather 'affinity space' (Gee 2004), where fellow users can freely and collectively play with the meme is usually the best venue for its popularity enhancement and further propagation. In particular, the parodied reworking by User A on the original lines makes meticulous and humorous adaptations to the very immediate context of the post; the two comments by User D and F then create the very local and concrete meanings of 'duang', specifically inferable among the community members, i.e. common or previously mentioned practice of the police officer. While these three instances localize the meme to the community, another major part of the comments are dedicated to the connection with the B site community, as in the comments of Users B, C and E, all of which are amusingly delivered and associated with the police officer himself. Most probably, these users are also members of the ACGN community, and their comments helped the meme and the Bilibili culture to be spread in the new location, the effect of which would be illuminating for the other 'uninitiated' users on this occasion of interaction.

II. Individual obsession with the meme

The urge to keep up with the viral trend was also patent at individual level, and a good deal of the posts passionately recorded the events where the knowledge of 'duang' was passed on to the users themselves. In so doing, these users themselves voluntarily became 'contagious hosts' of the meme and go on to 'spread the knowledge'. For example,

Excerpt 4.2 (Feb. 25, 21:09)

A: 哈哈哈哈哈哈哈！！！是头发的特技！！！很黑很亮！！DUANG~~~~DUANG~~~~~哈哈哈哈啊哈！！是化学的成分！假的假的！！DUANG~~~~DUANG~~~~~#一秒钟就跟上了时代的步伐，多亏我有妹子#	A: hahahahahahaha!!! It's the special effect of hair!!! Very black very shiny!! DUANG~~~~DUANG~~~~ hahahaha aha!! They're chemical ingredients! Fake, it's fake!! DUANG~~~~DUANG~~~~ #catch up with the times in a second, thanks to my gals#
>B: duangduangduang!	>B: duangduangduang!
>C: 跟我学英语，特技：duang 😂😂😂😂	>C: Learn English with me, special effect: duang😂😂😂😂
>A: @B: 哈哈哈哈笑死我了哈哈哈哈	>A: @B: hahahaha I'm laughing to death hahahaha
>A: @C: duangduang哈哈哈哈	>A: @C: duangduang hahahaha
>D: 一开始我是拒绝的	>D: I refused it in the first place
>A: @D: duang~duang~	>A: @D: duang~duang~

In this interaction, User A posts about her excited discovery of the latest meme, showcasing the meme in her own way. The post is saturated with heightened emotion, with repetitions of laughter and exclamation marks, which not only highlights the meme as extremely funny but also expresses her own unreserved approval. More interestingly, the hashtag, which usually serves various metalinguistic functions in tweets (Zappavigna 2015), clearly states her source of knowing the meme (probably her 'gals' from the ACGN community) and articulates her attitude towards it as 'catching up with the times', i.e., engagement with the meme is trendy and desirable. To respond to such ebullient discovery, three friends of hers comment with their knowledge of the meme as well as their agreement to its merits. Note the ways the interactants express their agreement and approval, including simple articulation and repetition of 'duang' (User B), highlighting the meme's notable element (User C), and some sort of minimal parody (User D).

III. Negotiation in the crossings

In many noticeable cases, the diffusion of 'duang' into other conspicuously distinct communities would be carried out in a way that tried to negotiate or redefine the meme. For instance, the blogger Guan Xin Sam, who is verified as a professional translator and has posted profusely and influentially on intercultural and language matters and anecdotes, also engaged with the meme when it began to show virality on Weibo.

Excerpt 4.3 (February 25, 21:34)

GXS:说说duang…不知你读有没有读出一股冬阴功味儿来…那么连着读duang taa nai duang jai试试，泰国味儿出来没…又比如暹罗却克里王朝拉玛一世，本名就是Thong Duang…中国的二胡传到暹罗后，演变成了当地乐器Saw Duang…即便是在美国的街上看到牌子上有什么Duang或duang什么的，基本也是遇到泰国菜馆了…	GXSam: Let's talk about duang… don't know if you sense some tom yum flavor in it… then try to read duang taa nai duang jai, does it taste like Thai food then… For another example, the name of Rama I, the king of Siam, is Thong Duang… the Chinese instrument Erhu, when it was first introduced to Siam, evolved into the local instrument called Saw Duang… If you see something Duang or duang something written on a billboard in the US, basically you must be running into a Thai restaurant…
>A: 抓住一切段子扫盲的管大👍	>A: The Guan Da [Chief Guan] who takes advantage of every meme to eliminate illiteracy (to educate people)👍

>B: duang是指成龙霸王洗发水的广告台词，有人把他重新剪辑恶搞，具体大家去搜索......我是来科普得	>B: duang is in the lines of Jackie Chan's commercial of the Bawang shampoo, someone has made a parody by re-editing it, just go and search it for details... I'm here to give you the knowledge
>C: ดวงตาในดวงใจ	> C: ดวงตาในดวงใจ [Thai, transliterates as 'duang dtaa nai duang jai']
>D: 哈哈哈哈哈哈第一哥和Yardthip妹子的心中之眼😱😱😱莫名穿越感😂	>D: hahahahahahah Bro First and Sister Yardthip from the Eyes in the Heart 😱😱😱 Unexplained feeling of time travel😂
>E: 我刚想吐槽来着。。不是一个人。。🐶	>E: I was just gonna mock it.. [I'm/You're] not alone.. 🐶

The above comments were also selected from the most liked ones to the post. Other than merely promulgating and utilizing the meme, this excerpt shows how a relatively more specialized community – in this case, a blogger-centered circle of cultural and historical anecdotes – engages with and positions itself in the virality.

Firstly, this post demonstrates how '*duang*' (or the viral status of '*duang*', to be more specific) gets decontextualized from its original scenario, used mostly symbolically to topicalize the true message conveyed in the post. In other words, GXS utilizes the meme, taking advantage of its increasing salience on social media, without being involved in the actual use of '*duang*', an ambivalent position of his (dis)engagement with the meme. In so doing, the blogger displays not only his keen awareness of online virality, but also, more emphatically, the knowledge of different cultural phenomena and artefacts. Such metalinguistic strategy enables him to move from the '*banal*' online popular culture and sensations to the more refined elite culture and a more international perspective, which is partly echoed with User E's attitude, who "was just gonna mock [the meme]".

The effect of the post was also multifarious on his followers, who displayed notable heterogeneity among themselves. A good proportion of the comments was about Q&As concerning the meme, which is illustrated by the comment by User B, explaining the meme in detail. Hence, the blogger's participation into the meme, no matter how detached or critical, in effect encouraged its propagation among his followers and increased its spreadability across communities. On the other hand, we can also notice 'community-specific' practice around this 'imported' meme. For instance, User C translates the series of foreign words in the original post back into a string of Thai characters, a code that can only be figured out and made sense of by those who possess the specific knowledge of the Thai language; User D follows up on the reference to a Thai TV show mentioned in the original post and contributes further personal attitudes (unexplained feeling of discrepancy, which may in fact imply her own identification with and appreciation of the blogger's 'whimsical' association). This latter group of followers, which may only amount to a small proportion, was however quite vocal and visible, highlighting the in-group characteristics and identities of the very circle against the backdrop of the general virality.

4.4.3 Out-spread of the meme

Since the virality of 'duang' got boosted on February 26, the number of posts to share, comment on or play with the meme increased exponentially from the previous days, and so did the participatory nodes that channeled the viral cascades for the wider public on the entire Weibo. As recorded by many data analysts (cf. Huang 2015) as well as Sina Weibo's own data platform, the diversity of the participatory nodes, i.e. accounts who posted or reposted posts containing this meme, also rocketed tremendously, with many 'big-V' bloggers with large follower bases as active players in this game.[66] However, this meme may have at this point lost its exclusionary value and attractiveness to members of the ACGN community. For instance,

66. One way to demonstrate the diversity of nodes: during the viral peak period, 47 of the top 50 media accounts on Weibo of different industries and reader-orientations (evaluated by Sina Weibo with consideration of their influence and number of followers) engaged with this meme in one way or another.

Excerpt 4.4 (February 26; 21:44)

A: 首页从昨天开始已被duang~梗霸占！求你们，别duang了，我脑子要爆了（是脑袋的特技~）😱放过成龙大哥吧😱	A: The front page has been occupied by the duang~ meme since yesterday! I'm begging you, don't duang any more, my brain is going to explode (it's the special effect of brain~) 😱 let go of Bro Jackie Chan😱
>B: 恭喜成龙加入全鬼畜明星套餐😂	>B: Congrats to Jackie Chan on entering the all-star Guichu menu (casting) 😂
>A: @B: 😂😂我的天	>A: @B: 😂😂My gosh
>B: @A: 于葛炮，元首，金坷垃三人组一样齐名	>B: @A: (He) is equally famous as Gepao, the führer, and the Jinkela Trio[67]
>A @B: 感觉成龙大哥更厉害一些	>A: @B: Feels like that Bro Jackie is more powerful
>B @A: 我是坷垃粉😂😂	>B: @A: I'm a Jinkela fan😂😂
>A: @B: 我什么也不是🤔我是正常人	>A: @B: I'm nothing🤔I'm a normal person

Based on the rather community-specific knowledge (such as Gepao, the führer, and the Jinkela Trio) in their interaction, both of the users are likely to be members of the Guichu sub-community. As a proper insider of this meme, User A has soon become fed up with it, articulates her negative attitude and urges the halt of the meme. This stretch of interaction may reveal the other side of the cross-community diffusion of memes, i.e. a community-specific meme may very soon lose its luster for the core practitioners once it well transcends the boundaries of the community, and becomes overwhelmingly general or popular, i.e. not special any more.

Arguably, the diffusion of a meme within a certain community can only last for a limited period of time before it's replaced by newer memes or the members' curiosity wears out. It may be the uneven diffusions of the meme within different communities and individuals that make the overall diffusion continue for an extended duration. As for the case of '*duang*', whose virality rapidly decayed in

67. Gepao (or Canon Ge) refers to the voice-actor Ge Ping, the führer refers to the Hitler character in the German film Der Untergang, and the Jinkela Trio refers to the three foreign characters in a commercial of a fertilizer product called Jinkela. These characters have become frequent sources in Guichu mash-up videos.

less than one month (as indicated in Section 4.1), it is then again the remarkable general popularity, virtually permeating all corners on Weibo, that became its own fatality. After that, the meme of '*duang*' stopped being a viral item in the ACGN community and became preserved in stock, which was to be utilized in future mash-up products only in a sporadic and creative way, just as User B notes as "entering the all-star Guichu" hall of fame.

To sum up, I have in this section outlined the major diffusions of 'duang' on Weibo from the perspective of community activities, formed around the use and spread of the very meme. Such interactions within, between and beyond the various sub-communities constitute, over the general public of Weibo, a variety of qualitatively different cascades of the meme's viral spread, where users of different community affiliations contribute, hence differentially, to the contingent meanings and functions of 'duang' as forms of their community practice. Therefore, such community-related practices and interactions are one of the most crucial contexts to make sense of any instance of 'duang's' meaning variation in virality, which I will expand on in the following section.

4.5 Virality of 'duang' as meaning-making processes

To zoom in onto each instance of 'duang', they are always 'entextualized' in that they are always being recontextualized into a new text, as well as 'resemiotized' in that it always involves (a complex set of) diverse semiotics for meaning-making (cf. Leppänen et al. 2014). In fact, such entextualization and resemiotization is not merely about alteration and creativity; the other side of the process is its relationship with the 'original', i.e. its recognizability, and its relationship with other entextualized and resemiotized 'derivatives', i.e. its intertextuality.

In what follows, I will demonstrate how the various kinds of meaning transformation of '*duang*' take place within the tension between such creativity and recognizability, during which process norms are being negotiated, new indexical meanings are emerging, and reflexive identities of the users are performed. But let's first look at the salient form of meaning negotiation that is directly related with the virality of '*duang*', which I call the virally-induced use.

4.5.1 Collective negotiation of meaning

While the isolated use of 'duang', without linking to the video or offering contextual information, has been mainly categorized as introductory and participatory in an original post (self-initiated), there're in fact a great deal more of such use in interactions or reposts, such as the repetitive and exclamatory uses in (Excerpt 4.5). A very noticeable venue for this use on Weibo is the comments section of many public accounts, where the virality is prominently 'staged' and such use clearly performs functions closely related with, or rather afforded by, the virality per se. Let's first take a look at an example – the comments to a post made by the official account of Shouji Taobao (Mobile Taobao, the largest e-commercial platform in China). Despite the fact that the blogger (SJTB) is an institutional account which doesn't attract much interpersonal interaction from its followers,[68] the utilization and parodying of the meme (Excerpt 4.5), however sloppy it may seem, in fact manages to gather a large wave of comments, mostly in the form of repetitions of 'duang'.

Excerpt 4.5 (February 26; 9:59)

A: #身已动，年未远# 当我第一次知道要发好玩的微博的时候，其实我是，是拒绝的，我跟老板讲，我拒绝，因为其实我根本不搞笑，老板跟我讲，发完看效果，转发很好，很多，很牛X，发了一天之后呢，转发duang~~~~就上去了！就像加了特技！！duang~~duang~duang~	A: #Departure is taken, festivity is still around# When I was first told to post something fun, in fact I, I refused it, I told Boss, I refused it, because I'm not fun at all, Boss told me just to wait for the effect after posting, [it turned out that] the reposts were very good, very many, very d*** awesome, after posting for a day, the reposts duang~~~~ increased! Just like adding special effects!! duang~~duang~duang~

Figure 4.8 shows the first 10 comments to this post (in a reverse order). Notice the unanimity in form of (at least) the first 7 comments – nothing but (repetitions of) 'duang'. Arguably, such use corresponds both to the blogger's parodic exclamation of

68. Compared with individual marketing accounts who usually post (made-up) jokes and sensational anecdotes, institutional accounts often get much fewer comments and reposting from their followers, especially when the posts are perceived as advertising.

'duang~~duang~duang~' in particular, and in general to the current viral trend of this very meme. Moreover, these comments are also posted in a collective manner, i.e. the scope of such] repetition extends to the previous comments, as if the commenters are aligning with each other while engaging in such performance. Also note the '+1'[69] in comment 5. It's a typical practice of displaying the commenter's agreement (sometimes, simply co-presence) with other users, just as how 'firsting'[70] more or less works, which is a means of 'phatic communion' (Varis and Blommaert 2015) by which people try to stay involved in the virality. Apparently, these users are not commenting on the original post or each other's comments with any informative content, yet they are indeed interacting positively with each other, and with the larger social media audience as well, by virtue of such phatic activity, in order to be part of this current memic culture. In so doing, the repetitions of 'duang', which resembles uttering greetings to each other if this phatic communion is vividly envisioned, may instantaneously be enhanced with such a function and may engender derivatives for further personalized usages and effects.

Figure 4.8 First 10 comments to this post (in a reverse order)

69. '+1' is one of the ways that Chinese internet users show agreement or affirmation as to other comments. It functions similarly as 'ditto', 'I second that' or 'same here' in English-language forums.

70. According to Varis and Blommaert (2015: 35), 'firsting' refers to the users' preoccupation to be the first to comment on or 'like' an update on social media.

There is another form of 'duang' that is less frequent in original posts but abounds in interactions where the virality is intentionally 'staged', i.e. the substitutive use of 'duang' to integrate with any existing phrases, expressions, lines, scripts, etc., in a playful way. This activity is usually formed around a post (usually by influential bloggers) with a vivid and humorous example of such substitution, which serves as a temporary and carnivaleque 'affinity space' (Gee 2004) for other users to reply and repost with their own contributions. For instance, on February 26,[71] one influential blogger Huanmie Yaoseng (lit. 'disillusioned monster-monk'), who is verified as a popular author and playwright of various TV shows, published a funny post by substituting characters in a well-known Chinese poem with 'duang', which immediately set off a huge wave of imitations of substituted poems. Those participatory comments that were found funny and creative by other users were massively 'liked' (and thus prioritized in the displayed comments) and reposted, expanding the diffusion of such carnivalesque substitutive wordplay even further.

Obviously, these above two forms of '*duang*', the repetitive and substitutive, are both occasioned by the meme's escalating virality here. Although the users seem to differ in degree as to how they involve themselves with the meme and how much effort they put into it, their 'agency and activity types' (Varis and Blommaert 2015) share a similar nature in terms of engagement on social media, that is, they're both convenient and easy ways for the users to play with the meme, make use of it in a minimal way, and temporarily relate with each other with very little effort – both phatic means to maintain relationships of conviviality. Moreover, such collective, phatic and playful practice does have bearings on '*duang*'s' diffusion. Having been continuously practiced in this way, the repetitive and substitutive uses have taken on such conviviality-invoking and relationship-smoothing effect as part of their meaning potential, or rather orders of indexicality (Silverstein 2003), in more engaged and interpersonal interactions, as we'll see in the following.

---

71. Accessed from http://www.weibo.com/2796627290/C602xDUEe on March 20, 2015.

4.5.2 Meaning transformation in interaction

As we have discussed so far, an analysis of the spread of 'duang' should take into consideration its forms of use, functional types, communities of diffusion, as well as its main virality-induced types of activity, and possibly some more dimensions, in order to examine its meaning variation in diffusion. But each instance of 'duang', as amply shown in the collected data, involves further meaning transformation, e.g. entextualization and resemiotization, in interactions, always actualized in the tension between the need for personal relevance (pursuit of creativity) and the fixedness of meaning (formation of recognizability). In what follows, I will investigate both the meaning transformation and orders of indexicality in the meaning-making process whenever 'duang' is used. Admittedly, the two aspects are always co-existent and should never be separated, but for the sake of convenience and clarity, I will illustrate them with different examples.

Entextualization

The functional types categorized earlier are not just different usages adopted by Weibo users simply to be creative or variable, but each instance of variation has indeed gone through a complex and dynamic process of entextualization, which will be better revealed from an interactional angle. For example,

Excerpt 4.6 (March 5; 15:14)

A: #元宵节#外面才真的是duang duang [2 personal photos]	A: #Lantern Festival# The outside is really duang duang
>B: 指甲duang	>B: The fingernails are duang
>A: @B: 回去现场给你Duang一个	>A: @B: When I'm back, let me Duang yours immediately

In Excerpt 4.6, the entire interaction could be said to center on 'duang', with all the crucial information in each comment expressed by the meme. User A first describes how the outside looks like on the Lantern Festival, which is supposedly opposite to the 'inside' where she poses for the two pictures. As she sits idly and comfortably inside with a glass of juice and desserts to enjoy, the state of the outside, indicated by the descriptive 'duang duang', may probably be festive, lively or even raucous, towards which A's specific attitude and stance could be interpreted variably. However, B's reply evades what's said in A's message yet apparently echoes with it by virtue of 'duang'. B (observantly) picks up the information from the pictures instead – the glaring fingernails, which lie in fact in the center of the second picture – and describes them as in a state of 'duang'. B most probably wants to give User A a compliment about the fingernails (possibly as shiny and beautiful), so B's somewhat echoic use of 'duang' implies her interpretation of the previous instance of 'duang' as likewise positive and impressive. Apparently, such an interpretation of compliment is attained by A, demonstrated by her offer to commit an act of 'duang' for B later – which can be understood as 'to realize such an impressive state', i.e. to polish B's fingernails. In this short stretch of interaction, the meaning-in-use is being dynamically entextualized by the two users collectively and interactionally, and thus the different function types of 'duang' can make real sense to them.

In a more subtle way, the entextualization process of '*duang*' is realized as intense construction and negotiation of the local meaning between interactants, even if the same functional type is deployed. For instance:

Excerpt 4.7 (Feb. 26; 00:33)

A: 泪流干，生活还是要继续，duang～加油...	A: When tears are dried, life is still going on, duang~ Fighting...
>B: 老大！你还有我！	>B: Boss! You still have me!
>A: @B: 	>A: @B: 
>B: @A: duang! duang!	>B: @A: duang! duang!

Although the function of the 'duangs' in this interaction is apparently expressive of the users' feelings and emotional states, we can observe that the meanings entextualized in the two instances are tussling with each other, or rather, the two users negotiate the issue at hand by entextualizing 'duang' with their differentiated emotions, which is done in a really implicit way. While User A utters 'duang' as an emotional component to go with her frustrated realization of life (the omission mark after 'Fighting' also confirms such tangible helplessness), User B obviously tries to cheer her up and show support to A. Just when B's offer is somewhat dismissed,[72] she strengthens her response with the exclamatory 'duang!', a use that is echoic in function as expressive, but different in meaning – probably a passionate display of affirmation and sympathy.

When the viral sign of '*duang*' is entextualized by an individual user in any instance, it always undergoes a dynamic process, where its function corresponds in a way with a recognizable usage, and its meaning and effect are locally and interactionally negotiated, as illustrated by the above examples. While social media encourages individual creativity, largely prompting the diversification of functional types, we also notice that such creativity is always conditioned by recognizability, i.e. being echoic either in a local stretch of interaction or in terms of the current viral trend in general. Most importantly, it is the collective and interactional construction that renders the linkage between creativity and recognizability as meaningful, and the two aspects as an organic whole.

Resemiotization

As discussed in the previous sections, the word 'duang' is an integration of the audible and the textual, which also aptly reflects the multi-modal nature of social media communication. An actual Weibo post containing 'duang' may encompass a variety of modes and modalities that all have important bearings on the meaning-making process. In practice, users would take into consideration any multimodal information that they deem relevant in order to process and make meaning of a post, which may result in more complex and inevitably differentiated uptakes and interpretations. But what's important is that we're able to observe and investigate this process of 'resemiotization' (e.g. Scollon 2008), where components of meaning are accumulated and construable though the sign's "movement and transformation across different modes and modalities" (Leppänen et al. 2014: 115). In the following excerpt, we will see how a blogger makes use of various semiotic resources into a post of 'duang' and how this resemiotized text is variably received.

72. Although the emoticon refers to waving or bidding farewell, it is in fact multifarious in use. It's most commonly used to express disagreement, dismissal or even contempt, with a subdued tone.

The blogger is verified by Weibo as a manga artist with a follower base of more than 40,000. In the original post, three different functional types of 'duang' are used, which also meaningfully relate with each other, and a single reading of any one of them may not be sufficient. The 'duang' in the text is apparently an adjective to describe the positive quality of the happy business, accompanied by a cute bunny emoticon '' in the start. The 'duang!' sticker on the upper right of the picture resembles an exclamatory or fanfare use of the meme, while the other two shaky (with surrounding symbols to indicate such movement) 'duangs' seem to emulate the flashy or vigorous state of the delicate painting on the pebble. These visual instances of 'duang' are all in tender colors and have obvious effects of cuteness, lovability and excitement. While the mood and emotion that permeate this post (interlinked by the multi-modal 'duangs') seem unquestionable, the relationship between the central idea of the text (the happy business) and the central idea of the picture (the cute painting on a pebble) is largely elusive.

Excerpt 4.8 (February 28; 21:59)

A: 今天发生了一件 很duang的喜事～	A: Today a very duang and happy business occurred~
[A picture of a cartoon character painted on a rock]	[A picture of a cartoon character painted on a rock]
>B: 啊啊啊啊啊啊啊啊龙猫！！！！！	>B: Ah ah ah ah ah ah ah ah Totoro [a Japanese anime character]!!!!!
>C: 你要结婚了吗。。。	>C: Are you getting married...
>D: duang	>D: duang
>E: 好萌，画的好好，好想学！	>E: So cute, you paint so well, I so wanna learn!
>F: 有女票了？	>F: Got a girlfriend?
>G: 想要hellokitty	>G: I want hellokitty
>H: 厉害DuangDuangDuang	>H: Awesome DuangDuangDuang

As discussed earlier, the meaning variation of 'duang' relies largely on the abstracttion, generalization, and metaphorization of its certain characteristic and quality. This is all the more notable when other semiotic resources come into play, and shows an unfinished and continuous nature on social media. This blogger has probably utilized this ongoing resemiotization process, by meshing the semiotic materials and pivoting around the abstracted meaning of 'duang'. In consequence, different readers may arrive at different resemiotized products that retrieve a distinct permutation and development of the semiotic materials. For example, the comments by Users B, E and G all choose to focus on the painting, while Users C and F attempt to infer from the 'happy business' in the text, and Users D and H simply echo with the use of 'duang'. Such ambiguity may hinder the audience from grasping a definite and clear message from the post – which may rightly serve the blogger's purpose, but it's able to deliver the intended feelings and emotions – which may be all that she aims for.

Problems of audience and inference

The above examples have highlighted the interactional and collective meaning-making of 'duang' in any instance of its entextualization, which also poses the question of how multiple interactants can effectively converge on the same uptake of the message as intended by the blogger. It is a frequent issue for CMC studies (e.g. Herring et al. 2013) as to how various pragmatic 'rules' and 'conventions' may be obtainable and transferrable so that 'successful' inference in online communication is possible and guaranteed.

Interestingly, the affordances and restrictions of the various technological realizations are evaded, coped with, and made the best of by the users, which gives rise to new forms of interaction (phatic, creative, playful, etc.) and communicative norms (Herring 2013). More important, such 'new' pragmatic norms have incorporated (the possibility of) multifaceted audiences (Tagg and Seargeant 2014) where a single message may be uttered to and construed variably by all reachable online users, and the very blogger may or may not be aware of all the 'context collapsing' and 'context crossing' (Baym and boyd 2012) that his/her message could have possibly led to.

As shown in the previous discussion, the users would usually 'get away' with the ambiguity by implicit or non-serious inferences of the 'convivial' uses of '*duang*' in more public encounters on social media. However, there are more interpersonal and serious interactions where any 'impressionist' construal of '*duang*' would not suffice for an effective inference of its meaning and purpose, so more informative exchanges (or common ground) are usually necessary.

In the following excerpt (4.9), the intended audience of the post is obviously the transportation service app @Kuaidi Taxi, as has been made evident by the poster through tagging and addressing a question to the account. The post would also be shown in her 'friends'' (anyone who has followed her account) Weibo feeds. The hashtagged '*duang*' used in the original post, a more public interaction directed at an unknown interactant, is more construable in terms of its functional types – it may work both as an attention-grabbing device and a means to connect with the current viral trend to intend for bigger exposure of the post. However, User B's comment, nothing but '*duang~*', seems highly elusive – only except that it may be echoic to the hashtag in the original post – not just to any other online users but to the intended interlocutor, User A herself, who immediately enquires about B's purpose with some bewilderment (indicated by the multiple 'doge' faces). B's reply, a clarification of her own purpose as merely 'calling' probably for fun, somehow diverts the course of the interaction, by foregrounding the interpersonal and phatic communication between friends, instead of the originally intended interaction that is more serious, informative and publicly-oriented.

Excerpt 4.9 (March 1; 21:33)

A: @快的打车 不带这样的 这也不偏阿 都没人抢 #duang#	A: @Kuaidi Taxi [a Uber-like app] How can it be, here is not a remote place, why wouldn't any driver pick me up #duang#
>B: duang~	>B: duang~
>A: @B: 你想干嘛	>A: @B: What do you want
>B: @A: 叫下你	>B: @A: Just calling you

While a single Weibo post may be seen by multiple online audiences, the very act of posting by the blogger may be more directional, which renders the 'correct' inference of the use of 'duang' only exclusive to its intended audience. For instance:

Excerpt 4.10 (February 26; 01:07)

A: 刚开始用樱花水彩上色 其实我是 是拒绝的 直到上色后 我发现 水彩干的速度duang duang duang	A: When I began to use Sakura Watercolor to paint, I actually, actually refused, until I used it, I found, the drying speed is duang duang duang
>B: 哈哈哈哈哈哈哈哈 我当初用> 樱花也这样	>B: hahahahahahahaha I had the same problem when I used Sakura
>A: @B: 秒扔	>A: @B: Threw away in a second
>C: duang什么鬼	>C: duang what the hell

In the above excerpt, User A's original post partly parodies the 'duang' meme with her experience with a certain watercolor product. Unfamiliar users may easily construe this post as a funny and playful participation in the current virality, and more careful users may be able to infer the somewhat negative attitude from the dismissive ' ' emoticon, but only an 'inside' user can clearly get the message – whether the use of 'duang duang duang' means too fast, too slow, or something else. User B is such a user, who might be a close friend of A's or simply a member of the watercolor painting community, and clearly shows her sympathy for A with her own similar experience. In contrast, User C, possibly an outsider of the painting community, may be puzzled by the use of 'duang' without necessary knowledge or experience. Interestingly, User A doesn't respond to C's questioning, which might confirm the 'outsideness' of C.

While '*duang*' can be voluntarily spread by users with multiple memberships in their posts and interactions, the use of this meme can also be calibrated to differential audiences and invite different inferences by the same token of the meme. This implicit differentiation, which makes use of the versatility and ambiguity of internet memes, may underlie all types of online interaction and is realized as different pragmatic norms governing different online situations, e.g. public playful hubbub, phatic exchange between friends, or serious, intimate talk, etc.

Negotiation of norms

What 'duang' has vastly displayed on the one hand is its versatility and flexibility in meaning and function, but on the other, there's plenty of concomitant negotiative and regulatory work by peer users throughout the meme's diffusion – what Leppänen et al. (2015) call "bottom-up and interactional forms of normativity" which "involves ways of evaluating, judging and policing the semiotic conduct of oneself and others" (2015: 2).

Firstly, such practice of norm-negotiation is observable since the very initial period of the meme's spread, where users usually rely on their pre-existing knowledge and conventions to make sense of the novel meme so as to regulate its use. Take the following interaction (Excerpt 4.11), which occurred at a rather early stage of the virality, as an example.

Excerpt 4.11 (February 25; 22:41)

A: #duang什么意思#这都能成为热门话题 duang duang duang 😂	A: #What's the meaning of duang# Even this can become a hot topic duang duang duang😂
>B: 我的洗发液么…	>B: Is it My Shampoo…
>C: @B: 北方一直说duang	>C: @B: In the north we have always said duang
>A: @C: b站，成龙那个广告……	>A: @C: B Site, that commercial of Jackie Chan…
>C: @A: 之前知道么	>C: @A: Did you know it before?
>A: @C: 最近才火不是么-_-||	>A: @C: It's recently gone viral, hasn't it -_-||
>C: @A: 可是duang一直都是北方话	>C: @A: But duang has always existed in the northern dialect
>A: @C: 那我就不知道了 ╮(╯_╰)╭	>A @C: Well I don't know about that ╮(╯_╰)╭ [a shrug emoji]

Based on the entire interaction as well as her account subscriptions, User A is most probably a member of the ACGN community, and her original post can be understood as a somewhat proud and amused (considering the multifarious emoticon ‘😂’) discovery as an insider that a piece of in-group culture has gone generally viral. User B is probably a fellow member as well, for he immediately identifies this hashtagged topic with his own knowledge of the ACGN community. However, User C weighs in, by replying to B’s answer, with his own knowledge that he deems relevant, at which point we can see that two pre-existing norms – the ACGN community practice and the knowledge of speaking a certain dialect – are in a tug-of-war, with both sides unyieldingly attempting to persuade each other.

Secondly, such bottom-up norm negotiation is also carried out in an interactive, ongoing manner where users also exercise their agencies as regards the recognizability as well as the creativity of the meme. For instance, in the following interaction (Excerpt 4.12), User A posts an emotion-laden self-ventilation of her current (fatigued) state. The use of ‘*duang*’ to refer to her physical (and probably emotional) state seems rather ‘transformational’ (compared with our previous discussion as to such functional type of ‘*duang*’ usually to describe the dynamic, engaging and solid qualities), highly idiosyncratic, or perhaps ironic. When User B questions the phrase ‘very *duang*’, without commenting on the other information. User A abruptly dismisses this act of questioning, which only prompts B to further expand on the question by clearly invoking the ‘norm’. Apparently, B’s serious and normative arguments are ignored by A, who simply uses ‘*duang*’ as ‘how [she] likes it’. User B’s act of overriding A’s liberal and emotive use of ‘*duang*’ with the ‘*norm*’ may have been taken by A as a negation or challenge to her linguistic expressivity, or even further to her act of emotional disclosure, which is demonstrated by A’s somewhat frustrated reactions to B’s questioning.

Excerpt 4.12 (Mar. 8; 22:31)

A: 矫情预告：周末累得要死　胳膊只能保持自然下垂抬不起来　一句话都懒得说　饭还没吃💔非主流配图 duang～很duang	A: Sentimentality alert: Tired to death during the weekend, can't raise my arms but only let them naturally fall down, not in the mood to utter a single word, and haven't eaten anything💔 illustrated with a non-mainstream[73] photo duang~ very duang
[One personal photo]	[One personal photo]
>B: 很duang是个神马鬼~	>B: What the hell is very duang~
>A: @B: 滚出出	>A: @B: Get out
>B: @A: 人家是duang 哪有很duang~	>B: @A: People only say duang, who would say very duang~
>A: @B: 我愿意	>A: @B: That's how I like it

Normative negotiation has also been understood by the users as an essential part of the viral practice and thus reflexively exploited to create intentional discrepancy and playful effects. For example, when User A in the following excerpt uses a phrase "in a Dung Dung way", he may probably be aware of this misspelling, either because he intentionally misspells or he doesn't bother to correct it by making a new comment. This typo immediately attracts corrections from his friends, a series of normative moves. But instead of explaining the misspelling, User A comments on a higher level of the three users' comments, in a joking manner, as if he has already rightly anticipated such criticizing acts from them. A's meta-comment indeed highlights the fact that social media users also form higher orders of normativity as regards the 'right' or 'wrong' use of a certain meme, which reflects the user's own knowledgeability, sophistication and the ability to stay playful with each other whenever necessary.

73. The notion of 'non-mainstream' in China, especially for the young people, has a connotation of being unnecessarily flamboyant, eccentric, and exaggerated in appearance and taste.

Excerpt 4.13 (February 27; 15:53)

A: 这雪下的DungDung的，根本停不来……	A: The snow is falling in a Dung Dung way, it won't stop by any chance...
>B: duang	>B: duang
>C: 拼错了，duang	>C: Wrong spelling, duang
>D: duang	>D: duang
>A: 我就知道你们，忍不住想评论	>A: I just knew, you guys can't help but comment on it

Last but not least, another important aspect about the emergent normativity regarding social media virality is when to stop using the very meme. Although users may express their own attitudes and preferences towards the meme at various points, there're moments when users mindfully observe the trend of the meme and arrive at the conclusion that it's better to stop using it. This kind of reflexive disengagement with the meme also constitutes an important part of its normativity, usually expressed with outspoken attitudes.

For example, one important node of such reflexive disengagement came shortly after the viral peak when another new meme barged in. Some savvy trend-chasers immediately caught sight of it and acted accordingly, as in the following excerpt (4.14), which may simply imply 'let's stop playing with "*duang*" and start with the "dress meme" now.'

Excerpt 4.14 (February 27; 19:51)

A: 终于不duang了！烦死人！白金党抱我！	A: Finally people stop duanging! So annoying! The white and gold[74] people, hug me tight!

Less 'trendy' users may not disengage with the meme in place of another one, but simply because it's been overused and lost its freshness. In the following excerpt (4.15), User A's articulate intention of not using 'duang' clearly bespeaks her own norms regarding the appropriateness of using 'duang' at certain points. Considering the date of the post (nearly one month after the

74. Since February 27, another globally viral meme of the 'black and blue or white and gold dress' began to sweep the Chinese social media. By this time, the 'duang' meme had just passed its viral peak.

virality), User A's express reflexive account of using 'duang', on the one hand, implies her awareness of the normative timeliness of online memes as well as her evident knowledge about them, and on the other, indexes a sophisticated and humorous persona who freely juggles memes.

Excerpt 4.15 (March 22; 22:39)

A: 周末擦的一下就没了（我就不说duang的一下），我是歌手好喜欢李健古巨基，周末最后一小时愉快地PO少爷PO渐彪PO子江PO自拍，明天又周一啦	A: The weekend has passed in a jiffy (I just won't say in a duang), I love Li Jian and Leo Ku in I'm a Singer so much, in the last hour of the weekend, I'm happily PO [posting] the selfies of Shaoye, Jianbiao and Zijiang, tomorrow is Monday again 

To recapitulate, the above analysis and discussion has illuminated the multifarious meaning/function transformations of 'duang' as meaning-making processes by social media users, especially from the perspective of entextualization and resemiotization. During such processes, actual meaning variations are collectively constructed and interactionally negotiated by the users, where they actively modify their interpersonal relationships, police each other's communicative practices, enact different norms, and perform different reflexive identities.

4.6 Concluding remarks

In the attempt to holistically explore the phenomenon of viral neologisms with a focus on meaning variation, I have in this chapter investigated different aspects and dimensions of 'duang's' viral spread and opted for a variety of methods needed for the respective questions. With the comprehensive and complex list of meaning/function variations, I was able to examine the linguistic aspects and mechanisms whereby new meaning/function comes about in detail, and also grasp a larger picture of this process, such as the range of 'duang's' meaning variations and its processual characteristics, which I wasn't able to answer in Chapter 3. However, during the investigatory process, I was constantly forced to consult the interactional data I'd collected, without which my qualitative analysis and categorization would have been unwarranted. It is at this point that I decided to proceed further to the spread and use of 'duang' as actual interactions and therefore shifted my analytical focus from the linguistic to the sociolinguistic.

In the successive sections, I then followed the viral diffusion of '*duang*' and found its important relationships with the various online communities, in that the intra-, inter-, or mixed-community spread of the meme would have different bearings on the activation and preservation of '*duang*'s' meaning/function variations. More importantly, with regard to community practice, the viral spread of '*duang*' can be regarded as meaning-making and learning processes, where the meaning transformations of '*duang*' were constructed and negotiated in actual interactions. During the processes, a variety of identities were performed by the users, where different indexical meanings also emerged.

The shift in the focus of my explorations in this chapter enabled me to see the viral spread as a dynamic and complex process, and my analytical attempts with '*duang*' especially highlighted community practice and emergent orders of indexicality as two important and fruitful dimensions that warrant more in-depth investigations. Therefore, in the next two chapters, I will continue to follow the viral flows by focusing on these two dimensions.

Chapter 5
Enregisterment of an innovated phrase: Languaging and identities of Chinese fans of Thai TV

5.1 Introduction

5.1.1 Fandom of Thai TV in China

Since their official debut on Chinese TV in 2003, Thai TV dramas have gained increasing popularity among Chinese viewers and progressed from the margin towards the mainstream (Zhang and Yu 2016). The relatively late development of Thai dramas also shows unique characteristics compared with the already popular Japanese and Korean TV in China – its main method of broadcasting has changed from being purchased and aired by Chinese TV stations,[75] to being streamed on online video platforms, and to its latest development of online production. Correspondingly, the composition of the growing fan base also changes from mainly TV viewers to social media users, and the main venues for fandom practices are therefore various social media sites. There is also a notable shift of themes, understandably comparable to its change of viewership and platforms, from melodramas to the genre of

75. It should be noted that nearly all of the stations are state-owned, and all public TV programs should be officially checked and licensed before broadcasting.

'xiaoqingxin'[76] (lit. 'young, pure, fresh'), which usually takes the form of 'campus romance'. The attractiveness of Thai dramas to Chinese viewers, according to Zhang and Yu (2016), includes its proximity to and compatibility with Chinese (especially Buddhist) values, its unique and diverse cultural features, and the multi-racial appearances of the actors.

5.1.2 Sites of fandom

Most recently, the main fandom sites of Thai TV and films are video-hosting sites (including Youku, iQiyi, Bilibili, etc.) that themselves are incorporating social media functions, where watching the shows and interacting with other users may take place simultaneously. The 'danmu'[77] ('barrage comments' hereafter) functionality also enhances fans' interaction, by creating a 'pseudo-synchronicity' (Zheng 2016) of the participants' comments to the same video from all times. Moreover, the fans also utilize various social media platforms to carry out fandom practices, and two important sites are the Baidu Tieba – where usually the fanpages are hosted and routine group interactions are carried out, and Sina Weibo – where more interpersonal interactions and relationships are extended among the fans. When more and more Thai series are imported through online platforms, it also poses great challenges for the translation work, as Chinese-Thai bilinguals are significantly fewer than English, Japanese or Korean bilinguals in China. Social media are therefore crucial for the localization of the series, where bilingual talents are mobilized and gathered as part of the fandom, through which the Chinese diasporic communities in Thailand are even connected (Shan 2015). The grassroots nature of the translating/subtitling teams, which, like all such self-organized 'fansub groups' in China (Liu and De Seta 2014), constitutes a crucial

76. 'Xiaoqingxin' is a popular internet neologism, which used to be an approximate translation of 'Indie Pop' in the first place (Yang 2016), but gradually becomes fixated on 'anti-consumerist' films and television that usually depict innocent romance between young lovers, which has an increasing Pan-Asian presence. 'Xiaoqingxin' is also used to refer to the aesthetics and cultural taste of the urban youth from middle-class families in China.

77. Danmu, literally barrage of comments (to compare the abundance of comments to a barrage of bullets), is an overlay of comments that are shown on the screen when the video is being played, usually in a moving manner.

part of the fandom practice, makes them especially accessible.

Currently, the most popular all-purpose fandom site for Thai TV is Bilibili.com, which is also the powerhouse of the 'Otaku' circle in China, or the ACGN subculture. It should be noted that the ACGN community is not a homogenous whole, considering that the four big letters represent quite different things, but there're indeed multiple ways that its sub-communities relate to each other. For example, one particular genre, that of 'Boys' Love' (BL), or young male same-sex romance, is especially popular and has permeated different sub-communities, e.g. the Japanese *shoujo* ('young women's') manga and anime, Chinese local web series, and Thai '*xiaoqingxin*' TV series – the focus of this chapter.

5.1.3 The 'fuxiang' ('rotten') genre

The genre of BL is originated from Japan, which has also gained popularity in its Asian neighbors (Martin 2012), and a special concept to refer to its end-users – 'rotten women' – also takes root in the newfound colonies. While the Japanese word 腐女子 (fujoshi, lit. 'rotten women') is originally a pejorative term to mock the female readers of BL-themed manga and anime, their Chinese counterparts seem to have happily embraced this identity (Jacobs 2015). Chinese users usually shorten the term to 腐女 (funv, lit. 'rotten women'), or simply 腐 (fu, lit. rotten) to include readers of both genders, and also use the notion 'rotten' to describe such cultural orientation and aesthetics, which becomes an interchangeable term with BL. The 'rotten' orientation has developed especially steadily in the ACGN community in China. According to a recent large-scale survey in the Chinese ACGN industry and community (iResearch 2016), 24.3% of all the ACGN users identify with the attribute 'rotten', making it the fourth most identified attribute overall. However, 'rottenness' is significantly gendered, as only 4.1% of male users identify with such an attribute, but a whopping 56.6% of female users do, making it the foremost attribute of female ACGN users. In recent years, the rotten orientation has also seeped into the Chinese popular culture, which may only be noticeable on the internet, as all the traditional media are guarded by the authorities. For instance, more than half of all the web series in

2016 on various major video platforms are rottenly-oriented.[78]

The trans-national spread and development of the BL theme is also actualized in its incorporation with the local cultural traditions and aesthetics, which begets new forms and sub-cultures. For example, the indigenous complex and multiple system of sex/gender identities of Thailand (Nanda 2014), which has already incorporated rich traditional cultural meanings, may become dynamically intertwined with the Japanese BL genre and whet the curiosity, probably in an ambivalent way, of consumers in other countries.

5.1.4 The Thai TV series

The TV show that I focus on is a low-budget, teen TV drama titled Ladyboy Friends (LF), featuring a classful of boys and ladyboys at a Thai high school. This show was first aired in Thailand on February 15, 2015, and was translated by the fansub team Tianfu Taiju (lit. 'Tianfu Thai Shows') into Chinese and uploaded on Bilibili.com on February 19. Ladyboys are probably one of the features that Chinese people immediately associate with the country of Thailand, which still belong to 'low culture' (Totman 2003) and have only a very limited representation in Thai cultural products. Interestingly, the Thai title was translated as 'A different kind of beautiful boys' in Chinese, which intentionally evaded the reference to the characters as ladyboys.[79]

Its first wave of popularity came around the end of February, 2015, when a Weibo user posted a set of screenshots from the show[80]. With the characters' appearances (as ladyboys), exaggerated gestures and makeups, and especially the hilarious Chinese subtitles, this post was reposted for more than 34,000 times. People's curiosity was greatly whetted by such 'extraordinary',

78. News article: The webseries this year belong to rotten women. Accessed from http://www.duxuan.cn/doc/6955441.html on August 2, 2016.

79. According to an interview (March 13, 2015) with the fansub team, there was struggling as to the translation of the title. The team was first shocked by the appearance of some characters in the show and thought that 'a different kind of beautiful boys' would highlight such contrast and shock as well as hide the word 'ladyboy' which may still sound weird in titles. Accessed from http:// Ent.163.com/15/0313/11/AKJ72TH800031GVS.html on March 19, 2015.

80. Accessed from http://www.weibo.com/1622747357/C6mPRaj1N on March 19, by which time the post accumulated 34925 reposts, 16418 comments, and 11928 likes.

'aesthetically challenging' characteristics (as repeatedly shown in the comments to the post), and LF soon became a playful sensation on Chinese social media. Within one month, it rose to the most watched TV show on Bilibili, with more than 1 million views for each episode (Shan 2015), and its fan page at *Baidu Tieba* attracted more than 40,000 members during the first month by April 5, 2015. As jokingly summarized by Wang Nima, a popular online comedian and webshow host,[81] the series' sudden huge fame consists in that "All the ugly ones are *sibi*-ing ('bitch-fighting'), while all the handsome ones are *gaoji*-ing ('bromancing')[82], and the fansub team has done a really great job."

As LF became a great hit in China, its production team soon announced cooperation with a Chinese media company. Since then, its marketing and promotion on Sina Weibo became much more visible, and many members of the cast also opened their own Weibo accounts to interact with the fans.

The fansub team 'Tianfu Taiju', which specialized in translating and subtitling Thai films, TV and web series of 'rottenly-oriented' and '*xiaoqingxin*' themes,[83] achieved a great success and gained tremendous accolades among the fans, for their work on LF. The most prominent features of the subtitles were the adoption of up-to-date internet vernacular and the exuberant use of various euphemized swear expressions, making the '*sibi*' verbal fights especially humorous and engaging. Some viewers questioned the accuracy of the translation with the original lines in Thai, but most Chinese viewers welcomed the adaptation, calling such non-serious, playful translation 'top-notch skill in using Chinese', and 'crucially contributive to the show's popularity in China'.[84]

Therefore, a great deal of 'rewriting and manipulation' (Cai 2015) was involved in the very fansubbing practice, which largely

81. Accessed from http://v.youku.com/v_show/id_XOTEwNTA4OTky.html on March 16, 2015.

82. Both 'sibi' and 'gaoji' are Chinese online slang words that have emerged in recent years. 'Sibi', literally 'to tear the cunt', is a metaphor to describe the nasty fights between women, which has evolved to refer to any type of quarrel or disagreement. 'Gaoji' is a neologism borrowed from the original Cantonese slang to mean 'doing/playing gay', which is now used jokingly to refer to any kind of intimate activities between people of the same gender.

83. Tianfu Taiju on Baidu Encyclopedia, accessed from http://t.cn/RVRQSxD on June 14, 2015.

84. These two remarks were among the comments to one of the fansub team's Weibo posts, accessed from https://www.weibo.com/2117871375/C6AZrxNLb on March 3, 2015.

relied on the fansubbers' creative, extraordinary and 'discrepant' using and enmeshing of linguistic resources. The extraordinary subtitles also stimulated the LF fans to discuss and play with the language, adding another dimension to the fandom practice. This can be regarded as an exceptional case of linguistic practice that involves all kinds of codes – Thai, Chinese, various varieties and styles of Chinese, etc., which I will approach from the perspective of 'languaging'.

5.1.5 Languaging and enregisterment

The various innovative and playful activities the Chinese fans engaged with, including commenting and playing on the translations, using the Thai phrases from the lines, 'buffalaxing',[85] etc., may on the surface resemble 'code-mixing' or, even more broadly speaking, 'code-meshing' (Canagarajah 2011), considering they indeed shuttled between codes of different language repertoires. However, as most of them were not Chinese-Thai bilinguals, it seems to defy our traditional understanding and definition of using 'language'.

In fact, the practice of partial appropriation of codes from another language has been amply studied. For example, the use of the Spanish phrase "Hasta la vista, baby", which was made popular by Schwarzenegger's character from the film *Terminator 2*, by Anglophone monolinguals, or 'Mock Spanish' (Hill 1998), directly invokes the congenial, carefree or macho persona for white male speakers, but indirectly indexes the highly negative racializing stereotypes of Chicanos and Latinos as well as the 'whiteness' as an unmarked normative order.

Rampton (1998) calls the practice of switching into other people's language, i.e. using a language that is generally felt to belong to another social group, 'language/ code-crossing', based on his studies of the crossing and stylization practices among multi-ethnic adolescents in South Midlands of England. He applies the Bakhtinian notion of voice to consider such complex linguistic practice as 'vari-directional double-voicing' (1998: 302): the young

85. Buffalaxing is the parodic practice to give "subtitles for what the producer thinks the oral material in the video [of a different language] sounds like in his/her own language" (Leppänen and Elo 2015: 111).

speakers simply use stylized social voices of other ethnic groups (e.g., when a boy of African descent banters with friends using a couple of Panjabi phrases) without really identifying with them. Such practice enables them to say things in a playful, lively, mischievous, or even transgressive way, which they would never do in their own language, i.e. in their own social voice.

In these cases, the semiotic entities which the speakers cross-codingly opt for as 'social voices' and 'stylization' seem to defy our traditional conceptions of 'language' or 'language varieties'. Linguistic phenomena as such are abundant, and ever-increasing, under globalization where the flows of information, people, commodities, ideas, etc. generate new contacts and encounters, prompting some sociolinguists to shift the focus and level of analysis "from 'language' (primarily an ideological and institutional construct) to resources (the actual and observable ways of using language)" (Blommaert 2010: 102). The notion of 'languaging' is therefore the alternative perspective to investigate the dynamic and ongoing process where speakers make use of semiotic resources and features to make meaning, interact with each other, and change the world (Møller and Jørgensen 2009). In the current superdiverse societies, languaging is practiced in even more complex forms, which have been variously studied for instance as 'polylanguaging' (Jørgensen et al. 2015), and 'translanguaging' (Creese and Blackledge 2010; García and Li 2014).

Here, the concept of *register* offers special insights into such practice. Agha expands the traditional notion of 'register' as a certain way of speaking in a particular social situation (e.g. Halliday and Hasan 1989) to "cultural models of action that link diverse behavioral signs to enactable effects, including images of persona, interpersonal relationship and type of conduct" (Agha 2007: 145). Registers, or sometimes called "register formations" by Agha, are themselves ongoing processes and only characterizable as "repertoires used in utterances by particular sociohistorical population" (2007: 149) in a reflexive manner. When a certain linguistic feature becomes associated with a register, it's therefore 'enregistered', which Agha further defines as "processes and practices whereby performable signs become recognized (and regrouped) as belonging to distinct, differentially valorized semiotic registers by a population" (2007: 81). In this light, the aforementioned resource-oriented and feature-based practices of languaging also rely on the enregisterment of the features that are associated and associable with the stereotypic values of their 'normal' speakers, namely the laid-back Latino stereotype in the case of 'Mock Spanish' or the funny Panjabi image in case of the 'crossing'.

One important implication of the perspective of enregisterment is that the associative and indexical links between a linguistic feature and its social meaning may be systemically related, and have the possibility to become, by virtue of enregisterment, relatable to a certain register. This is especially helpful when we investigate the emergence of new languaging practices, such as the Chinese fandom languaging on Thai, where many of its crucial indexical links are in the forming and yet to be characterized.

5.2 Methods and research questions

5.2.1 Online participatory observation

When I first came across the viral Weibo post that joked about the extremely unattractive ladyboys of the show, I was very curious and watched the first two episodes on Bilibili.com. By that time (March 5, 2015), LF had already attracted a large number of viewers and comments. I was especially intrigued by the active participation of the users by means of the 'barrage comments' that largely outnumbered other shows during that time, and then decided to conduct online observations within LF's fandom.

This study is a digital ethnography (Varis 2016) about the fandom practice, which is also based on, and motivated by, my own participation as a member in the fandom. Moreover, my longitudinal participation and observation (see Table 5.1), with self-reflections along the process, make it possible to record each and every detail involved in the constantly changing and developing practice and to reflect on their nuanced significance. It is through this 'digital ethnographic monitoring' that I have been able to analyze this emerging new phrase which has important bearings on the fandom.

Table 5.1 Digital ethnography of the fandom

Stages	Duration	Tasks
Focused observation (airing of Season 1)	March 5-April 20, 2015	– Situated myself as member of the fandom; – Participated in & monitor the fans' routine language practices; – Determined & located the very phrase to investigate; – Collected relevant data; – Conducted participatory interactions[86] with members.
Intermittent observation (hiatus between seasons)	April 21-September 5, 2015	– Expanded the observation outside of the core fandom; – Monitored the occurrences of the phrases whenever possible.
Re-focused observation (airing of Season 2)	September 6-November 30, 2015	Observed and monitored the discursive practice at the three major fan sites.

All the ethnographic data were then compiled into two major datasets. DO3 contained all the observational and reflectional data of the researcher as a participatory member, and all the interactional data among the fans were collected into DC3.

5.2.2 The innovation of 'chesaika'

Figure 5.1 Screenshot of 'chesaika' (in circles) in the barrage comments

86. No 'official' interviews were conducted to elicit the participants' accounts of the practices. Instead, interpersonal and group interactions with various members, with the researcher being an in-group member, is arguably a way to obtain necessary ethnographic data.

When I was watching Episode 4 on March 7, 2015 (five days after its release on Bilibili, the show had already gathered 30k barrage comments), I noticed when one character in the show uttered a sort of exclamation which was translated as 'stinky bitch' in the subtitles. Several approximations of this sound in Chinese appeared in the barrage comments, including拆塞卡 (chāi sāi kǎ), 车塞卡 (chē sāi kǎ) and扯赛卡 (chě sài kǎ). Soon afterwards, whenever this phrase was uttered in the show, there would be several comments (see Figure 5.1) flying across the screen to mimic the pronunciation. I also noted that the translation of the phrase was not consistent from one occurrence to another, including zhen hansuan ('so pathetic'), xiao biaoza ('little bitch'), chou biaolian ('shameless'), xiao jianren ('little cheapie'), etc. in the first five episodes alone.

Within one week or so, I began to sight this phrase '*chesaika*', written in Chinese, in other places than Bilibili, including fans' microblogs, comments to fan-made videos on other video-hosting sites, interactions on the fan page on Baidu Tieba, etc. On March 17, someone posted a question on Baidu Zhidao (the biggest Q&A website in China), asking "What does *chesaika* mean?", and the best voted answer was "*Chesaika* is Thai for *xiao biaozi* ('little bitch')"[87]. It seems that at this point 'chesaika' had become a meaningful and functional phrase for the fans, and it began to diffuse rapidly in the fandom. Therefore, I decided to particularly focus on this phrase.

Based on these observations, I will investigate the following questions in order to have a full grasp of the spread of '*chesaika*' within the very fandom and beyond, namely,

-- How should 'chesaika' be understood from the perspective of languaging?
-- What kinds of personae and images are enregistered by the use of 'chesaika' and what are the identities being performed?
-- How should the languaging and enregisterment be understood in relation to the diffusion of an innovated neologism?

5.3 Languaging around the innovated phrase

The innovation of the phrase 'chesaika' is prima facie a case of

87. Accessed from https://zhidao.baidu.com/question/1639826713402419700.html on May 1, 2015.

individual transliteration. While transliteration has been a major method to translate foreign notions into Chinese (Hu and Xu 2003), it has also become an accessible and powerful instrument for ordinary internet users to get playful and creative with languaging on a global scale, which are also notable characteristics found on those successful and/or viral linguistic innovations on the internet (Nishimura 2015).

The original instances of '*chesaika*' are just idiosyncratic ways to write the Thai phrase in Chinese characters which make no literal or figurative sense to anyone. Therefore, its initial spread works like a meme that does not have "clear, transparent and shared meanings before [it] goes viral" (Blommaert 2015: 19). What makes '*chesaika*' contagious and drives its diffusion within the fandom may be its exotic sound and the amusing ways the characters in the show utter it, as one fan commented "*Chesaika* is my favorite line, I just can't help laughing whenever they say it!" (W031107[88]). But more importantly, it is the collective languaging that continues to render '*chesaika*' a meaningful, sharable and spreadable sign within the fandom and beyond.

5.3.1 Linguistic components

Various linguistic aspects of this phrase came about through collective negotiation within the fandom. The phrase's orthography, as said earlier, had undergone a series of negotiations as to a dozen of different forms before it was mostly fixed on the three Chinese graphemes 车塞卡. On a side note, any single Chinese character is at once a grapheme and a phoneme: i.e., it represents both sound(s) and meaning(s). Therefore, the orthographic negotiations were not only concerned with which phonetic approximations would be closer to the original Thai phrase, but also involved an interesting parsing of the candidate forms' literal meanings, all of which were in fact nonsensical (in various degrees) in Chinese.

The users also carried out collective fan activities to negotiate the phonetics of '*chesaika*'. For example, there were several threads on the fan page that encouraged users to submit their own

88. Each piece of data (comment, message, or post) was labelled in DC3 in the form of 'site (Weibo, Bilibili, Tieba) / date (mmdd) / assigned number'.

recordings to actually perform the phrase and compete with each other. The following thread in the screenshot is titled "everyone, each of you say chesaika, and see who performs most similarly to the original", and more than 100 participants have posted their recordings as replies.

Figure 5.2 Screenshot of the 'voice contest' on the Tieba fanpage

In the comments, the users freely and playfully discussed the various features of the original pronunciation as well as the imitations that had the most merits. The competition in such activities was in fact important and effective for the establishment of a widely accepted and 'localized' pronunciation of the phrase. Moreover, they also enhanced the sharedness and attractiveness of this phrase which was on the rise at that point, in effect promoting its further diffusion within the fandom.

The semantic aspect of '*chesaika*' may be very tricky, as the users had 'equated' it with 'little bitch' in Chinese since the very early stage, based on its translations in the subtitles. Most of the early Weibo posts and Tieba interactions containing '*chesaika*' were enthusiastic displays of acquiring the phrase (such as Excerpt 5.1) on the one hand, as well as the curious inquiry about its meaning on the other (Excerpt 5.2).

Excerpt 5.1 (W031202)

A: Today I learned another new word from Sister A (a LF character), chesaika

Excerpt 5.2 (T031107)

A: What is your best line in the show?

> B:Chesaika

> C:What does this phrase mean

> B:reply to C: it seems to mean little bitch

The unquestioned acceptance and spread of the phrase's semantic equivalence with 'little bitch' in Chinese was in fact crucial for its virality at least within the fandom, which enabled the fans to use it and spread it more quickly and effectively. However, such misunderstood equivalence, or careless meaning assignment may reflect the fans' agency and cultural identities in a more profound way, which I will elaborate on later.

5.3.2 Pragmatic functions

Two lines of development of the phrase's pragmatic functions can be observed. First, its widely recognized equivalence with 'little bitch' made it likewise functional as an interpersonal address term as well as an expletive. More importantly, 'chesaika' was mostly only equated with the 'euphemized' version of 'little bitch' in practice. The Chinese word for bitch or whore is 'biaozi'. By adding the diminutive prefix 'xiao' (lit. 'little') and rounding the last vowel from [i] to [a] to simulate the intimate colloquial speech style, 'xiaobiaoza' ('little bitch') is much euphemized and 'softened' in tone than 'biaozi' ('whore'), which itself has become a popular (or even viral) word on Chinese internet. This euphemization will also be expanded on later.

Second, the fans also collectively derived pragmatic functions of 'chesaika' from its actual utterances on the show by the characters. This was usually achieved by means of the barrage comments, where the viewers left all kinds of comments, whenever 'chesaika' was uttered, as to any related information in the show, which helped them infer the contextual functions of this phrase in the original scenes. Moreover, various fan-made artefacts, such as fan fiction works, mash-up videos, and all kinds of drawings and images, also appropriated the phrase 'chesaika' in a variety of ways. For example, the following is a meme of 'chesaika' built on the 'image macro'[89] of a LF character, who is nicknamed 'Sister A' by the fans. The pragmatic meaning of 'chesaika!' is quite inferable from the character's angry face with a fierce snarl, as if he (she) is swearing with the phrase in great intensity. At this point, we could say that 'chesaika' had gathered notable pragmatic potential for heightened expressivity, from a bottom-up manner, even without articulate codification of the phrase.

Figure 5.3 A 'chesaika' image meme used in the fans' interaction (T031409)

5.3.3 Sociolinguistic status

When the languaging on 'chesaika' was being exercised, the fans also engaged with the negotiation of the phrase's social 'significance' inside and outside the fandom. The phrase underwent a series of valorization processes (Agha 2007), that is, it was considered more important and valuable for the fandom community, reflected by two crucial incidents at the 'official' level. For one thing, the

89. In internet culture, an image macro is a picture superimposed with text for humorous effect. (Wikipedia, accessed from https://en.wikipedia.org/wiki/Image_macro on May 1, 2016.)

fansub team, possibly the summit of the fandom hierarchy, also participated in the diffusion of the meme. As shown in Excerpt 5.3, the official account of the fansub team (@Tianfu Taiju) interacts with a passionate fan user, by replying her post and recognizing 'chesaika' as a proper phrase, therefore elevating its 'sociolinguistic status' at a higher level – i.e. the phrase was no longer a mere fan-made gibberish.

Excerpt 5.3 (W031602)

User A: I'm begging you, the subtitling team @Tianfu Taiju!!!!! I can't stand it, I have to find a student of Thai from the School of Foreign Languages!! It's killing me when I wait for the subtitles!!! I only understood chesaika!! Chesaike!!!

> Tianfu Taiju: Haha, I also know that phrase, chesaika

> User A: @Tianfu Taiju: ah ah ah ah ah ah ah ah ah ah ah ah ah ah ah ah ah ah ah ah ah ah ah ah ah ah ah ah ah, I have been replied! I must now express my love to you!! You're the conscience of the subtitling industry!!

This official recognition was even more obvious when the fansub team actively used this phrase in their Weibo posts, which also opened up a space for further metalinguistic discussion and interaction. In the following post (Excerpt 5.4), the fansub team uses 'chesaika' when talking about other TV shows, and the use of this phrase has actually moved beyond the proper fandom of LF (though there may be a great overlapping of members).

Excerpt 5.4 (W031803)

Tianfu Taiju: #Tianfu Thai Shows# Listen to how the two characters laugh together, so vociferous to my ears. Chesaika, be quick and give me the new video file (to work on)

> B: Chesaika, you beast, let go of that little boy, and give him to me...

> C: Chesaika, what is the best way to translate it?

> D: @C: It means xiao biaoza (little bitch)

Moreover, as the phrase was becoming increasingly viral among the fans during the production of later episodes, since the 11th episode on, the fansub team began to translate the Thai phrase directly in the Chinese characters 'chesaika' in the subtitles. This practice also caused great repercussions among the viewers. The barrage comments would display a gush of excited and amused comments when the specific piece of translation appeared in the subtitles. Obviously, the fans were excited at the fact that their collective fan-made innovation became officially validated.

Another important 'status' issue of '*chesaika*' is how the phrase invoked discussion of its source language, Thai. In this regard, the fans' metalinguistic discussions should be examined in relation to their metapragmatic models concerning aspects of the Thai language. As shown in their interactions, what really mattered for the fans' 'translanguaging' (García and Li 2014) is the taken-for-granted or playful attitudes that willy-nilly accepted the phrase as a substantial part of the Thai language. For example, one user called the phrase "core frequent word in beginner's Thai language" (W031703), while another made memes (e.g. Figure 5.5) that simply asserted 'competent' use in Thai.

Figure 5.4 A 'chesaika' meme used in the fans' interactions (T031702)
Translation: In Thai, you're just a chesaika

It should be noted that even by declaring their 'acquisition' of Thai, the users were not equating this engagement with Thai to learning or using it in the traditional sense. For instance, in the following Weibo interaction, although User A seems to be excited and confident about acquiring the Thai phrase, she nevertheless cringes when a pedagogical question as to learning the language is posed to her. Hence, what really mattered for the fans was the playful and creative nature of translanguaging where language users picked up whatever features or resources (Blommaert 2010) they found interesting in a confident way, instead of the language system in the normative sense.

Excerpt 5.5 (W031802)

A: Finally, besides sawadeeka, kopkunka, and all kinds of ka, I get a new Thai word chesaika!!!
> B: Are you coming to my class to learn sawadeeka or what
> A: @B: Thai seems too difficult 😰 I can't learn it

5.3.4 Contestation on languaging

However, there were also fans who subscribed to the more conventional linguistic ideologies that emphasize the 'correctness' or 'purity' (Jørgensen et al. 2015) of languages even in superdiverse encounters, who questioned and challenged the fandom languaging practice, especially as to the semantic equivalence of the phrase with 'little bitch'.

Some serious fans consulted other people with knowledge of the Thai language for further explanation of the phrase. When they found that this phrase was probably mistranslated, they also turned to the fansub team for clarification. The fansub team didn't shun away from the fact that the phrase was indeed mistranslated, as the following interaction shows:

Excerpt 5.6 (W033005)

User A: Translator-san,[90] please help clarify. I have a Chinese-Thai classmate and she says that she doesn't understand 'chesaika'!!!
> Translator: It means I'm despising you in a condescending way
> User A: @Translator: Oh I see! I had gone to various sources to find the meaning hahaha
> Translator: @User A: Approximately looks like this เชิดใส่ค่ะ 😳

The spread of the phrase on the internet also attracted the attention of Thai users living in China, some of whom also posted in the fanpage about the real meaning of the Thai phrase and wanted to correct the widely spread misunderstanding. According to a Thai student studying in Beijing (T041401), the Thai phrase เชิดใส่ค่ะ

90. '-san' is the honorific suffix in Japanese to address someone of higher status or with respect, which has also been widely used by Chinese internet users, usually transliterated as 桑 (sāng).

(Romanized as chēd sai kha) literally means 'to raise (one's) head'. This phrase may have probably been grammaticalized as a stance marker, which is usually uttered to express the speaker's contempt or displeasure at someone else. Note that the ending particle 'kha' is always used by female speakers (or self-identified females, such as ladyboys) at the end of a sentence.[91]

Apparently, this phrase was used entirely 'incorrectly' by Chinese LF fans, not to mention that the phrase was also frequently uttered by male fans, ignoring the gender restrictions in the Thai language. However, LF fans generally didn't react much to this kind of 'corrections', and the languaging practice of '*chesaika*' still continued in its unique way.

The above analysis from the perspective of languaging illustrates how the fans agentively and collectively cross the boundaries of 'languages', innovate the phrase out of different semiotic resources, arrive at meaningful and functional components that constitute the phrase as a spreadable sign, and actively promote its viral diffusion within the fandom. But what kinds of creativity and criticality (García and Li 2014) does such languaging have and what cultural identities of the fans have underlain the practices? The claim that '*chesaika*' converges with 'little bitch' both in meaning and in use is in fact a metasemiotic statement (Agha 2007) to describe the innovated phrase's significance, which offers us a suitable point of entry.

5.4 'Chesaika' as a social voice

Firstly, what are the qualities of the show that the fans find 'mysteriously attractive' and 'extremely enchanting' and make them "can't get it out of [their] mind at all" (T033009)? Recall the two major themes of the show, as facetiously characterized by Wang Nima – 'sibi' bitch-fight and 'gaoji' bromance. But what do the fans really see in 'gaoji' and 'sibi'?

While the native Japanese BL (i.e. young male homoerotic) subculture has received limited academic attention, its increasingly global influence and derivatives in recent years have given rise to

91. This fact has also been confirmed via personal communication with Professor Nantawan Chuarayapratib at Thammasat University, Thailand.

a great many studies in various cultures and localities (e.g., Korea: Noh 2004; U.S.: Zanghellini 2009; pan-Asia: Martin 2012; and the greater China region: Jacobs 2015). A common research question to nearly all such studies is: What do these readers, mostly female, really consume?

Many investigations have converged on the liberating and empowering functions of the 'female gaze' (Zanghellini 2009) at the most intimate activities between men, which is at the same time a licensed type of voyeurism, a subversion of the patriarchal sexual and gender ideology, as well as an opportunity to reimagine the conventional cultural scripts. However, the actual consequences of the BL fandom are still contested: whether it's feminist and critical in nature – thus potentially emancipatory for women (Nagaike 2012), or does it succumb to the sexist male-dominated ideology where such abnormal fantasies are simply driven by "sexual jealousy and competitiveness" (Martin 2012: 373)? Either way, what has been conspicuous all over the cases is the young women's collective articulation and reworking against the dominant culture, and especially in the Chinese context, an unprecedented display of "Chinese women's erotic power and positive outlook on [...] nonnormality, and sexual abundance" (Jacobs 2015: 136).

Just as the practice to gaze, the practice to curse among women, especially when it comes to the conventionally derogatory sexist slurs, has also been under heated discussion. On Chinese social media, while the social type of 'cute girls' (Zhang 2012), among other beauty standards, is still of wide currency, there're also many women who try to break loose from the 'sweet, polite, and well-behaved' (Zhang 2012) image, and instead utilize the 'sharp-tongued' talk as well as 'cursing' (Zhang and Kramarae 2012) to 'de-emphasize the gender difference' in social encounters. The traditionally victimized group may also voluntarily adopt the disparaging slur for a recuperative effect and significance. For example, Rahman (2012) argues that the use of the 'N word' among African Americans can have "illocutionary functions related to showing approval or a proactive self-empowerment" (2012: 141). In other words, the sexist derogatory slur may also enregister the subversive and self-affirming type of persona.

Following the above discussion, the concept of '*sibi*' bitch-fight, a highly sexist term to demean and belittle women, and the theme of '*gaoji*' bromance, a counter-normative cultural practice, may index the same image of identity for the LF fans – the proactive, self-empowering, and unrestrained female, who can assert and exercise her own values and tastes without hindrance. Here, when the fans inhabit the social voice of '*chesaika*' of the ladyboy characters, what they enact is a highly powerful and expressive persona. This has always been clearly felt throughout the series, especially evident in the fansub team's intentional translation that has shown such character – their well-designed 'maneuvers' to 'spice up' the subtitles and make the '*sibi*' fights more powerful and appealing to the audience.

When '*chesaika*' becomes 'equated' with the already emergent practice of 'bitching', it is therefore 'troped on' (Agha 2007) the urban young female liberal ideological construct, which itself may still be forming and possibly inclusive of ambivalent elements (Kleinman et al. 2009). Therefore, when the trope of '*chesaika*' is entextualized in an utterance by the fans, it has the potential to directly index such a self-asserting and powerful image, which is why there are a great number of instances where '*chasaika*' has been used to express powerful and intense feelings, a mere expletive, as in the following two examples.

Excerpt 5.7 (W031301)

A: Darn, there's always a power outage when you're least prepared, my cellphone has only 10% of battery left, and my hair is still wet. Chesaika!

Excerpt 5.8 (W050301)

A: What the fuck! Can it be any worse! My heart is full of anger! Can't be good! Chesaika!

This 'empowered' persona may have interesting consequences. While most of such a powerful social voice is performed and enacted through exclamatory and expletive use instead of the typical epithet usage of 'calling someone a bitch', there're still some interesting and prominent cases of the latter usage, one of which is how the fans interacted with the director of the show.

Firstly, in terms of the global media industry, Chinese viewers have long been passive end-users of imported cultural products from (mostly) Western countries. With the advancement of digital technologies that allow fans to engage with the production process (Booth 2015), the Chinese users have also enjoyed increasing participation in the cultural industry, especially with web-based series that largely rely on their fan bases (Wang 2015). LF, as well as many new Thai series (Zhang and Yu 2016), may be one of the new opportunities that Chinese fans have to have a say or certain influence on the production process. This may be especially true for the case of LF, as evidenced by the fact that the show was in fact sponsored by a Chinese media company that also engaged closely with the ACGN fandom. Such practice of 'active prosumption (a portmanteau of consumption and production)' on social media (Leppänen and Elo 2015) is surely felt by the fans as empowering. In consequence, the fans' direct and indirect interactions with the production process are just rampant on all kinds of social media platforms of various members of the production crew (Instagram, Facebook and Twitter[92]), the sponsoring Chinese company, as well as the fansub team.

Interestingly, since very early on, the phrase "Director is a chesaika" was frequently noted in the fans' comments (earliest instance collected T031001), when the fans were discussing how the director displeased them with the storylines, mostly in terms of the unsatisfying relationships between the characters which the fans passionately fantasized about. Later, the fans began to simply refer to the director as '车导 ('Director Che')',93 and the fans would directly address him this way in their comments to his Facebook, Twitter and Weibo accounts, mostly when they were complaining about the storylines and specific plots. Note that most of such comments were written in Chinese while none of the members of the production crew was bilingual in Chinese. As previously said, although the BL genre enables the (female) fans to challenge

92. As all of the three platforms are inaccessible in China, the fans have to use VPN services or even more complicated measures to overcome the technological restrictions.

93. This appellation undergoes further translanguaging: in Chinese practice, professionals are usually addressed in the form 'occupation + surname'. In this case, the first character of 'chesaika', che, is simply taken to be the 'surname' of the director.

certain types of sexual ideology and create their idealized romance, various localized forms of this genre may incorporate other existing cultural scripts. Some elements of LF have obviously offended the Chinese fans, which they called 'unnecessarily tragic and poignant' and 'simply poisonous', and which obviously deprived the fans of their sense of empowerment and satisfaction from fantasizing about the characters' homoerotic romance. The following Weibo comment is an obvious illustration in point, where the fan's harsh reprimand reflects such ideological conflicts.

Excerpt 5.9 (W031502)

User A: If I were the director, in order to make the plot more attractive, I would make Wut and Frank happily together in the end: Director Che, you really have too low an EQ (Emotional Quotient), in fact I began to love this show just because of the translations. Your lack of sensitivity has drained my last interest in this cheaply-made show.

The fans' collective demand and vehement criticisms forced the director to make an open statement in English (see the following), apparently aiming at the Chinese and other international fans. Although the statement was rather difficult to comprehend due to its nonstandard use of English, the fans might still be able to get the gist that the director was unyielding and the storyline was already set.

> I have my way. It is my story. I took all the characters as I put into it. The character of the people around me down. Create a character for it to come to life. If the story is changing. It got me on this? The Lady Boy Friends The Series "It is my story." And one of the performers at the show it. It also has the role as my own. (The Director's statement, published on LF official Facebook Page, accessed from https://www.facebook.com/556505651146136/posts/636384659824901 on March 19, 2015)

Probably, the use of 'chesaika' to refer to the director, especially in the fans' committed negotiations, highlights their dissatisfaction with the lack of self-empowerment and is just in line with their ongoing identity register formations that proactively demand agency and disinhibition through such prosumptive practices.

5.5 'Chesaika' as a group marker

More importantly, once the use of 'chesaika' is readily associated with the 'sharp-tongued' register, its entextualized use may have a higher order of indexicality (Silverstein 2003), i.e. 'informed' people can not only construe what kind of social persona the trope indexes, but they can also infer the social and cultural meanings of such a strategic and purposeful use. For example, the use of racially discriminatory slurs among young black rappers may serve as the vehicle of rapport for them to strengthen in-group solidarity (Brontsema 2004), and the use of sexist offensive slurs among young female activists in a mutually supportive environment may help invoke shared experience and increase the feeling of empowerment (Gaucher et al. 2015). Similarly, the use of 'chesaika' in practice is also indexical of the very LF fandom composed of like-minded people with similar tastes and online experiences. Interestingly, such indexical value has been recognized and made into an overt in-group reference label.

Since mid-March 2015, the LF fan page on Baidu Tieba officially changed the epithet of its subscribed users from the default name, which is simply 'member', to '*chesaika*'. The following screenshot shows the fanpage's description in its profile, where the term for its members is designated as '*chesaika*'.

Translation:

About this fanpage

Admins:

User A

User B

Vice admins: 7 people

Members: Chesaika

Genre: Southeastern Asian TV series

Figure 5.5 Description of LF fanpage on Baidu Tieba[94]

94. Accessed from https://tieba.baidu.com/f?ie=utf-8&kw=不一样的美男 on May 10, 2015.

Members of the fanpage also accepted this epithet, in that they not only addressed each other as 'chasaika' (70 thread titles were found in the fanpage that have this phrase as address term), but also used 'chesaika' simply to refer to people in their interaction there. The establishment of 'chesaika' as an in-group address term was also demonstrated by the fan practice at other fandom sites. For example, on Bilibili.com, users also called each other 'chesaika', which was usually seen in the barrage comments, such as "Greetings to the other 1212 chesaikas", as users can see the number of total viewers who are watching a certain video simultaneously, which, again, is another technical infrastructure that in fact increases the feeling of belonging to the same online community.

'*Chesaika*' has also been used outside the LF fandom. Like any other viral sign that may simply diffuse regardless of its content, '*chesaika*' does offer a brief moment for out-group users perhaps to wonder at its meaning or feel amused about its quirk, just as how it infected the LF fans in the first place. However, once the phrase is imbued with indexical values (or enregistered) in the fandom community, it becomes highly tropic whenever the in-group members use it. For instance, the following excerpt is a stretch of interaction I stumbled upon when I was randomly reading the comments on a Chinese folk music band's channel[95] at the music-streaming site NetEase Cloud Music. My attention was immediately drawn to the extended interaction between two users (A and B), who were probably strangers to each other. As shown in the following excerpt, the first comment made by A is obviously intended to express her appreciation and loyalty to the band, and the use of '*chesaika*', a term obviously irrelevant to the very music band community, to address her idols here may be a very personalized way to show playfulness and endearment. This illustrates how User A proactively projects the trope of '*chesaika*', someone who is sassy and 'bitchy' and loved by the fans, onto the two singers. Coincidentally, this act of entextualization was sighted by another fan, who immediately picked up the phrase as a salient

95. Accessed from: http://music.163.com/#/program?id=9324096 on April 4, 2015.

marker for A's membership.

Exerpt 5.10

1) A: You two chesaikas, I'm gonna vote for you at Modernsky (a music festival)😂
2) > B: You must have watched Ladyboy Friends 😂😂😂
3) > A: Got caught by you 😂
4) > B: 😂😂What a coincidence
5) > A: Have watched it for several times and can't stop, what should I do 😂
6) > B: Me too!!!!!! Can't give up on the JN (couple)!! 😂😂
7) >A: Ah ah ah you're just like my family!! Although I'm totally pissed off by Jet the 'forever straight'
8) > B: Episode 14 is so tormenting!!! Newnew is crying so hard and I was totally unwell😭((by the way, is it really OK that we talk about this in the comments under their channel😱😱
9) > A: Indeed, what a jerk Jet is!! (but I find it quite alright😂)
10) > B: giggle, who hasn't loved a jerk when one was young😂 Luckily Jet is a handsome jerk!!

What may also be picked up, though not explicitly said, by User B, may be a funny, expressive and 'rotten' fan identity that other in-group members can share experience with. This is illustrated by the rather extended and passionate stretch of 'fan talk' (Deller 2014), right after the confirmation of membership, which is full of inside knowledge (e.g., the 'JN couple; in turn 6), jargon (e.g., the phrase "forever straight" in turn 7 to refer to the stubborn stance in a romantic relationship) and presumed group values (e.g., the agreement on 'jerk' in turns 9 and 10) and instantaneously marks off the fandom from within another online community.

5.6 Concluding remarks

In this chapter, a thorough effort has been made to explore what may seem to be a case of word borrowing in popular culture. With the analytical focus on community practices, the innovation and spread of 'chesaika' in fact involves

1) Multiple dimensions of 'translanguaging', where the fans agentively and creatively draw from various semiotic resources

to make the sign into a meaningful object of practice;

2) Dynamic processes of 'enregisterment', where the seemingly innocent sign becomes a metapragmatic trope for the desirable social persona that the very fandom endorses, namely, the self-affirming, self-empowering, and disinhibited modern female; and
3) Complex community practices, where the in-group and out-group use of the trope enregisters differential identities for the fandom members and enact different identities.

On the whole, this chapter provides a detailed and comprehensive ethnographic investigation of the spread of a meme in relation to online communities, revealing such new forms of social formations that are composed of loosely connected or even users who are totally unknown to each other, nurtured with various processes of cultural and identity enregisterment, and maintained by the transmission of various memes. In the next chapter, I will move the exploration higher and enter into the ideological realm that inevitably influences all meme diffusions.

Chapter 6
Chinese internet vernacular (re)defined

6.1 Introduction

6.1.1 Internet vernacular, memes, and online culture

The Chinese notion of 'wangluo yuyan', which directly translates as 'internet language', has become widely used on a meta-semiotic level by scholarly experts and the general public alike, to refer to the 1) types of neologism or internet-based discourse patterns, 2) words and expressions that are deemed specific and original to internet communication, 3) styles of speaking that are typical among the 'young people online', etc. In other words, the referents of 'internet language' in the Chinese social discourse range from the 'medium-based', the 'repertoire-based', and the 'user/practice-based' focuses, which interestingly corresponds with the shift of approaches in the studies of language use on new media throughout the years (for an overview, see Akkaya 2014).

From the 'repertoire-centric' (Agha 2007) perspective, this language variety has been most of the time treated as a particular register of object discourse, characterizable by means of its typical words and expressions. In such a reductionist manner, this register is composed of an ever-growing number of 'wangluo reci' (lit. 'internet hot words') which derive from 'wangluo geng'[96] (lit. 'internet memes')', with old ones falling out of use. The composition of the viral memes during the past 20 years has undergone qualitative changes (see Chapter 1), from the 'computer geek' jargon, to allusions to sensational incidents, and to the numerous slangs originated from all kinds of niched sub-communities (Yu 2014; Chen 2016). Therefore, all these subaltern, changing, and heterogeneous memes render the language register as vernacular in nature. Moreover, since 2008, Baidu, the largest search engine in China, has published the annual ranking of the top 'internet hot words' as a way to commemorate those memes that have risen to fame from various sub-cultural margins (Zhang 2015) and have thus contributed to the emerging 'online vernacular culture'.

Therefore, the use of (up-to-date) linguistic memes online are taken to be the most salient criterion for identifying one's utterances as the Chine Internet Vernacular (CIV). In fact, as found by many researchers of Chinese internet (e.g. Herold 2015), the blending of on- and offline discourses is ubiquitous among young people living in urban areas, who also constitute the absolute majority of internet users in China – 73.1% according to the latest official report (CNNIC 2017). With the continued growth of the Chinese internet population and the rate of internet penetration – respectively 710 million and 51.7% by July 2017, the register of CIV has gained steady ground in recent years and interacted with the mainstream culture, backed up by the expanding 'online culture', and is argued to become an important everyday 'national vernacular' (De Seta 2016). However, the features that characterize CIV as a register are much more than the memes *per se*, but consist mostly in the 'vernacular practices' of the users, which I'll elaborate on in what follows.

6.1.2 Between 'internet', 'standard' and 'popular'

The recognition of a certain 'deviate' register – where the internet vernacular is certainly such a case – always presupposes the

96. The Chinese word 'geng' (the correct form should be 'gen'), which originally refers to the standing jokes in traditional Chinese crosstalk comedies, has been increasingly used to describe the virally spread expressions and jokes on Chinese social media, and thus becomes a rough-and-ready equivalent of the English notion 'meme'.

ideological construct of the 'standard' register, in relation to which all the other speech varieties are evaluated normatively. In the Chinese context, such meta-semiotic (d)evaluation is especially vocal as CIV has become the target of 'language regulation' since very early on. To regulate language use on the internet is in line with the Chinese government's pronounced strategy of 'informatization' of the country, which serves as a means of boosting economic growth, as well as enhancing a 'socialist harmonious society' (see China's Internet White Paper 2010[97]). In such official accounts, the use of 'internet language' is associated with the online culture that is increasingly 'de-authoritative', 'blurred of principles and regulations' and 'at the risk of cathartic negative sentiments' (Zhang and Wei 2011). The National Medium- and Long-Term Language Work Reform and Development Plan (2012-2020),[98] published by the Ministry of Education, makes it clear that "online public opinions and sentiments should be monitored" and "social language practice should be regulated" to "maximize the harmonious factors and minimize the disharmonious factors... as creative ways of administering [people's] language practice." Since then, there has been a good number of governmental papers, investigatory reports, etc., official and semi-official, every year to monitor and regulate the development and spread of the current internet language and public sentiments.

The official discourse and ideology, however, only seems to complicate the meta-semiotic evaluation in 'the people's language practice': an additional dimension of antithesis between the authoritative and the online public may also be at work. It is speculated by some media scholars (e.g. Zhang and Wei 2011) that the 'underdeveloped civil participation' and 'undue anxiety of individual rights' may amplify the public antagonism towards any governmental decisions. Moreover, when it comes to the issue of internet vernacular, the voice of its proper users – the online public – is very likely to be overrepresented and slant the 'public opinion in reality'. For instance, back in 2010 when the proposal of censoring

97. China's Internet White Paper (2010), published by the Information Office of the State Council of China, accessed from http://www.scio.gov.cn/tt/Document/1011194/1011194.htm on May 10, 2016.

98. Accessed from http://www.moe.edu.cn/publicfiles/business/htmlfiles/moe/s7246/201301/146511.html on November 10, 2015.

internet slang words made up of non-standard orthography (e.g., obsolete Chinese characters or Latin alphabet) became a matter of public debate, the online public were in favor of the internet vernacular by a landslide, possibly 'overriding the opinions of non-netizens' (2011: 11). In consequence, this antithesis has always been noticeable, which makes the regulatory efforts even more tense and the evaluation of the internet vernacular more ideologically-charged.

6.1.3 Relationship with the 'mainstream'

As we have discussed previously, the extension of CIV has undergone prominent changes throughout the years as a (partial) result of the changing technological and socio-political framings on the Chinese internet. The increasingly diversified memes which have largely outnumbered the previous technical jargon and politically suggestive hidden transcripts may, on the one hand, reflect the increasing 'pan-entertainment' and 'light political' orientations (Chen 2016) in CIV. On the other, the recent growing number of (sub-)community vocabularies incorporated into the entire register is also the consequence of the development of social media, where users who participate in different online communities of practice are much more likely to interact and exchange their language use.

As such exchanges continue, the register of the internet vernacular is less and less distinct from the mainstream culture. In fact, this register has become an epitome of the most popular and fashionable subset of the mainstream culture, in which sense it implies an inter-generational distinction, instead of a center-periphery one. This 'mainstreamization' is especially highlighted when official discourse attempts to utilize elements from this register. For instance, *People's Daily*, the mouthpiece of the Chinese Communist Party, 'acknowledged', adopted and adapted more than 50 internet hot words during 2009-2013 (Wang 2015). It is also noted that intense ideological reworking is involved in such 'official appropriation', with its tangible endeavors to standardize the words and regulate their use. In other words, the online public and the authorities are yet to be reconciled vis-à-vis the register of CIV.

6.1.4 Using CIV as reflexive social processes

To investigate the Chinese Internet Vernacular, I mainly adopt Agha's (2007, 2015) theories on register formations. Agha's reflexive perspective declines a mere repertoire-based approach to a register, instead, using the internet vernacular should be studied as "(a) the reflexive processes through which samples of the thing come to be differentiated from other discursive behaviors or (b) the social-interpersonal processes through which expressions of [the very register] undergo change in form and significance for different members of a language community" (2015: 306).

Specifically, the existence of a certain register depends on its 'value boundary' – how it's evaluated meta-pragmatically in a positive or negative way by different groups of evaluators. In the actual use, a register boundary is usually 'inhabited' by 1) voicing from a different register (for example, when I comment that "you're trolling in the thread", every word in the sentence is from another register – standard English), by 2) invoking the very criterial personae (and being successfully recognized as such) associated with the register in public life, which Agha also calls 'meta-pragmatic typification', and/or by 3) setting and drawing the 'baseline of evaluation' – a perception that some unified *standard* exists from which the register is differentiated and *derogated*.

The presupposition of the *standard* in a larger language community also enables the register speakers to work on the evaluation and mediate forms of their interpersonal footing at a micro level. For instance, shifting baselines of the *standard* or other relative registers can strategically render part of the in-group speakers 'more legitimate' or 'less competent' and thus create sub-groups and distinctions. Stereotypes, stigmas and other value constructs upheld in the *standard* can also be invoked from within the register to bring forth a new hierarchy.

To sum up, the Chinese Internet Vernacular, presumed here as a social register for further analysis, has interacted with both the mainstream and the official discourses over the years, and has thus developed certain (changing) relationships with them. From a practice-based and ethnographic perspective, I will try to investigate how ordinary Chinese internet users look at this register *as an ideological framework*, how they relate themselves to it *as interactional processes*, and how they practice it *as a repertoire* in their daily online communication. For this, I will focus on the various features that have emerged as prominent evaluations of CIV over the past few years, and enquire into the following questions:

I. What are the main (discursive) activities that ordinary social media users carry out regarding the various (negative) evaluations, and what are the aspects and dimensions involved in such activities that metapragmatically constitute CIV as a register?
II. How do users construct, negotiate and perform (different) identities, in terms of metapragmatically typified voices and styles, when they engage in the evaluative activities of CIV?
III. What are the ideological constructs that are invoked, keyed and switched to in users' activities with CIV, and how do such metapragmatic processes (re)define CIV as a register?

6.2 Methods and data

This study makes a tentative effort to probe into the daily practice with the register of CIV and users' attitudes and opinions. Towards this end, a digital ethnography of mixed methods was adopted to collect data. Specifically, 1) I conducted online participatory observations and close monitoring of internet users' daily language practice on various social media platforms in order to develop emic understanding of the practice, locate possible points of interest, and record necessary data. And 2) I also organized offline focus groups and individual interviews, asked the participants to reflect on their practice of CIV, and elicited other qualitative data related to it.

6.2.1 Online data

The online data collection spanned a period of two years (November 2014-December 2016), where a large miscellany of posts, forum threads, comments, discussions, etc. mainly on Weibo were recorded and sorted (in terms of major themes, attitudes, and speech events, etc.). As more data were gathered, some recurrent themes, opinions, speech acts were identified as important to the notion and practice of CIV, and five groups of data were finally selected for detailed analysis. The following table summarizes the main data used in this chapter.

Table 6.1 Summary of online data (Corpus DC4)

Sub-dataset	Data type	Sources	Contents
D1	Forum discussion	Zhihu.com[99] Thread: *What popular words have been overused?* Collected in December 2014	332 replies as answers 2,688 comments to the first 10 answers
D2	Weibo comments	Sina Weibo Post: *The 2014 Online Vulgarism Ranking 'released'* Collected in June 2015	1,963 comments collected 1,381 valid[100] comments for analysis
D3	Weibo comments	Sina Weibo Post: *Popular Language and Popular Disease* Collected in November 2016	6,074 comments collected 4,438 valid comments for analysis
D4	Weibo comments	Sina Weibo Posts: Blogger WQXL's complaint about *doujiling* Collected in December 2016	124 comments collected 92 valid comments for analysis
D5	Weibo comments	Sina Weibo Five posts of different bloggers containing the phrase *HRYTC* Collected in December 2016	604 comments collected 212 valid comments for analysis

The above datasets were parsed and analyzed differently due to their volume of data and central themes. Datasets 2, 4, and 5, due to their large amount of comments and divergent voices, were first processed with corpus software to extract the keywords, major themes, and opinions, and then a feasible amount of comments were randomly sampled for detailed analysis.

99. Zhihu is a popular question-and-answer platform in China, similar to Quora.com and Yahoo Answers.

100. Reposts, replicates, tagging, and within-comment replies were excluded to increase the feasibility of the data parsing and analysis.

6.2.2 Offline data

The focus group interviews were conducted during the period June-July 2015. The target participants for this study were the young Chinese who frequently used internet in their daily life (the majority of the 'internet population' in China, according to CNNIC report 2017). All of the participants selected were among the age group of late teens to early 30s.

There was no predetermined criteria for selecting participants, but I did intend to conduct a purposive sampling (Bryman 2008) in terms of gender, educational background, and social status in order to cover a spectrum of participants as wide as possible. Whenever possible, I organized the participants into focus groups and carried out casual, semi-structured interviews with them. They were *casual* in that I introduced myself to the participants as a researcher at a foreign university who was especially intrigued by the recent boom of CIV words and phrases, and would like to know more based on their own experiences and understandings; and the interviews were *semi-structured* in the sense that I tried to cover topics including 1) their daily online experience, 2) their attitudes towards certain internet language items, 3) their construal of certain expressions, 4) their opinions about other groups of internet users, etc. The following is a summary of the participants and their basic demographic information.

Table 6.2 Summary of participants in DF2

Sub-dataset	Participants	Gender & Age group	Social status
Focus group (F1) (June 6 2015) *Shenzhen, China*	Erin[101]	Female, 25-34	White-collar employee
	Alex	Male, 25-34	White-collar employee
Focus group (F2) (June 15 2015) *Chongqing, China*	Celine	Female, 25-34	White-collar employee
	Uno	Male, 25-34	Civil servant
Focus group (F3) (June 16, 2-15) *Chongqing, China*	Sweety	Female, 15-24	Graduate student
	Paula	Female, 15-24	Graduate student

101. All the names appearing in this paper were chosen by the participants themselves after being informed of the confidentiality.

Sub-dataset	Participants	Gender & Age group	Social status
Focus group (F4) (June 30, 2015) *Beijing, China*	Sophie	Female, 15-24	High school student
	Tony	Male, 15-24	High school student
	Sabrina	Female, 15-24	High school student
Focus group (F5) (July 2, 2015) *Beijing, China*	Mr. G	Male, 25-34	Graduate student
	Miss E	Female, 15-24	Undergraduate student
	Soothing	Female, 25-34	White-collar employee
Phone interview (P1) (July 3, 2015)	Lixiaoduo	Female, 25-34	University lecturer
Focus group (F6) (July 4, 2015) *Beijing, China*	Bebert	Male, 25-34	Graduate student
	ZY	Male, 15-24	Undergraduate student
	XF	Male, 15-24	Undergraduate student
	Aurore	Female, 25-34	Graduate student
Focus group (F7) (July 6, 2015) *Beijing, China*	Panso	Female, 15-24	High school student
	Daisy	Female, 25-34	High school teacher
	Bella	Female, 15-24	High school student
Focus group (F8) (July 30, 2015) *Tilburg, Netherlands*	Leona	Female, 15-24	Graduate student
	Olivia	Female, 15-24	Graduate student

Based on my longitudinal observations for over four years, various evaluations and perceptions have been attributed to CIV, which would usually attract users' heated discussion and interaction. In what follows, I will discuss four of such evaluations of CIV, around which some salient metapragmatic processes of the users have emerged from the data, revealing some important forms of reflexive practices of the participants with CIV. As the data were gathered from various sources over the past few years, I will also expand on how specific datasets were drawn on and processed for the analysis.

6.3 Construction of the value-boundary: The case of vulgar

Most of the vocal evaluations about the register of Chinese internet vernacular are by and large negative ones, from a highly institutionalized, standard-oriented, and normative perspective, to distinguish this discourse from the rest of the language. This is understandable as this register naturally corresponds with the online public sentiments and thus falls under the close official monitoring and scrutiny. As the authorities release evaluations of the register every now and then, which would usually become sites of heated discussion, we are able to observe the antithetic evaluations where the 'value-boundary' is being drawn that defines the very substandard register. Two Weibo posts (Datasets 2 and 4) that publish such official opinions on internet language were selected with their comments in order to investigate the attitudes and opinions of the practitioners of CIV.

On June 2, 2015, the official account of *Caijing Magazine* published a Weibo post[102] about the recent release of the top vulgar internet language by the 'public opinion monitoring office of People.cn' and attached a picture (see Appendix IV. a) of the entire list to the post:

> **[The 2014 Online Vulgarism Ranking 'released': '*nima*'[103] tops the list and '*tufeiyuan*' is on] Today, the public opinion monitoring office of People.cn has published the Investigatory Report of Online Vulgar Language, which ranks the online vulgar words used in original Weibo posts. '*Nima*' is first in the ranking, and '*diaosi*', '*doubi*', '*nimei*', '*caonima*' are all on the list. See the following list, today, have you been vulgar** 

This post immediately attracted vehement discussions by Weibo users. By the time of collection, there were already 1,963 comments to the post. All the valid comments were processed and annotated using the software NLPIR (ICTCLAS 2015) before I extracted the keywords and calculated the frequencies so as to form a general overview of the discourse in question. Among the 30 most frequent keywords, 14 of them are words from the very 'vulgar list', which were apparently referred to when the users discussed the list in the

102. Accessed from http://www.weibo.com/1642088277/CkJeJyYZE on June 18, 2015.

103. See Appendix IV. a for the explanations of these 'vulgar' CIV words.

comments. The other 16 keywords (see Appendix IV. b) may help us form a general and rough idea of what main aspects the users' comments are concerned with. For instance, there are several keywords that are in clear opposition to each other, such as 'civil language' versus 'vulgar language', and there are also keywords that reflect a strong sense of normativity, such as 'monitoring office' and 'ought to'. In what follows, I will look into these aspects in detail.

6.3.1 Irreconcilable disagreement

To investigate the general attitudes of the users about the 'vulgarity' of internet language, I singled out all the comments containing 'vulgar' (314 comments in total) and coded them into roughly four attitudinal categories, namely,

1) Supportive, where the users are positive about the post and regard (at least one of) the words on the list as vulgar and should be avoided;
2) Opposing, where the users disagree with the post and negate the concept of 'vulgarity' or don't consider the words as vulgar;
3) Uncertain/questioning, where the users question, challenge, or express doubt about the words or the concept of vulgarity, without indicating a clear attitude; and
4) Sarcastic, where the users make sarcastic (self-)statements about the words, especially in terms of vulgarity, which usually take the forms of self-confession or apology.

As shown in Table 6.3, only a small part of the users (15.3%) are genuinely in favor of the negative evaluation of the 'internet vulgarity', while twice as many users are outspokenly against such evaluation. A minor fraction of the users tries to qualify or challenge the official evaluation, while still keeping a certain level of affinity with the standard, and interestingly, the biggest group of users are sarcastic about it, dismissing such evaluation by implication. Such results are similar to the previous online polls regarding the regulatory evaluations of internet language (Zhang and Wei 2011), where internet users rejected such negative framings by a landslide.

Table 6.3 Distributions of attitudes on 'vulgar'

Attitude	Counts	%
Supportive	48	15.3
Opposing	95	30.3
Uncertain/questioning	46	14.6
Sarcastic	125	39.8
Total	314	100.0

Obviously, such antithesis on the vulgarity of internet language is a reflexive negotiation between practitioners of two ideological frameworks, the standard vs. the online, in order to draw the 'value-boundary' between the two discourses and define the register of internet language. In what follows, I will analyze how the meta-pragmatic judgements by different internet users, both online and offline, actually work on such 'boundary-drawing'.

6.3.2 Self-valorization

Different from the above negotiation of value-boundary that attempts to argue over the 'position' of internet language in relation to the standard, there're also many users who implicitly presuppose the uniqueness of the register and try to justify the in-group valorization by highlighting such uniqueness, or insider's knowledge. For instance, the "our meme" in Excerpt 6.1 and the comparatively in-group lexicon of 'meng-ized' (as well as the meek tone in face of the authorities) immediately foreground the opposition between the two registers.

Excerpt 6.1

How is this vulgar, it's just because cctv (metonymic of the authorities) doesn't understand our memes (D2/0022)[104]

Excerpt 6.2

These are already menghua (lit. 'made cuter', ca. euphemized) words, don't be too harsh, we won't say them offline, just cut us some slack online... (D2/0298)

104. The message data used in this chapter are labelled in the format (sub-dataset/ assigned number), while the offline interview data were cited in the format (sub-dataset/ participant).

6.3.3 Trope of personae

Agha (2007) refers to the 'trope of personae' as the systems of stereotypical social indexicals that link a certain repertoire to particular kinds of social personae that can be inhabited and negotiated through the use of expressions from the repertoire. While the social personae of internet language can be as general as anyone who uses the internet, the users would depict a vividly 'otherized' persona in order to argue how the value-boundary should be drawn so as not to be included by such a negative persona.

Excerpt 6.3

> Reading all these comments, I'm really speechless! A bunch of rubbish who think that by speaking one or two vulgar internet phrases would make you trendy and fashionable, actually you're no different from those hateful rascals on the street with a cigarette dangling in the mouth! (D2/0186)

Excerpt 6.4

> Leave nobility to all kinds of bitches, it (nobility) doesn't fit us (D2/0752)

The above two examples express opposite attitudes about the criticism of internet vulgarity by both invoking negative social personae: in Excerpt 6.3 the user's detailed depiction of 'hateful rascals on the street with a cigarette dangling in the mouth' as those who would use the vulgar words online, by orienting to the ideology of the standard and the high culture, immediately lowers such a discourse register with the socially stigmatized community of 'street thugs' and their 'despicable' culture; whereas in Excerpt 6.4, the user's curt characterization of 'all kinds of' noble bitches, however, indexes a different ideological framework, that of morality, to overshadow the one of 'the standard language', and by implication renders the criticism hypocritical, pretentious, or scheming.

However, in offline interviews, the participants would usually be less assertive about the 'vulgar' quality of CIV and would express a mixed account of a social personae typified as using such memes on and off the internet. For instance in Excerpt 6.5, Bebert's understanding of the vulgar quality in the following example is typical of the interviewees' formulation, in that unlike online participants who would defy and dismiss the *standards* outright, they try to ameliorate various aspects of the social persona using such vulgar language, with a somewhat tacit acknowledgement of established social standards and etiquettes. While the participant Bebert recognizes the vulgarity, in accordance with the *standard language* ideology, he also attempts to highlight the much desirable qualities, such as intimate and playful, that are troped on the catchphrases. By accounting for the use of the memes as exercising a rather positive persona, he implicitly tries to elevate the evaluation of CIV as a register.

Excerpt 6.5

> It is strange that most internet catchphrases are vulgar words, which then again don't feel quite so when articulated. It seems that many of such vulgar words have 'washed white' through being popular online. Because I'm not a person who curses a lot, I did feel a bit of uneasy and careful first using such words, especially on Wechat, but when you do use them, they don't feel as vulgar as they look. The vulgarity has already been bleached, and instead becomes a feeling of closeness and teasing between people. And that kind of intimacy and unseriousness has now to be expressed through such words. (F6/Bebert)

6.4 Negotiation of baselines: The case of deficient

Another persistent evaluation of CIV in the official discourse is its overwhelming feature of rapid and vast reproduction – the intrinsic characteristic of memic diffusion as we've discussed in previous chapters – which has usually been downplayed from the standard perspective as lexical monotony and verbal inadequacy. Such a comment is usually formulated in a way to deride the internet users' Chinese language aptitude, and the following post is a recent case in point. On November 1, 2016, the People's Daily published a commentary, titled 'Popular Language and Popular Disease', to criticize the epidemic of overusing online buzzwords, finding fault especially with the current viral phrase 'lanshou, xianggu',[105] where the author calls the spread of such 'nonsensical' phrases as the 'language deficiency syndrome'. Besides 'lanshou, xianggu' (LSXG henceforth), the article also specifies several other

105. Literally 'blue thin, shiitake', partial homophonic (with a Guangxi accent) to 'feeling sad, want to cry'.

deficient internet phrases, and by contrast proposes a couple of 'desired' phrases that are more elegant and cultured. People Daily's official Weibo shared this article in a post[106] with some additional comments, which attracted more than 6k comments of quite vocal attitudes by the time of collection.

Our ancestors use '*maobipan'an*'[107] and '*yushulinfeng*'[108] to describe beautiful appearances, while we can only say '*gaoshuaifu*' ('tall-rich-handsome') or '*baifumei*' ('fair-rich-beautiful'); people in the past use '*woxinshangbei, mozhiwoai*'[109] to express their sorrow, whereas we only know 'LSXG'... If one day you can only produce '*gaofushuai*' or '*aiqiongcuo*' (short-poor-ugly) whenever you speak, will you be shocked by your own expressive deficiency?

6.4.1 Clashes of orientations

On the 4,438 valid comments (out of the total 6,074 comments collected), a similar corpus-processing was conducted with the software ICTCLAS (NLPIR 2015) to obtain the top keywords and most frequent words from the dataset (see Appendix IV. c) in order to form a general picture. Based on the keywords list, we can see that many of the comments and discussions are carried out around the 'deficient' and 'desirable' phrases suggested by the original post, and their respective sociocultural underpinnings, e.g. 'hot words' (rank 14) vs. 'traditional culture' (rank 8), as well as attitudinal evaluations, e.g. 'brainless' (rank 18) vs. 'pretentious' (rank 10). To narrow down the focus of analysis, I singled out all the comments containing 'deficien*'[110] to investigate the commenters' opinions and attitudes on the issue. Of all the 173 comments, four attitudinal categories, similar to the operation on the 'vulgar' dataset, were roughly distinguished.

106. Accessed from http://www.weibo.com/2803301701/EfvfRytSz on November 2, 2016.

107. To resemble the appearance of Pan'an, a gorgeous man in Chinese history.

108. A jade tree in the wind, an idiom often used to describe a young man's talent as well as his outstanding physical appearance.

109. These two phrases are originated from the poem 'Cai Wei' ('Homecoming after War') in the ancient Chinese collection 'Shijing' ('Classic of Poetry') (compiled ca. 600 BC). They can roughly translate as 'My grief overflows. Who knows? Who knows?'

110. The Chinese characters 'pinfa' can either be a noun ('deficiency') or an adjective ('deficient').

Table 6.4 Distributions of attitudes on 'deficient'

Attitude	Counts	%
Supportive	53	30.6
Opposing	63	36.4
Uncertain/questioning	30	17.4
Sarcastic	27	15.6
Total	173	100.0

As shown in the above table, the majority (about 70%) of the commenters are either antagonistic or suspect of the 'deficient account', if sarcasm and questioning are both taken to be means of negative attitudes. Compared with the criticism of vulgarity, apparently more (cf. 15.3% as to vulgarity) users are positive about the normative judgement on the verbal deficiency of the internet vernacular, especially the phrase LSXG, while considerably fewer users are sarcastic about it (cf. 39.8% as to vulgarity). Supportive users are generally concerned, or even irritated, about the preemption of common people's everyday vocabulary by CIV; whereas many sarcastic comments in effect highlight the phrases and patterns in the Chinese official discourse that are equally, if not more, repetitive and monotonous, and therefore no less deficient. Explicit opposing opinions, the relative majority, target especially at the authorities' imposition of certain lexicons and their 'shang gang shang xian'[III] approach; while a group of less antagonistic users (still with tangible negative attitudes) question the expressive efficacy and popular acceptance of the 'suggested' lexicon and generally regard them as anachronistic.

The notion of 'verbal deficiency' as a value judgement of CIV provokes likewise intense metapragmatic discussions, similar to the case of 'vulgar'. Interestingly, the ways that online participants frame their comments and discussions, where the opposition between CIV and the *standard* is usually highlighted and reiterated, are in stark contrast to how offline participants reflect on their CIV

III. 'Shang gang shang xian', lit. 'as a matter of political principle', a Chinese idiom used primarily during the Cultural Revolution (1966-1976), is originally invoked to criticize something or someone as anti-revolutionary. In recent years, this idiom is increasingly used in a negative way, meaning to make a big deal, or to make a mountain out of a molehill.

practices. Partly because controversial or opposing opinions are generally more likely and vocal in online news[112] comments (Ziegele et al. 2014), and the Weibo post at issue is announced by the central voice of Chinese authorities, we thus see a spate of scathing and defensive comments for CIV.

On the one hand, there're many Weibo participants who share or support the claims in the post by expressing their (usually helpless or vexed) feelings about the 'shrinking' vocabulary. In most of their accounts, in line with the official opinion, CIV stands opposite to the standard language, especially the written form. Within such a highly normative frame, the literary form of Chinese, which is usually exhibited with the extended use of idioms, allegories, allusions, and other generic features formed throughout the Chinese literary history, occupies the summit of the hierarchy and reflects the most authentic and refined elements of the Chinese culture (Xing 2000). Such an 'elitist' orientation, even though classical literary Chinese has long been left out of common use,[113] has persisted as an important criterion for marking one's 'culturedness', and has also seeped into the curricula of all levels of language education (Zhang 2006). Participants who frame their (everyday) language practice within this ideological construct practically view CIV as an inferior, degraded subset of the common language and the (excessive) use of CIV as the incompetence to draw elevated lexicon from the standard – therefore verbally deficient. In this light, social media communication is 'blamed' for such personal degeneration in linguistic competence. For instance, the following user views his own use of CIV (e.g. 666[114]) as the loss of the standard form (realized by using idioms), and deplores (possibly in a joking way) the resultant cultural inferiority as an 'illiterate'.

Excerpt 6.6

I once could describe the beautiful sceneries with phrases such as 'rushiruhua' [lit. 'like poetry like painting'] or 'shanhezhuangli' [lit. 'magnificent mountains and rivers']

112. The Weibo account is linked directly with the newspaper's website and shares most of its daily news articles, making the comments within its posts more like public news comments.

113. In the early 20th century, a major language reform during the 'New Culture Movement' (1910s-20s) was implemented to replace the classical Chinese with the vernacular form as the national standard to be used for all common purposes.

114. An internet neologism meaning 'awesome' or to show appreciation.

when I travelled, now I can only say 666 wherever I go, I've become a damn illiterate. (D3/289)

In contrast, opposing and doubtful users try to evaluate CIV as a register in the opposite direction – by invoking the boundaries between CIV and the standard as well as warding off the negative evaluations with self-assertions. In particular, the Weibo participants, as in-group practitioners of CIV, try to differentiate it from other registers (e.g. the written, the authoritative, the outdated, etc.) by invoking respective ideological antitheses and baselines which I will expand on in the following.

6.4.2 Differential invocations of baselines

"Characteristic of the current time" is the most used phrase (77 counts) by Weibo users to evaluate 'LSXG' and CIV in general, where the 'officially exalted' idioms and expressions in the post are considered at best "outdated and out of touch (D3/1011)" and more harshly as "stinking of the grave of musty old books (D3/309)." Although a certain CIV item still evokes varied attitudes among the users (LSXG is a perfect example, as many users express their aversion towards the meme), there's a general conviction of the timeliness and usability of CIV among them – i.e. appropriate to the very interactional frame of contemporary Chinese social discourse. For instance:

Excerpt 6.7

Language and orthography are always developing, the appearing of new words and new buzzwords will only make our language richer, not deficient. Internet buzzwords usually reflect certain social trends at certain times, they're lively, they're folksy, and those buzzwords that survive a long period of time and get generally accepted, have especially shown their vitality. The so-called deficiency caused by buzzwords is nothing but groundless worries. (D3/107)

Another important baseline for evaluation that the participants usually invoke is the serviceability of the common language, where the aesthetic and value judgement of the common people is elevated higher than the official standards. For instance, in Excerpt 6.8, the actual idiom used is 'renmin qunzhong xiwenlejian' (lit.

'the people/ the masses love to hear and see'), which is a common, if not overused, phrase resorting to the populist political and cultural ideology. However, such ideology in Chinese society has always been offset by the rigid and indiscriminate censorship (Hou 2015) that at various times runs starkly counter to what the common people really 'love to see and hear'. And such conflict of baselines around the 'deficient' quality can also be regarded as extension of such ideological clashes.

Excerpt 6.8

> They're loved and used by the common people. You don't like them, what the hell do you think you are? (D3/972)

Besides the clashes in baseline invocation, many offline participants in fact have shown a noticeable tendency for a reconciliation between different language ideologies. For instance, in the following example, all of the three participants are well educated and active social media users. This excerpt of interview begins when Soothing elaborates on how she finds many people's use of memes deficient, or 'don't know how to express themselves'. Apparently, all of them hold the standard language to be the unquestionable baseline, and in accordance their evaluation of CIV is directly negative, such as Mr. G's 'yusizao'.[115] But when I ask them to elaborate on their feelings about their own use, they then try to work on a sort of balance between the standard and CIV, highlighting some criteria as alternative baselines for actual communication, such as Mr. G's account of the replacement of a 'literate culture' by the 'popular culture', as well as Miss E's emphasis on CIV's merit of 'wide applicability'.

Excerpt 6.9 (F5)

Soothing:	Right, right, that's it. In fact, a lot of people are like this nowadays. A lot of internet buzzwords are [popular] just because they don't know how to express themselves, then they would say everything with the same word...
Mr. G:	Yusizao (a contracted form of 'one's Chinese language teachers died too soon')...
Soothing:	I... I have that feeling, maybe it's just, just me.
Researcher:	Do you feel the same?

115. This phrase itself is an internet catchphrase that people use to tease others for their language inadequacy or lack of proper language comprehension abilities.

Mr. G:	Occasionally yes, it's just, um... how should I put it... it's just a feeling that... the literary culture has been replaced by the popular internet culture.
Researcher:	How do you feel about that then?
Mr. G.:	It's really hard to say, I think, I don't detest it
Miss E.:	I do feel that, too. For example, sometimes, something happens, and every time [I would say] 'ah, I'm intoxicated as well'. And I wouldn't try to think of any other expressions, say, something more specific...
Soothing:	Indeed! Me too...
Miss E.:	Whatever the encounter is, always 'I'm intoxicated as well', then I would feel, I seem to have lost the words to describe...
Soothing:	Indeed! We have lost our own language...
Miss E.:	Well... maybe not that terrible... maybe it's because of its really wide applicability...

In sum, as the above discussion has shown, in the case of the negative qualification of CIV as deficient, the participants would invoke different baselines, orienting to different language ideologies in order to make sense of the use of CIV in their daily life. However, as such ideological constructs may clash with each other, e.g. the 'literate' versus 'popular', the participants are also actively involved in the construction and negotiation of their own identities whenever CIV memes are opted for. By ascribing the various effects of ideological significance to CIV, the participants have metapragmatically arranged it in their daily repertoires as a functional register (in parallel with other registers), which in effect ameliorates the evaluation of CIV.

6.5 Performance and interactional microspaces: The case of memes

As discussed above, social media users have engaged metapragmatically with the two negative evaluations of CIV, where they also construct and negotiate their social identities. Moreover, another keyword – meme, or in Chinese 'geng', which I have already discussed at length in previous chapters as sign vehicles of viral transmission, has also involved intense ideological activities when users engage with it reflexively, and thus becomes an indispensable component of CIV. In what follows, I will discuss how the participants act on the notion of meme to position their footing, perform their (desired) identities, and manage inter-personal (power) relationships at various microspaces, both online and offline, and reveal that the participants are in fact engaging with different ideological frameworks through such 'meme practices'.

6.5.1 Meme practice as nexus of rapport

In previous chapters, I have shown in detail how memes, such as 'duang' and 'chesaika', are adopted and innovated by certain cohesive online communities who make use of the memes as important in-group markers for community building and maintenance. In fact, based on my longitudinal observations, especially in the participants' offline interactions, various memes, or rather using memes as a daily practice, has already become an important means of maintaining rapport within social groups or between individuals.

For instance, the participant Lixiaoduo, a university lecturer, frankly says that making use of the current memes has made things easier for her in her teaching, which creates an atmosphere of like-mindedness between her students and herself.

Excerpt 6.10

> (By using the memes) in everyday talk, especially to my students, it not only helps me express my thoughts more smoothly, but also it lets them understand my feelings better. Besides, it brings me closer to the students, and by occasionally saying one meme or two, it at least makes the students think my mindset is not far from theirs. (P1/Lixiaoduo)

Besides the instrumental adoption of updated memes, it is more interesting to note that in some cases, the 'memes' per se do not even matter as much as the very activity of using them for a group of people. When I was interviewing the participants, a group of high school students, about their daily experience with online memes, to my wonderment, many of them voluntarily came up with the phrase 'bingmeiyou' as an example. On a side note, 'bingmeiyou' (lit. 'nevertheless not') is a perfectly normal and plain phrase in standard Chinese, with a tinge of literariness. When I asked them why they would think so, some of them began to recall various personal experience with it.

Excerpt 6.11 (F4)

Sabrina:	About 'bingmeiyou', it's just that, in our high school, it started from one or two boys, they started to say it, 'bingmeiyou', and then they wouldn't stop, and we were so confused. Were the two boys out of their mind? Why did they keep saying it? And then I was 'brainwashed', and after I said it for a couple of times, I just couldn't stop. Whatever I say, I would use 'bingmeiyou' to start with, 'bingmeiyou'!
Tony:	Actually, it's just... saying such and such, and then, 'bingmeiyou'.
Researcher:	So you said you were first annoyed by the use of 'bingmeiyou'?
Sabrina:	Indeed, I just felt it was weird in the beginning! It's just, why so weird? And then, because they just kept saying it, and I simply followed suit...
Tony:	When chatting [online], you would first design something, and then make a 'shrug' emoticon [makes a physical shrug at the same time], and then add a black bracket, just like this [and say 'bingmeiyou'], it's just a gesture...
Sophie:	I think this is just an ACGN meme!
Tony:	Is it? [giggles]
Sabrina:	I really think so! I was using ACGN [memes] with them.

In this stretch of interview, Sabrina tries to recall how she came to use 'bingmeiyou' as a meme. Like any other internet buzzwords, 'bingmeiyou' reached her through viral contagion, only except that in this case such contagion was offline. Just when Sabrina finishes her own account of the meme and its usage (i.e. starting every sentence with the meme) as a 'lay' user, Tony weighs in and gently hints that the 'correct' position of the phrase should be after, instead of before, the main sentence. Tony, an ACGN enthusiast, then goes on with a detailed demonstration of the phrase's proper usage, but simply compares the phrase to 'just a gesture', instead of a meme. However, Sophie and Sabrina, neither of whom considers themselves as an ACGN practitioner, insist that it should be a proper meme in the ACGN community. It is therefore arguable that such ascription of the catchphrase as a community-specific meme in an ad hoc manner, be it a proper meme or not (as what Tony judges), constitutes an important 'meme practice' for the girls to achieve and maintain rapport in the social group that they wish to identify with (in this case, the ACGN community).

Based on the above two examples, the participants have relied on such 'meme practice', the quick and casual utilization of shared and current memes (or simply oft-heard phrases), as important form of 'phatic communion' (Malinowski 1923) in their daily interactions, i.e. the trivial yet significant means of maintaining harmonious groupness and sense of smoothness within a certain 'light' (Blommaert 2018) or temporary community. It has arguably become an indispensable social identification mechanism, or rather a routine reflexive activity, for ordinary people to maintain their social relations in the age of social media, i.e., within a common chronotopic context.

6.5.2 'Stop doujiling': Negotiation of power relations

In the above discussions, we get to understand the users' own accounts of the negative evaluations of CIV as reflexive negotiation and valorization of their social identities, and their routine use of memes as phatic communion for the maintenance of their light and temporary forms of group interaction. However, it is also notable that users sometimes make rather negative evaluations when certain CIV memes are used in social media interactions, on which occasions the use would usually stir up intense negotiations of social norms and inter-personal relationships.

Before proceeding, there is an important notion '*doujiling*', roughly translating as acting witty, which is used when a certain use of memes is regarded as impertinent or insolent. Wuqiong Xiaoliang Weibo (*lit.* 'Infinitesimal light microblog'), posted three pictures of his baby daughter smiling glowingly, and the post reads, "My wife just sent me these pictures. She [his baby] is so happy when I'm away." Later he retweeted the original post[116], adding that "I've blocked and deleted all those saying 'because the Uncle Wang[117] next-door has come'. My family never taught me to make such jokes to others." What the blogger does is apparently an act of 'calling out' or 'public shaming' the 'transgressor', who has made a

116. Accessed from https://www.weibo.com/1393017020/FyogUtu79 on December 5, 2016.

117. 'Uncle Wang next-door' is a recent neologism on Chinese internet that jokingly refers to the paramour of a cheating wife, and the birth father of the child.

detestable comment on the blogger's previous post.

Before proceeding, there is an important notion 'doujiling', roughly translating as acting witty, which is used when a certain use of memes is regarded as impertinent or insolent. For instance, in a Weibo post by a popular blogger, Wuqiong Xiaoliang Weibo (lit. 'Infinitesimal light microblog'), he attaches three pictures of his baby daughter smiling glowingly, and the post reads, "My wife just sent me these pictures. She [his baby] is so happy when I'm away." Later he retweeted (footnote 117) the original post, adding that "I've blocked and deleted all those saying 'because the Uncle Wang (footnote 118) next-door has come'. My family never taught me to make such jokes to others." What the blogger does is apparently an act of 'calling out' or 'public shaming' the 'transgressor', who has made a detestable comment on the blogger's previous post.

Excerpt 6.12

> Really hate memes like 'Old Wang next-door', and 'the forgiving color'.[118] They are just extremely disgusting. (D4/32)

Excerpt 6.13

> This meme is not only low but also disgusting, don't know why so many people like to use it, those who like to use it must all be nasty guys (D4/76)

The users accuse such 'acting witty' action as rude, vulgar and disgusting, obviously transgressing norms for politeness and decency between people. And we can see that the many reflexive activities such as de-valorization and the construction of a negative persona (such as the 'nasty guys' in Excerpt 6.13) work in a different direction on CIV memes here. Moreover, in the comments, many users in fact share their moments of such transgression on social media, for instance:

Excerpt 6.14

> It is still OK if people of the same sex use such memes, but if the opposite sex conducts such sexual harassment for the sake of humor, no wonder s/he's single for life (D4/52)

118. 'The forgiving color' may refer to the color green, which comes from the phrase 'green hat', a common expression to refer to someone who is cuckholded.

Excerpt 6.15

> This meme can only be a joke between friends who are very familiar, while unknown internet users can only be called being an asshole (D4/90)

Interestingly, the above two comments show how some users retrieve, and in effect deconstruct, the supposed purposes of using some vulgar memes between users. For example, the use of the meme with a strong sexual connotation may suit the purpose of shortening the interpersonal distance between two users of opposite sexes that is created by the Chinese social norms and etiquettes on gender and sexuality, and in effect elevates the meme-user's position, apparently a male here, in the power relationship constructed in the very stretch of the interaction. However, the comment in Excerpt 6.14 in fact tries to subvert such gender-related power relation by defining it as 'sexual harassment'. In a similar vein, the user construes the original purpose of using the meme as creating a specific power relation by transgressing the social norm of interpersonal familiarity, and she simply deconstructs it by calling such meme-practice 'being an asshole'.

Therefore, at various interactional microspaces such as the ones discussed above, participants purposefully use memes to construct a specific interpersonal power relation by imposing or presuming certain norms (such as the gender-relation and interpersonal familiarity above), which can only be established and maintained if the norms are shared between the interactant users. More often than not, users are very sensitive to the minute change of invoked norms, or 'nano-hegemonies', at every move of online interaction, where an immediate and interactional deployment of meaning is exercised. This results in the user's quick and sensitive perception of the meme use as a specific, transparent action, such as 'sexual harassment', 'being an asshole', instead of 'acting witty' or 'just making a joke'.

6.6 Endless spinning of reflexivity: The case of sarcastic

Besides negative evaluative terms such as vulgar and deficient, sarcastic is also a recurring theme when users talk about CIV, and such evaluations are epitomized in the phrase "yinyang guaiqi jubao le", whose word-for-word translation is 'yin yang weird tone, (I) have reported (you)'. Basically, 'yin-yang guaiqi' means sarcastic or cynical. However, to a Chinese ear, it sounds more like 'crooked', or 'twisted', especially given that this phrase is mainly used to accuse others of making sarcastic and rude comments. Hence I will stick with the translation 'have reported your twisted comment' (henceforth HRYTC) as a more suitable translation.

As discussed above, the evaluations of CIV involve intense boundary negotiations where internet users collectively construct CIV as a register in opposition to the standard language, the official ideology, and/or language practice of the older generations. However, among social media users themselves, the CIV styles, such as sarcasm, have become the target of heavy contestation and differentiation. This increasing phenomenon results partly from the divergence of the so-called 'online population' into a myriad of inter-connected niched online communities. While the sarcastic style embedded in CIV may firstly be derived from the netizens' struggle against and resistance to the official discourses (e.g. Du 2016), things began to shift when community-specific neologisms sprung up and spread to other corners of the cyberspace. This is especially salient in the so-called '*sibi*' culture, or 'bitch-fighting', where members of different (rival) communities, such as different online fandoms, interact aggressively with each other.

6.6.1 HRYTC in use

When there's increasing sarcasm from out-groups or other users, they're usually accused of making 'twisted comments'. And the fans usually make use of the 'report function' of Sina Weibo in a 'crowdsourcing' manner. That is, the more reports and complaints are filed, the more likely an abusive comment is believed to be taken down by Weibo. Hence, HRYTC is the phrase they often use, not only to state the fact that they have indeed reported the post at issue, but also to accuse the posting user of posting such sarcastic and malicious message.

Interestingly, around early 2016, I observed an increasing use of this phrase in the interactions under many governmental Weibo accounts, especially the official accounts of the Communist

Youth League at various administrative levels that mainly target adolescents and young people. Not surprisingly, this coincides with the official internet strategy of raising and cultivating 'an army' of voluntary patriotic youths ('little pinks') on Chinese internet, both at home and abroad.[119] Besides, the Youth League has also adopted the strategy of converging with the online fandom culture in order to mobilize all kinds of fandoms and appeal to more young people, that is, people who were born in the 80s, 90s, and 00s (Wu 2016).

6.6.2 Indexical values of HRYTC

When sarcasm as a pragmatic effect is articulated, its indexical referent to a certain in-group value and identity is also implied, in that users of the phrase must be aware of their own stance as well as that of the target user while making such an accusation. Therefore, the use of the phrase would always presuppose the opposition of values, stances and/or ideologies, and in effect brings such tension into actual contestation, in other words, its indexical entailment (Silverstein 2003).

This contestation usually results in the accusation of 'taking sides': that is, the articulation of 'HRYTC' immediately points to the user's oppositional value or even political orientations. Such value differentiation is very prominent in the various high-profile 'battles' that the Communist Youth League's official Weibo waged against the perceived 'ideological rivals', who are being vocally critical of the government and thus usually accused of being 'unpatriotic'. It is through these battles that the phrase 'HRYTC' gained wider popularity as an indexical marker. Of course, such accusations are voiced from both sides.

During such large-scale ideological verbal battles, many Weibo bloggers, who like to make sarcastic and cynical comments against the motivational and patriotic posts of the governmental bloggers, have been especially targeted by the 'little pinks', the supporters of the governmental bloggers and by extension the official ideology, with the 'HRYTC' phrase. For example, the blogger '*daguguguji*' (with

119. Such a policy has been clearly stated in many governmental reports and documents, for example, the report of the '2016 National Working Conference on Internet Publicity', accessed from http://www.qstheory.cn/laigao/ycjx/2016-01/15/c_1117775218.htm on January 20, 2016.

a follower base of 3.18 million users), who's notorious for his cynical, acerbic and outlandish style, was once called out by the Youth League's official Weibo and therefore fiercely attacked by its supporters.

Interestingly, I soon observed a variety of further reflexive activities being carried out on such 'indexical referent' of one's (presupposed) political orientations or agendas. That is, some users began to reflexively act on such indexical referents of the phrase, in terms of playfulness and subversive resistance.

6.6.3 2nd-order indexicality: Playful resistance and subversion

When the indexical values of the HRYTC phrase become the target of the users' reflexive practice, a second-order indexicality – that is, how users individually and collectively evaluate, comment on, and play with the 'stance indicating' and 'opposition-inducing' meta-functions of the phrase – begins to emerge and take effect. While the users are working to transform the indexical values of the phrase, it is also noticeable that new norms are rapidly emerging, and brief moments of knowledge transmission are also quickly formed. In what follows, I will discuss three forms of such subversive and playful reflexive activities that users contribute to the second-order indexical meanings of the phrase.

I. Parody

As discussed in previous chapters, parody is one of the most common viral activities social media users engage with, which gives rise to collectively and interactionally negotiated meanings to overshadow the phrase's first-order indexical referent. Furthermore, in order to publicize their own parodic uses, many users began to share their 'tweak' on the HRYTC phrase in their casual chats with friends, as a sort of taunting remark for each other, to poke fun at or dismiss each other playfully. Figure 6.2 is a post that displays User A's screenshotted conversation with a friend of hers, where she obviously parodies the accusation with HRYTC between the two friends for a trivial matter, both highlighting the absurdity of the phrase per se and expressing her feeling of unease in an amusing way. Such example of entextualized parody of the HRYTC that also fulfills other interpersonal functions in fact abounds in my collected data, and constitutes a good proportion of the phrase's viral spread.

Excerpt 6.16 (D5/122)

> User A: hehe, sounds twisted, never mind, let me report first
> [A screenshot of the teasing conversation between two friends]

II. Derivative memes

Another way of such playful and subversive use is by turning the phrase into image memes. The following Figure 6.1 is one vivid example. It is an edited picture based on the report and complaint page of the Weibo mobile app. While the original page contains seven reasons to report, which are common offences and transgressions in online communication, the eighth reason on the lower right corner (circled in red), i.e. 'HRYTC', is apparently added by the user him/herself. This image meme was observed to appear mostly in comment sections of Weibo posts, where the users can interact with each other by posting both texts and pictures. In actual interaction, this meme is mostly intended as a fun-making device, as it can never fulfill the actual report function, but it does highlight certain aspects of the message or comment in question that can be accused or challenged in a joking way.

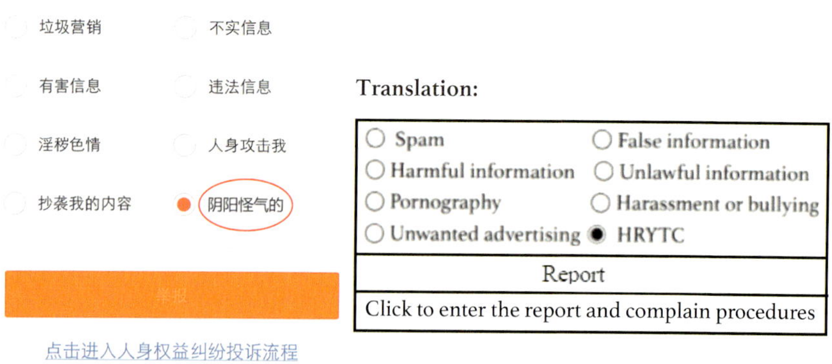

Figure 6.1 A derivative meme in one user's comment (D5/12)

III. Voluntary 'pre-emptive' use

While some bloggers became targeted as typical 'twisted' (i.e. cynical, sarcastic) commenters, who thus attracted a lot of 'anti-users' who would refute and condemn the bloggers fiercely in the comment section, their own followers began to embrace the phrase and use it in a 'pre-emptive' way, that is, to use it to describe oneself and in effect pre-empt its accusatory meaning/function. It's comparable to the African Americans' voluntary use of the N-word (Rahman 2012). For instance, whenever the blogger 'daguguguji' posts anything, there would usually be some of his own followers commenting 'HRYTC', which usually gathers many likes and shares. It has become a persistent and routinized in-group signature and convivial practice among the followers, just like 'firsting' in many comments.

In this way, the indexical values of imposing political or ideological opposition have been somewhat resisted or even subverted, and channeled into a sort of community practice where the in-group users vent their discomfort at the accusation and collectively construct their shared values and identities. Therefore, at this point, it is arguable that the third-order indexicality is emerging.

6.6.4 3rd-order indexicality: In-group marker

When this newly formed in-group norm, i.e. by reflexively appropriating and subverting the phrase's second-order indexicalities, becomes disseminated sufficiently within these knowledge-related communities, this phrase was then used as an additional 'in-group' marker, or at least, a marker for similar ideological orientations. But without sufficient contextualization cues, the so-called 'reflexive calibration' (Silverstein 1996) of the use would be very bumpy. That's why there are many interesting instances of failures or gaffes of such in-group indexicality.

Excerpt 6.17 (D5/41-43)

A: "I've reported your twisted post"
> B: Has the blogger stepped on your G-spot?
> C: @B: Obviously he's an ally, look at the quotation marks

Excerpt 6.18 (D5/70-72)

A: What a twisted comment, I'd better first report you

> B: There's no dog's head, screw him!

> C: Attention, attention! He's no ally, no ally. Over.

The two examples above are both stretches of interactions taken from Weibo comments. In the first one, after User A posts a comment to a topic putting the HRYTC phrase within quotation marks, User B immediately refutes A by taunting that he's being unreasonably irritated, as the phrase "step on one's G-spot" mocks one's unreasonable irritability on Chinese internet. However, another user, C, then replies to B's refutation, reminding him of the quotation marks and calling User A an ally – an outright affirmative of the 'in-group' identity, indicating that such use of HRYTC is apparently a subversive wordplay. In contrast, Excerpt 6.17 shows how the users identify HRYTC in its original use by finding that "there's no dog's head." By 'dog's head', User B refers to the doge emoji (), whose dismissive and subversive functions in interaction have been discussed in previous chapters. Therefore, both quotation marks and the doge emoji are extra contextualization cues to help calibrate the indexical values of the phrase as a playful in-group identity marker. Also note that these two instances are common learning processes in actual social media communication where uninitiated users may get to know the normative functions of the phrase by interacting with other users, or simply watch and learn.

6.6.5 Endless spinning

Such in-group calibration may also backfire among possible in-group members, and it may also fail to achieve its purpose against oppositional opinions. However, social media interactions have amply shown how the users can reflexively strengthen a phrase's desired indexical values in various non-linear transformations, but such activities have to be negotiated in interaction. What we may expect is further and continuous development of the phrase's indexical meanings, with higher orders of indexicality emerging as the users' dynamic and complex interactions keep going.

What drives and sustains this ongoing process consists in fact in our capabilities to get a grip on, as well as our ever-present orientations to, norms, structure, and the meaningful orderliness in our everyday activities, or what Garfinkel (1967) calls 'practical reasoning':

> As Ethnomethodological studies analyze everyday activities as members' methods for making those same activities visibly-rational-and-reportable-for-all-practical-purposes, i.e., 'accountable', as organizations of commonplace everyday activities. The reflexivity of that phenomenon is a singular feature of practical actions, of practical circumstances, of common sense knowledge of social structures, and of practical sociological reasoning. (Garfinkel 1967: vii)

Indexicality is therefore invoked whenever any particular action is being accounted for as such by the socially competent member in his/her very accounting practices. As illustrated by the case of HRYTC, reflexivity is key to understanding every instance of the repetitive and/or creative use of a CIV item as accomplishing meaningful, orderly and 'accountable' actions, which derives the driving force for the meme's diffusion and variation in the users' meaning-making activities on social media. When a certain indexical function of the meme is reflexively constructed as an accountable action, it inevitably invites further reflexive participation and interaction, and engenders more reflexive meanings and functions in the processes – the infinite spinning of memes as we have observed on social media.

6.7 Concluding remarks

While the previous chapters have focused on and investigated the actual spread and variation of CIV neologisms on social media, this chapter put the very notion of CIV into question. From the perspective of 'register formation' (Agha 2006, 2007, 2015), I proceeded to look into Chinese social media users' practices and understandings of the various CIV memes they engage with every day, as reflexive processes. Centering especially in the four major characteristics of CIV, especially from the official discourse, i.e., vulgar, deficient, memic, sarcastic, I have revealed the important metapragmatic processes underlying the participants' engagement with CIV, which not only constitute as the mechanisms and driving force of meme variation, but also effectively redefine the CIV as a changing register.

Firstly, the active participation and engagement of social media users with the negative evaluations of CIV by the official discourses were investigated as important metapragmatic processes where the users collectively construct and negotiate the formation of CIV as a register, through various reflexive practices such as drawing the value-boundary between CIV and other language registers, engineering desirable social personae associated with the CIV use, differentiating finer baselines of *in-situ* CIV use, etc., all of which work towards a positive redefining of the register of CIV. At the same time, such reflexive processes are also coupled with the users' construction and negotiation of their desirable identities within the mishmash of multiple values and ideologies in contemporary society.

Moreover, the various reflexive accounts of memes and the memic quality of CIV were also investigated, revealing another significant metapragmatic process for the users, i.e. CIV practice as identity performance and footing inhabitation in microspaces of social media interaction. I then moved on to the discussion of the seemingly endless change even in CIV memes' folk perceptions and evaluations, and found that reflexivity is crucial for the emergence of high orders of indexicality that continuously sustain such metapragmatic activities. More importantly, both of these two processes, usually overtly carried out, invoke the users' identity diacritics, community affiliations, value systems as well as ideological constructs, so that the use of CIV memes at any given moment of interaction can be made accountable as a meaningful action, which then again serves at the reflexive object for further spinning.

At this point, my research journey of following the digital flows of various CIV memes has come to an important milestone. Now that I have overseen the general reflexive processes governing the spread and variation of CIV memes, I will then be able to sum up and theorize my findings in the next chapter.

Chapter 7
Conclusion

A vignette

On November 27, 2016,[120] a Weibo user with more than 1.5 million followers, named 'Nalan Xingji'[121] tweeted with only one line – 'The Expo of Parents' Wechat Screenshots', which immediately attracted thousands of users' voluntary disclosure of their parents' conversations and personal updates on the Wechat app. By the time of collection (February 2017), the post has accumulated 150k comments and 70k reposts, and still counting. This post has literally turned into a grand exhibition of the misconceptions and faux-pas of one's parents' use of Chinese Internet Vernacular (CIV) neologisms as well as the amusing miscommunication between the two generations.

Among all the top-voted comments, the following is one of the screenshots that had gathered more than 10k likes at the moment of collection (Figure 7.1).

120. Accessed from http://www.weibo.com/1893235105/EjswZnGtd on February 10, 2017.

121. On April 23, 2017, the original user transferred the account to his friend and the username was changed into 'Kafka on the kang'.

Translation

User A: A fun game to recommend, a poisonous game, Snake Battles, hahahahaha!

Dad: Why do you let me download a viral game?

Figure 7.1 One user's comment with the screenshotted conversation

The daughter sends a Wechat message to her father to recommend a smartphone game, describing the game as 'poisonous'. The neologistic sense of 'poisonous' – literally derived from the Japanese word 中毒 (chūdoku) frequently encountered in the ACG context, meaning addictive (Tang 2010) – has been used to refer to various viral content online, but an uninitiated Chinese person (yet with sufficient IT-related knowledge) would more likely associate it with a computer virus. This comment was immediately upvoted and shared among Weibo users as a hilarious exemplar of the discrepant use/understanding of CIV between the older and younger generations. Many users are also greatly amused by the father's use of the 'surprise' emoji, which is rather infrequently used among young people, inevitably invoking a rather serious frame of interaction, something quite incompatible with the light-hearted, playful ambiance of the online culture.

Let's recall the two vignettes that the book begins with. The seemingly convenient and 'superficial' imitation and adoption by my father and Yuxia's mother may possibly turn out in an awkward way in their interaction with the younger generation on social media, just like the screenshotted dad in Figure 7.1. But it doesn't really matter if the older generation stick with their own understanding and preference of the neologisms among the likes of themselves. And all this highlights the very central point of this book – the immediate variation and differentiation of CIV is intrinsic to its viral imitation and diffusion.

The very phenomenon of virality is possible only when people collectively choose to 'ride' it, but different (groups of) people are 'riding' the same virality towards different directions with different co-travelers – therefore making different journeys. So my very own research journey has been to follow such different rides with viral CIV signs and to investigate how and why they diverge and/or converge.

7.1 Locating the flows

When I first set out to explore the ubiquitous phenomenon of CIV, I was on the one hand dazzled by the range and extent to which the neologistic usages vary, and on the other preoccupied with the attempt to systemize and categorize such variations. I decided to first focus on the three 'very X very XX' phrases – i.e. 'very erotic very violent', 'very stupid very naive', and 'very good very powerful', which are CIV items that have undergone the 'viral cycles' (Zhang et al. 2016), had their shares of notable virality and possibly become sedimented in the common CIV repository. I conducted qualitative parsing and analysis of a corpus of rich and diversified uses, as well as individual and focus-group interviews.

My tentative efforts to characterize and categorize the usages mainly dealt with the departures and variations in the phrases from their original meanings, usually through the mechanisms of metaphorization, metonymization and conceptual abstraction, where the users have come to form a general 'pragmatic orientation' (cf. Mertz 1996), and would infer from various patterned affective and pragmatic interpretations – e.g. emotion expletive, perspective shift, topic-marking, etc. – under such circumstances. These findings, however, led me to conjectures in two directions.

First, as the neologisms had been widely spread and, at least at one point, virally adopted, their novel pragmatic functions may have been naturally and contextually (contextualized as ordinary online communication) strengthened, or *subjectified* (Traugott 1995; Traugott and Dasher 2002), onto them whenever these neologisms were used. This process is well comparable to the typical ways multiunit-strings are idiomized and pragmatically charged in Chinese (e.g. Wu 2011; Yue 2011), except that these neologisms went through the process in a more rapid and radical fashion, mostly because of the highly interpersonal nature and affective embedding on social media. However, such pragmatically and affectively enhanced functions, rather than getting consolidated onto the neologisms *per se* – probably due to their short-lived vitality online – lay the intertextual ground for more novel CIV items to come.

Furthermore, ordinary users' general tendency for the pragmatic orientation then again raised the question as to how such 'pragmatic calibration' (Silverstein 1996) is achieved and managed, i.e., how they enact and invoke the different indexical values so that the interpretation of the very discursive interaction is coherent for the users. In this light, the use of the neologisms serves as 'meta-utterances' (Hübler and Bublitz 2007) that, with varied explicitness, invoke certain interactional frames and invite other users to interpret the current stretch of interaction as intended discursive situations of, say, sympathy-seeking, sarcastic stance-taking, etc. The recognition and management of such functions apparently work at the metapragmatic level, and are largely sustained by the perceived virality of the very neologisms; however, such changed functions are packaged as meaning potential in the CIV phrases and are always underdetermined for the participants, when the local contexts of interaction are removed.

All these findings inevitably beg the question of meaning actuation in actual interactional events, which therefore helps me locate the digital flows to be researched of a CIV neologism's meaning variation – i.e., the viral trend of a particular meme which is made up of a myriad of momentary, local and intimate interactions by the users actually using it on social media.

7.2 Following the flows

When I was fishing for such flows as prompted by the very question inspired by the last case study, a very remarkable viral diffusion of 'duang', an ideophonic word innovated in a parodic mash-up video, began to inundate the Chinese social media. With sufficient pilot research, I was able to identify the two main digital flows throughout the meme's viral diffusion, that is, 1) its meaning and function variation throughout the viral diffusion (before it faded out of virality) on Weibo, and 2) its online milieus of use and spread, from the original cohesive ACGN community all the way to the most general public. Recall the four features and aspects of CIV I have introduced in Chapter 1. In the attempt to achieve a comprehensive grasp of the viral flows, I need to remix different quantitative and qualitative methods to operationalize the investigation of such a multi-layered phenomenon.

From the very beginning, the innovated word's viral diffusion was marked with tremendous variation and transformation. A typology of 11 major meaning and function usage types was qualitatively worked out from an ad-hoc Weibo message corpus in order to examine the range of variation and its relationships with the different stages of '*duang*'s' virality (i.e. initial, pre-peak, viral peak, post-viral). In proportion, the imitative and commentary uses – the typical viral behaviors (Shifman 2014) – plummeted immediately after the meme reached general virality, while its meaning variations sprung up dramatically, most of which were in fact revamped from, in terms of pragmatic effects and indexical values, various intertextual antecedents in the growing CIV repository. Generally speaking, '*duang*'s' meaning and function transformation is very sensitive to its virality, especially those usages that require greater cognitive efforts in inference, which shrank quickly when it passed the viral peak. My analysis therefore demonstrates the multifarious functional nuances a CIV neologism can gather despite its uniformity in appearance in viral participation, which is, at this moment of research, apparently motivated and conditioned by two inseparable forces: a) the perceived virality of the meme as well as b) the actual participations and interactions of the users. It is thus crucial to examine the accompanying viral contexts of such meaning transformations, in other words, to move from the linguistic to the sociolinguistic.

It is important to note that to follow the spread of '*duang*' as meaning transformation is necessarily a learning experience for every ordinary social media user (including myself as a researcher), where the diffusion and adoption of the innovated word is actualized as processes of transmitting the relevant knowledge. Different aspects and dimensions of knowledge exchange and transmission were involved instantaneously when the meme began to diffuse, where users interactively performed different 'knowledge-related' (Blommaert 2018) roles in any instance of entextualization and resemiotization. For example, while in some cases, the outward spread of the meme entailed voluntary 'spreaders' as active agents, or 'high-degree nodes' (Goel et al. 2016) that triggered large diffusional cascades; in others, frequent ask-and-answer exchanges were performed, so that not only the involved users but virtually anyone came, to various extents, to be in the know. Either way, intense interactive negotiations and co-constructions were always involved as to the meme's local meaning, understanding and normativity within a certain environment that certain users collectively constructed as relevant.

In consequence, such knowledge-related practices in the entextualization processes define, cross-cut, or even conflate online collectivities of different natures. Cohesive and sustainable online 'communities of practice' (Lave and Wenger 1990; Wenger 1998), such as the original '*Guichu*' video-remixing sub-community, a certain music band's online fandom, or even a circle of mutual friends,[122] were almost always highlighted and discussed along the viral diffusion, therefore marking off the users' distinct memberships. There were also less connected group interactions, in various degrees of attenuation, where the meme was locally entextualized to create an ad-hoc affinity space (Gee 2004) for users to temporarily engage with, the typical case being the interaction among a group of co-followers of a certain social media celebrity under a single message thread. The viral diffusion therefore created a myriad of nexuses, where participant users interactively identified with online communities of various kinds, negotiated their in-group identities, invested feelings and emotions, and collectively conventionalized certain types of situated and entextualized usages. During this process different orders of indexicality associated with distinct community practices formed and emerged. While the perception of virality pushes our thinking

122. Here, 'mutual friendship' is defined by the users' reciprocal following (or friending) on their social media applications.

towards uniformity and stability, the actual practices push our thinking towards diversity and change.

7.3 Zooming in on the flows

This diversity then needed to be addressed in depth. For this I chose an example which may look like a straightforward case of trans-cultural word-borrowing through the channels of globalized popular culture. To illuminate the pervasive niched community practices underneath the diffusion of viral neologisms, I looked into the spread of the phrase 'chesaika', by virtually entering the flows of the very TV fandom community where the neologism was innovated and propagated. Such participatory ethnographic experience enabled me to zoom in on the very mechanism and motivation for neologisms to become appropriated and appropriable for community practice, through the lens of 'languaging' (Møller and Jørgensen 2009; Blommaert 2010). At this point, the focus of my analysis entirely shifted from the sign itself as the residue of histories of interaction generating a more or less underdetermined potential for meaning effects (such as the functions and effects I discussed in Chapter 3) to the situated actions in which the indeterminacy of the sign is replaced with actual, momentary concrete effects. Or in other words, the shift from the linguistic system to the sociolinguistic one was completed.

In such languaging practices, users reflexively consider various semiotic features as resources that are useful in different ways because of their different presupposed indexical values. In the case of '*chesaika*', the fans interactively negotiated and highlighted the linguistic, pragmatic and sociolinguistic components that were differentially invoked from their 'original' contexts across multiple 'language varieties' (e.g. Chinese, Thai, regional dialects, CIV memes, etc.), so that a particular fan-made style was successfully codified with the novel phrase. This highly complex process is in fact a telling case of 'translanguaging' (Creese and Blackledge 2010; García and Li 2014) and sheds special light on the regional sociolinguistic dynamics (in this case, East and Southeast Asia) under globalization.

More importantly, such translanguaging and entextualizing practice with the neologism is only possible and meaningful when relevant norms and indexical values are ready and associable, in other words, when the fandom members can readily use '*chesaika*' to 'enregister' (Agha 2007) their collective taste, aesthetics and identity. From the perspective of 'enregisterment', it is found that the values and tastes of the "rottenly-oriented" (homo-erotic) sub-culture among young Chinese women become especially relevant, and have thus been metapragmatically typified as the social voice and style of a sharp-tongued, self-empowering, and uninhibited persona, and consequently troped on the very neologism.

The enregisterment of '*chesaika*' has also been found to proceed in various ways, fulfilling various social and interpersonal functions within and beyond the very fandom, including sustaining group interaction, exercising in-group camaraderie, expanding the fandom, marking off and carrying out fan-talk, etc. Therefore, the collective translanguaging of the innovated phrase, a specific type of meaning and function transformation through diffusion, serves as an important means to perform and enact the value, style and identity of a certain online community of practice.

7.4 Looking over the flows

After discussing the previous three chapters, I was in the position that warranted a revisit to the popular conceptualizations of CIV outlined in Chapter 1. How, then, does the virality of CIV memes that has been amply demonstrated in the case studies, both as a social epidemic and as entextualized interactions, impact ordinary social media users' perception of CIV as identifiable language varieties? For this question, I zoomed out a little bit and looked over all the participants' metapragmatic engagements and flows that I'd followed over the past three years, and put the very notion of CIV into question. From the perspective of 'register formation' (Agha 2006, 2007, 2015), I inquired into Chinese social media users' practices and understandings of the various memes they engage with every day as reflexive processes.

The recognition of CIV as a register mainly lies in its opposition to the standard language that is endorsed in the official discourses, which may be inherently derived from many neologisms' sociocultural and symbolic function as expression for self-empowerment (Yang 2009), collective anxiety and forms of resistance (Szablewicz 2014; Du 2016), and populist cultural identity (Yang et al. 2015). Such register-formation is especially marked vis-à-vis negative evaluations, such as vulgar or deficient, from the official discourse, provoking intense reactions and counter arguments from the majority of users, where they negotiate and draw the value boundaries, metapragmatically typify the styles, and collectively valorize and claim ownership of CIV as a distinct register. It is arguable that such metapragmatic practices with CIV memes constitute for the social media users one of the essential processes of collective identity construction and negotiation in contemporary society.

Such reflexive processes of CIV as register formation also have an interactional dimension for the participants, most noticeably shown in their explicit or implicit evaluations of CIV memes. The participants metapragmatically construct and negotiate the actual use/non-use of memes as specific actions, where certain memes are strategically deployed to perform the users' interpersonal identities, inhabit interactional footings and negotiate their power relations at every minute move on social media. On the one hand, the strategic deployment of memes highlights the 'phatic' (in the Malinowskian sense) function, which can also be reflexively projected on other semiotic signs, in order to keep a contemporary sense of conviviality for any kind of light communities. On the other, memes are also qualified with finer distinctions in interaction, with regard to various 'nano-hegemonies', or interactional norms governed by higher orders of metapragmatic constructs such as gender relations, interpersonal familiarity/politeness, etc., at every momentary interaction, which lead to different reflexive accounts of actions with the memes. These two seemingly contrastive meme practices in fact reveal how various instances of meme practice are made 'accountable' (Garfinkel 1967) by different users as homologized or diversified actions, i.e. how they differentially manage their identity performances at various interactional microspaces, online and offline, by the use and non-use of certain memes.

More importantly, focusing on the evaluation of CIV as sarcastic, I investigated how the participants manage the reflexive practices on social media in a reiterative and continuous manner. While the discursive construction of CIV sarcasm is regimented by the involved participants' ideological orientations and community identities, their further interactions within and beyond the very communities of knowledge would inevitably give rise to a re-evaluation and re-negotiation of the very sarcastic meme and action, in other words, the emergence of a higher order of metapragmatic indexicality. My analysis shows how this infinitive process of ordered indexicalities becomes a) essential for rendering the meme-practice 'accountable' as meaningful and organized actions, b) important for the continuous spread of the very memes, and c) serviceable for the convivial interpersonal and in-group activities on social media.

These metapragmatic processes not only effectively redefine CIV for social media users as both an ideological construct and interactional performativity, but are also found to be the driving force for the continuous and open-ended change of a meme throughout its virality.

7.5 Theoretical highlights

To sum up my ethnographic inquiries and findings, along the viral flows of various CIV diffusions, the moment a CIV neologism gathers viral momentum to spread on social media, it at once becomes the sign vehicle to undergo the countless entextualization, in all kinds of fashions and on all levels, until its virality wears out. Therefore, what we experience as noticeable meaning variation and transformation throughout the viral sign's diffusion may in fact be indexical to, under different circumstances, interpersonal communicative effects, collective dynamism and identification, and larger sociocultural conditions, all of which can be reflexively – be it inadvertently or strategically – performed, enacted and calibrated in social media interaction.

In what follows, I'll attempt to build up on the theoretical works that have largely informed me in navigating such dynamic and complex processes. In general, my exploration of theoretical frameworks proceeded from 1) approaching CIV as signs in themselves to actions and processes where the signs are involved, as well as from 2) meaning/function as indeterminate potential to that as performance and accountability in interaction. The building up of these theoretical heuristics also corresponds with the development of the remixed methods as demanded by each specific case study.

7.5.1 On virality

While studies concerning the ubiquitous phenomenon of social media virality are voluminous, the notion is usually defined by and approached with some structural and external factors, such as the speed of propagation and number of clicks (Bonchi et al. 2013), reach of diffusion and rate of sharing (Eckler and Rodgers 2014), or some behavioral constructs such as 'viral intentions' (Alhabash and McAlister 2014). It therefore follows that what matters is not the viral signs per se, but how they are employed to trigger viral cascades and form structural diffusions (Weng et al. 2013; Shakarian et al. 2015; Goel et al. 2016), so that certain patterns of virality can be predictable and profitable.

This line of research is somehow reflected in qualitative studies on virality (e.g. Shifman 2014), which regards viral signs as 1) means of online ritual communication where their most salient function is to invoke "meta-comments" (2014: 58) from the users so they gather momentum for further spread, and 2) not typically involving the sort of 'text modification' observed in egalitarian memes (Shifman 2011; Gal et al. 2015). By contrast, Varis and Blommaert (2015) argue that all kinds of signs and action types within virality involve likewise mechanisms of social media communication, i.e. re-entextualization and resemiotization. And virality brings about new opportunities and infrastructures for contemporary users to engage in new ways with new sociocultural effects, such as the feeling of conviviality by means of brief yet joint focusing.

My empirical findings have demonstrated that the phenomenon of virality is much more than the apparent sameness in diffusion, which also involves intrinsic and immediate variation and transformation, thanks to the users' entextualizing practices at various levels and dimensions. Therefore, beside the general convivial functions, each instance of entextualization can potentially, with sufficient interactional backing, enact and enregister a diverse range of sociocultural identities and interpersonal relationships, leading to various forms of implicit, yet not insignificant, feelings of collectivity and belonging. During such processes, various memic qualities of CIV neologisms become reflexive objects in themselves, typified and routinized as styles, social voices, and personae that are indexically re-evaluated, re-ordered and re-ascribed to specific identities. For instance, the opening vignette of this chapter just illustrates how the child's use a CIV meme and the dad's use of an emoji respectively invoke differentiated social identities that come into clash in one single interaction.

7.5.2 On communities and online sociation

So far, I've used the notion of community rather broadly to refer to the various forms of collective practice on social media. However, with all the previous discussions, it is necessary to clarify these conceptions and further distinguish their forms and relationships based on the empirical findings. Although the 'communities' were investigated in terms of their relationships with virality, they're not merely the most convergent clusters of transmission edges, as most diffusional studies conceptualize communities (e.g. Papadopoulos et al. 2012; Weng et al. 2013; Quinn et al. 2016). On the other hand, practice-based treatment of the notion, such as the application of 'communities of practice' (Lave and Wenger 1991; Wenger 1998) to online studies (see Angouri 2015 for an overview), largely focuses on the various forms of (sustained) engagement that produce norms and involve identity-making, which cannot characterize the contingent, temporary yet vehement forms of collective encounters occasioned by the viral participation.

In response to similar phenomena, the idea of 'light communities' (Varis and Blommaert 2015; Blommaert 2018) has been proposed as an analytical lens to describe and understand the broad range of 'less conspicuous forms of relationships and kinds of interaction' (Simmel 1950, as cited in Blommaert 2018) as opposed to the traditional notions of 'society' or 'community', with the former being variously sustained and rendered coherent by the feeling of conviviality. Therefore, social categories, physical loci, or such 'big diacritics' (ibid.) are no longer the necessary glue that forms social cohesion and interaction; instead, among other things, knowledge sharing and exchange, especially on social media, may create social spaces and inter-relations, which may well correspond to what Simmel calls 'sociation' – the basic forms of sociality and building blocks of society. According to Simmel (1971), sociation refers to those stable and patterned forms of reciprocal interaction between individuals who are "with-one-another, for-one-another, in-one-another, against-one-another, and through-one-another" (1971: 127). In other words, what various patterns of knowledge exchange create on the social media space are new forms of interaction and dynamism between individuals, and very likely, new forms of sociation.

More importantly, such sociation is almost infinitely fractal:[123] that is, the adoption of memes immediately creates communities-within-communities-within-communities and so forth, where the formation at one level can reoccur at other levels, can be broken down with finer-grained distinctions, and can almost be infinitely changeable in terms of allegiance/affiliation. As a result, one user can simply move from one such community to another and assume respective memberships in an instant. Recall the Excerpt 6.10 in Chapter 6, which is a good case in point. The teacher casually 'aligns' with her students through the use of a CIV term, which is by all means non-permanent, situated, strategic, but fulfills significant identity-related and interactional functions – in her view, for smoother interaction.

In this light, what my empirical findings highlight are the necessary components of the knowledge-related 'light communities', brought about by viral diffusion, and how such infinitesimal interactions and fractal community formation and alignment amount to sociation on contemporary social media. Such components, as variably demonstrated in my case studies, include: 1) As the knowledge (of a new meme) spreads outwardly, a

123. Here 'fractality' refers to the notion that Irvine and Gal (2000) define as "fractal recursivity", which is "the projection of an opposition, salient at some level of relationship, onto some other level" (2000: 38).

learning process of some sort is always involved, where users automatically enact the different roles of informer and (active or passive) learner, in a single act of interaction – meaning such roles may immediately change in the next act.

2) Such communities can take their temporary form in a variety of loci, provided by the very infrastructure of the online platform, such as forums, blog pages, or comments.
3) These temporary light communities are the most relevant and important mechanism in the immediate entextualization of the viral signs, which impact and inflect the local meaning/function variation in a non-linear manner (Blommaert 2015), i.e. its entextualized meaning is not directly predictable based on the sign's previous instances.
4) They are the important interfaces where different individuals negotiate their own identities of other sorts, for instance, of other social diacritics or communities of practice. They are therefore very important for the information diffusion among online communities of practice.
5) In comparison, online communities of practice, such as the '*Guichu*'[124] remixing sub-community or the Weibo pet-owner community in my studies, are on the same gradable continuum. They can conflate with each other or move further apart, and their relationships can be keyed strategically as 'interactional micro-frames' to signal desired identities online.

7.5.3 On reflexivity

Reflexivity may be an increasingly important yet largely nebular theoretical notion in sociolinguistics. It is an essential perspective for any study of language and society, in that reflexivity is "on the one hand, a universal characteristic of sociolinguistic meaning and, on the other hand, a variable quality of the social environment in which language use takes place" (Coupland 2016: 447). Besides, a growing number of sociolinguistic studies keep accentuating its significance for the contemporary world, not only in that reflexivity is key to addressing the complex system and orders of indexicality in language use, which in fact marks the central theme of the 'Third

124. See footnote 31.

Wave Sociolinguistics' (Eckert 2012), but also because globalization itself is sociolinguistically marked by the 'heightened reflexivity' (Coupland 2010) which common people daily engage with to cope with the increasingly superdiverse sociolinguistic condition.

This entire project is also marked by an increasing commitment to reflexivity, not only in terms of the research trajectory where all questions and findings were reflexively grounded and motivated, but also in terms of the shift of my analytical focus, i.e. from language products to language practices, and from signs to accountable actions. At this point, it is necessary to revisit the Ethnomethodological Program, where the notion of reflexivity constitutes as the very basis of the social order (Heritage 1984). In Garfinkel's (1967) original theorization, reflexivity essentially characterizes the 'socially competent members'' accounting practices of all the everyday activities going on around them, which are in fact displayed in their own actions. He provides detailed explanations of such reflexive, in other words 'self-explicating and self-organizing' (Czyzewski 1994), character of members' actions:

> Their [studies'] central recommendation is that the activities whereby members produce and manage settings of organized everyday affairs are identical with members' procedures for making those settings 'account-able'. The 'reflexive', or 'incarnate' character of accounting practices and accounts makes up the crux of that recommendation. (Garfinkel 1967: 1)

> They [members] treat as the most passing matter of fact that members' accounts, of every sort, in all their logical modes, with all of their uses, and for every method for their assembly are constituent features of the settings they make observable. Members know, require, count on, and make use of this reflexivity to produce, accomplish, recognize, or demonstrate rational-adequacy-for-all-practical-purposes of their procedures and findings. (Garfinkel 1967: 8)

Through the reflexive accounting practices, members not only interpret and embody their everyday experience as organized activities, but also construct their meaningful and relational identities in interaction. And in the same manner, i.e. with the same cognitive capabilities and reflexive orientations, the ethnomethodologist – the researcher – reconstructs the members' practical reasoning displayed in and through their interactional activities. More importantly, reflexivity is also scaled (Blommaert 2005, 2010) in that all the virtual scales, such as all the levels and dimensions of various possible knowledge-based 'light communities'. In other words, the infinite fractality of the communities, would impact the participants' activities and the corresponding accounting practices with a single meme, making possible the emergence of orders of indexicality in a potentially infinite way.

As revealed in my findings, reflexivity is key to both generating and understanding the variation and transformation of the viral CIV signs, and the spread and adoption of them should be basically understood as reflexive activities. First, the memes are used as 'meta-utterances' at the discourse-pragmatic level, as interactional and contextual variables to activate a sort of 'pragmatic calibration'. Secondly, reflexivity always works between recognizability and variability in any instance of entextualization, providing a most important driving force for a sign's continuous replication, as well as variation. And moreover, heightened awareness, or rather identity sensitivity, of each of the niched communities on social media is also reflexively typified with distinctive or stereotypic tastes, styles, or sub-genres of CIV, which serve as the resources for users to opt for and enregister. In short, reflexivity is the essential process driver as well as the communicative orientation that renders the use of CIV memes as meaningful activities in social media interactions which in return engenders new orders of indexical meanings and functions in an infinite way, a process that promotes and sustains the continuous and open-ended spread and variation of the memes.

7.6 Payoff of the Remix Approach

Looking back on my entire research trajectory, I didn't opt for the Remix Approach in the first place, but only came to embrace it when I gradually changed the way I viewed CIV, namely from merely a collection of linguistic items to a much larger ensemble of objects, activities, processes and ideologies. Therefore, the choice of the Remix Approach is the natural methodological correspondence with such epistemological foundations of language use on social media.

The Remix Approach is not confined or limiting in any sense, leaving open the possibilities for further, ad-hoc development of research designs and methods. This approach is thus especially capable of uncovering the minute yet exciting aspects and dimensions of sociolinguistic phenomena that may have been overlooked otherwise. Just as my investigations of CIV have highlighted, the ever-changing, open-ended nature of virality also characterizes our contemporary superdiverse society, where the complications and interrelations between the multiple social, cultural, linguistic dimensions and processes could only be understood as 'accountable' (in the Garfinkelian sense) organizations of everyday life through such an ethnographic and reflexive approach.

References

Agha, A. (2006). Registers of language. In A. Duranti (Ed.), A Companion to Linguistic Anthropology (pp. 23-45). Malden, MA: Blackwell Publishing.
Agha, A. (2007). Language and social relations. Cambridge/New York: Cambridge University Press.
Agha, A. (2015). Tropes of slang. Signs and Society 3(2), 306-330.
Akita, K. & Usuki, T. (2016). A constructional account of the 'optional' quotative marking on Japanese mimetics. Journal of Linguistics 52(2), 245-275.
Akkaya, A. (2014). Language, discourse, and new media: A linguistic anthropological perspective. Language and Linguistics Compass 8(7), 285-300.
Alhabash, S. & McAlister, A. R. (2014). Redefining virality in less broad strokes: Predicting viral behavioral intentions from motivations and uses of Facebook and Twitter. New Media & Society 17(8), 1317-1339.
Androutsopoulos, J. (2013). Online data collection. In C. Mallinson, B. Childs & G. V. Herk (Eds.), Data Collection in Sociolinguistics: Methods and Applications (pp. 236-249). London: Routledge.
Angouri, J. (2015). Online communities and communities of practice. In A. Georgakopoulou & T. Spilioti (Eds.), The Routledge Handbook of Language and Digital Communication (pp. 323-338). London; New York: Routledge.
Baym, N. K. & boyd, d. (2012). Socially mediated publicness: An introduction. Journal of Broadcasting & Electronic Media 56(3), 320-329.
Bian, Q. & Gao, B. (2012). Cong weiguan dao xingdong: Qinggan quce, Weibo hudong yu lixing fugui [From watching to action: Emotion, micro-blogging and reason]. XInwen yu Chuanbo Yanjiu [Journalism & Communication] 19(6), 10-17.
Blommaert, J. (2005). Discourse: A Critical introduction. Cambridge/New York: Cambridge University Press.
Blommaert, J. (2007). On scope and depth in linguistic ethnography. Journal of Sociolinguistics 11(5), 682-688.
Blommaert, J. (2010). The sociolinguistics of globalization. Cambridge, UK/New York: Cambridge University Press.
Blommaert, J. (2015). Meaning as a nonlinear effect: The birth of cool. AILA Review 28(1), 7-27.

Blommaert, J. (2018). *Durkheim and the Internet: On Sociolinguistics and The Sociological Imagination*. London: Bloomsbury Academic.

Blommaert, J. & Backus, A. (2013). Superdiverse repertoires and the individual. In I. de Saint-Georges & J.-J. Weber (Eds.), *Multilingualism and Multimodality: Current Challenges for Educational Studies* (pp. 11-32). Rotterdam: Sense Publishers.

Blommaert, J. & Dong, J. (2010). *Ethnographic Fieldwork: A Beginner's Guide*. Bristol/ Buffalo: Multilingual Matters.

Bonchi, F., Castillo, C. & Ienco, D. (2013). Meme ranking to maximize posts virality in microblogging platforms. *Journal of Intelligent Information Systems* 40(2), 211-239.

Booth, P. (2015). Crowdfunding: A Spimatic application of digital fandom. *New Media & Society* 17(2), 149-166.

Brinton, L. J. (2002). Grammaticalization versus lexicalization reconsidered. In T. Fanego, J. Pérez-Guerra & M. J. López-Couso (Eds.), *English Historical Syntax and Morphology: Selected Papers from 11 ICEHL, Santiago de Compostela, 7–11 September 2000. Volume 1* (pp. 67–97). Amsterdam: John Benjamins.

Brontsema, R. (2004). A queer revolution: Reconceptualizing the debate over linguistic reclamation. *Colorado Research in Linguistics* 17(1), 1-17.

Bryant, A. & Charmaz, K. (2007). Grounded Theory research: Methods and practices. In A. Bryant & K. Charmaz (Eds.), *The SAGE Handbook of Grounded Theory* (pp. 1-28). London: SAGE.

Bryman, A. (2008). Of methods and methodology. *Qualitative Research in Organizations and Management* 3(2), 159-168.

Buchstaller, I., Rickford, J. R., Traugott, E. C., Wasow, T. & Zwicky, A. (2010). The sociolinguistics of a short-lived innovation: Tracing the development of quotative all across spoken and internet newsgroup data. *Language Variation and Change* 22(02), 191-219.

Cai, X. (2015). Fansubbing humor: A mainland China case study. *Journalism and Mass Communication* 5(9), 435-453.

Canagarajah, S. (2011). Codemeshing in academic writing: Identifying teachable strategies of translanguaging. *The Modern Language Journal* 95(3), 401-417.

Cang, L., Liu, Z. & Li, C. (2012). *Liuxingyu zheshe de wangluo wenhua [Online Culture Reflected in Online Buzzwords]*. Beijing: Tourism Education Press.

Chen, Y. (2016). Lun wangluo yuyan de fanyulehua yu qingzhengzhi qingxiang [On the pan-entertainment and light political orientations of internet language]. *Xinwen Zhishi [News Research]* (4), 6-9.

CNNIC (2009). 2009 CNNIC annual report. Retrieved from CNNIC website: http://english.cnic.cas.cn/ap/201009/t20100907_58610.html

CNNIC (2017). The 39th statistical report on internet development in China Retrieved from CNNIC website: https://cnnic.com.cn/IDR/ReportDownloads/201706/P020170608523740585924.pdf

Coupland, N. (2010). Introduction: Sociolinguistics in the Global Era. In N. Coupland (Ed.), *The Handbook of Language and Globalization* (pp. 1-27). Chichester, UK: Wiley-Blackwell.

Coupland, N. (2016). Five Ms for sociolinguistic change. In N. Coupland (Ed.), *Sociolinguistics: Theoretical Debates* (pp. 433-454). Cambridge: Cambridge University Press.

Creese, A. & Blackledge, A. (2010). Translanguaging in the bilingual classroom: A pedagogy for learning and teaching? *The Modern Language Journal* 94(1), 103-115.

Croft, W. (2000). *Explaining language change: an evolutionary approach*. Harlow, England/New York: Longman.

Czyzewski, M. (1994). Reflexivity of actors versus reflexivity of accounts. *Theory, Culture & Society* 11(4), 161-168.

Dawkins, R. (1976). *The Selfish Gene*. New York: Oxford University Press.

De Seta, G. (2016). *Dajiangyou: Media practices of vernacular creativity in postdigital China*. (Unpublished dissertation) The Hong Kong Polytechnic University, Hong Kong.

De Smet, H. & Verstraete, J.-C. (2006). Coming to terms with subjectivity. *Cognitive Linguistics* 17(3), 365-392.

Deller, R. A. (2014). A decade in the life of online fan communities. In L. Duits, K. Zwaan & S. Reijnders (Eds.), *Ashgate Research Companion to Fan Cultures* (pp. 237-248). London/New York: Routledge.

Dentith, S. (2000). *Parody*. London/New York: Routledge.

Diewald, G. (2002). A model for relevant types of contexts in grammaticalization. In I. Wischer & G. Diewald (Eds.), *New Reflections on Grammaticalization* (pp. 103-120). Amsterdam/Philadelphia: John Benjamins.

Dingemanse, M. (2012). Advances in the cross-linguistic study of ideophones. *Language and Linguistics Compass* 6(10), 654-672.

Dong, J., Du, C., Juffermans, K., Li, J., Varis, P. & Wang, X. (2012). Chinese in a superdiverse world. In N. de Jong, K. Juffermans, M. Keijzer & L. Rasier (Eds.), *Papers of the Anéla 2012 Applied Linguistics Conference* (pp. 349-366). Delft: Eburon.

Dong, X. (2016). Zhuguanxing biaoda zai Hanyu zhong de tuxianxing jiqi biaoxian tezheng [On characteristics of subjectivity in Chinese]. *Yuyan Kexue [Linguistic Sciences]* 15(6), 561-570.

Du, C. (2016). *The birth of social class online: The Chinese Precariat on the internet.* (Unpublished dissertation) Tilburg University, Tilburg, the Netherlands.

Eckert, P. (2012). Three waves of variation study: The emergence of meaning in the study of sociolinguistic variation. *Annual Review of Anthropology 41*(1), 87-100.

Eckler, P. & Rodgers, S. (2014). Viral advertising: A conceptualization. In H. Cheng (Ed.), *The handbook of international advertising research* (pp. 184-202). Chichester, UK: John Wiley & Sons.

Fan, Z. (2009). Shilun 'hen A hen B' Geshi [Discussing 'hen A hen B' Format]. *Hunan Keji Xueyuan Xuebao [Journal of Hunan University of Science and Engineering] 30*(1), 145-147.

Fitzmaurice, S. (2004). Subjectivity, intersubjectivity and the historical construction of interlocutor stance: From stance markers to discourse markers. *Discourse Studies* 6(4), 427-448.

Gal, N., Shifman, L. & Kampf, Z. (2015). 'It Gets Better': Internet memes and the construction of collective identity. *New Media & Society,* 1-17.

Gao, L. (2012). Synchronic variation or diachronic change: A sociolinguistic study of Chinese Internet Language. In J. Liu & H. Tao (Eds.), *Chinese under Globalization* (pp. 7-28). Singapore: World Scientific Publishing.

Gao, Q., Abel, F., Houben, G.-J. & Yu, Y. (2012). A comparative study of users' microblogging behavior on Sina Weibo and Twitter. In J. Masthoff, B. Mobasher, M. C. Desmarais & R. Nkambou (Eds.), *User Modeling, Adaptation, and Personalization: Proceedings of the 20th International Conference, UMAP 2012, Montreal, Canada, July 16-20, 2012.* (pp. 88-101). Berlin: Springer Berlin Heidelberg.

García, O. & Li, W. (2014). *Translanguaging: Language, Bilingualism and Education.* Basingstoke: Palgrave Macmillan.

Garfinkel, H. (1967). *Studies in Ethnomethodology.* Englewood Cliffs, NJ: Prentice-Hall.

Gatto, M. (2014). *The Web as Corpus: Theory and Practice.* New York: Bloomsbury Academic.

Gaucher, D., Hunt, B. & Sinclair, L. (2015). Can pejorative terms ever lead to positive social consequences? The case of SlutWalk. *Language Sciences 52*, 121-130.

Gee, J. P. (2004). *Situated Language and Learning: A Critique of Traditional Schooling*. New York: Routledge.

Gibbs, R. W. (2000). Irony in talk among friends. *Metaphor and Symbol* 15(1-2), 5-27.

Goel, S., Anderson, A., Hofman, J. & Watts, D. J. (2016). The structural virality of online diffusion. *Management Science* 62(1), 180-196.

Gong, Y. (2015). Media reflexivity and taste: Chinese slash fans' queering of European football. *Communication, Culture & Critique* 10(1), 166-183.

Halliday, M. A. K. & Hasan, R. (1989). *Language, Context, and Text: Aspects of Language in a Social-Semiotic Perspective* (2nd ed.). Oxford: Oxford University Press.

Heritage, J. (1984). *Garfinkel and Ethnomethodology*. Cambridge/New York: Polity Press.

Herold, D. K. (2015). The blended lives of young Chinese online. In L. Hjorth & O. Khoo (Eds.), *Routledge Handbook of New Media in Asia* (pp. 189-198). Oxford/New York: Routledge.

Herring, S., Stein, D. & Virtanen, T. (2013). Introduction to the pragmatics of computermediated communication. In S. Herring, D. Stein & T. Virtanen (Eds.), *Pragmatics of Computer-Mediated Communication* (pp. 3-32). Berlin/Boston: de Gruyter.

Hill, J. H. (1998). Language, race, and white public space. *American Anthropologist* 100(3), 680-689.

Hine, C. (2015). *Ethnography for the Internet: Embedded, Embodied and Everyday*. London: Bloomsbury.

Hou, Y. (2015). Lun Zhongguo xianxing dianying shencha zhidu de biduan he chulu [On the shortcomings of China's current film censorship and possible solutions]. *Dianying Wenxue [Movie Literature]* (5), 29-31.

Hu, L., Liu, Y. & Yang, C. (2014). Wangluo yuyan ershi nian fazhan zongshu [Review of Internet language development in the past two decades]. *Hunan Daxue Xuebao [Journal of Hunan University]* 28(5), 136-141.

Hu, Q. & Xu, J. (2003). Semantic transliteration: A good tradition in translating foreign words into Chinese. *Babel* 49(4), 310-326.

Hu, X., Qiao, C. & Fu, K.-w. (2017). Weibo. In L. Sloan & A. Quan-Haase (Eds.), *The SAGE Handbook of Social Media Research Methods* (pp. 593-609). Los Angeles/London: SAGE Reference.

Huang, C. (2015). Shuju wajue duang! duang! duang! de qianshi jinsheng [Data mining of the development of duang! duang! duang!]. Retrieved from Huxiu.com website: https://www.huxiu.com/article/109129/1.html

Huang, R. (2016). Xin Renzhi Yuyongxue shijiao xia wangluo liuxingci 'Duang' de tanjiu [Investigating the online buzzword 'Duang' from the perspective of New Cognitive Pragmatics]. *Yuwen Xuekan [Journal of Language and Literature Studies]* (2), 52-54.

Hübler, A. & Bublitz, W. (2007). Introducing metapragmatics in use. In W. Bublitz & A. Hübler (Eds.), *Metapragmatics in Use* (pp. 1-26). Amsterdam/Philadelphia: John Benjamins.

Hymes, D. H. (1974). *Foundations in Sociolinguistics: An Ethnographic Approach.* Philadelphia: University of Pennsylvania Press.

Hymes, D. H. (1996). *Ethnography, Linguistics, Narrative Inequality: Toward an Understanding of Voice.* London/Bristol, PA: Taylor & Francis.

iResearch (2016). Zhongguo erciyuan yonghu baogao (2015) [Report of Chinese ACGN users (2015)]. Retrieved from http://www.iresearch.com.cn/report/2412.html

Irvine, J. T. & Gal, S. (2000). Language ideology and linguistic differentiation. In P. V. Kroskrity (Ed.), *Regimes of Language: Ideologies, Polities, and Identities* (pp. 35-84). Santa Fe, NM: School of American Research Press.

Jacobs, K. (2015). Mainland Chinese women's homo-erotic databases and the art of failure. In L. Hjorth & O. Khoo (Eds.), *Routledge Handbook of New Media in Asia* (pp. 364-374). Oxford/New York: Routledge.

Jenkins, H. (2006). *Convergence Culture: Where Old and New Media Collide.* New York: New York University Press.

Ji, Y. (2012). *Wangluo bianyi yuyan xianxiang de zhenzhi yanjiu [Cognitive Studies of Language Variation Online].* Nanjing, China: Nanjing Normal University Press.

Jiang, Y. (2016). Chinese linguistics: Pragmatics. In S.-w. Chan (Ed.), *The Routledge Encyclopedia of the Chinese Language* (pp. 184-202). London/New York: Routledge.

Jørgensen, J. N., Karrebæk, M. S., Madsen, L. M. & Møller, J. S. (2015). Polylanguaging in superdiversity. In J. Blommaert, K. Arnaut, B. Rampton & M. Spotti (Eds.), *Language and Superdiversity* (pp. 137-154). New York/London: Routledge.

Jucker, A. H. (1997). The discourse marker well in the history of English. *English Language and Linguistics 1*(1), 91-110.

Kleinman, S., Ezzell, M. B. & Frost, A. C. (2009). Reclaiming critical analysis: The social harms of 'Bitch'. *Sociological Analysis 3*(1), 46-68.

Lakoff, G. & Johnson, M. (1980). *Metaphors We Live By.* Chicago: University of Chicago Press.

Lambrecht, A., Tucker, C. E. & Wiertz, C. (2015). Advertising to early trend propagators? Evidence from Twitter. *SSRN*, 1-54. Retrieved from https://ssrn.com/abstract=2419743

Lave, J. & Wenger, E. (1991). *Situated Learning: Legitimate Peripheral Participation*. Cambridge/New York: Cambridge University Press.

Leppänen, S. (2009). Playing with and policing language use and textuality in fan fiction. In I. Hotz-Davies, A. Kirchhofer & S. Leppänen (Eds.), *Internet Fictions* (pp. 62-83). Newcastle upon Tyne: Cambridge Scholars Publishing.

Leppänen, S. & Elo, A. (2015). Buffalaxing the other: Superdiversity in action on Youtube. In J. Blommaert, K. Arnaut, B. Rampton & M. Spotti (Eds.), *Language and Superdiversity* (pp. 110-136). New York/London: Routledge.

Leppänen, S., Kytölä, S., Jousmäki, H., Peuronen, S. & Westinen, E. (2014). Entextualization and resemiotization as resources for identification in social media In P. Seargeant & C. Tagg (Eds.), *The Language of Social Media: Identity and Community on the Internet* (pp. 112-138). Basingstoke: Palgrave Macmillan UK.

Li, L. (2009). 'Hen A hen B' jiegoulei duanyuci qianxi [Analysis on the phrases in the 'very A very B' structure]. *Caizhi [Intelligence]* (33), 149-150.

Liu, D. (2012). Shici de tancihua he tanci de qutancihua [Interjectionization of content words and deinterjectionization of interjections]. *Hanyu Xuexi [Chinese Language Learning]* (3), 3-13.

Liu, Q. (2010). Wangluo liuxingyu de gouci tezheng yu yuyan jingji yuanze [Word formation of online buzzwords and the principle of economy]. *Keji Xinxi [Science & Technology Information]* (11), 131-132.

Liu, X. & De Seta, G. (2014). Chinese fansub groups as communities of practice: An ethnography of online language learning. In P. Marolt & D. K. Herold (Eds.), *China Online: Locating Society in Online Spaces* (pp. 125-140). Oxford/New York: Routledge.

LSC Team. (2009). *2008 Zhongguo yuyan shenghuo zhuangkuang baogao [Language situation in China: 2008]*. Beijing: Commercial Press.

Lucy, J. A. (1993). Reflexive language and the human disciplines. In J. A. Lucy (Ed.), *Reflexive Language: Reported Speech and Metapragmatics* (pp. 9-32). Cambridge: Cambridge University Press.

Luo, C., & He, T. (2015). Jin shinian lai woguo wangluo liuxingyu de yanbian ji chuanbo yanjiu [An analysis of the evolution of Chinese internet catchwords and their effect on digital cultural communication]. *Henan Daxue Xuebao [Journal of Henan University]* 55(2), 108-115.

Mair, C. (2013). Corpus-approaches to the New English Web: Post-colonial diasporic forums in West Africa and the Caribbean. *Covenant Journal of Language Studies 1*(1), 17-31.

Malinowski, B. (1923). The problem of meaning in primitive languages. In C. K. Ogden & I. A. Richards (Eds.), *The Meaning of Meaning* (pp. 296-336). London: K. Paul, Trench, Trübner.

Markham, A. (2013). Remix cultures, remix methods: Reframing qualitative inquiry for social media contexts. In N. K. Denzin & M. D. Giardina (Eds.), *Global Dimensions of Qualitative Inquiry* (pp. 63-82). London/New York: Routledge.

Markham, A. & Buchanan, E. (2012). Ethical decision-making and Internet research: Recommendations from the AOIR ethics working committee (version 2.0). Retrieved from AoIR Website website: http://aoir.org/reports/ethics2.pdf

Markham, A. N. (2017). Remix as a literacy for future anthropology practice. In J. F. Salazar, S. Pink, A. Irving & J. Sjöberg (Eds.), *Anthropologies and Futures: Researching Emerging and Uncertain Worlds* (pp. 225-242). London/New York: Bloomsbury Academic.

Markham, A. N. & Gammelby, A. K. (2017). Moving through digital flows: An epistemological and practical approach. In U. Flick (Ed.), *The SAGE Handbook of Qualitative Data Collection* (pp. 451-465). Los Angeles/London: SAGE Reference.

Martin, F. (2012). Girls who love boys' love: Japanese homoerotic manga as trans-national Taiwan culture. *Inter-Asia Cultural Studies 13*(3), 365-383.

Mertz, E. (1996). Recontextualization as socialization: Text and pragmatics in the law school classroom. In M. Silverstein & G. Urban (Eds.), *Natural Histories of Discourse* (pp. 229-252). Chicago: University of Chicago Press.

Miao, J. (2009). 'Shanzhai' liuxing zhong yuyi fanhua yu shehui wenhua de gongbian [The co-variation of semantic generalization and socio-cultural change during the popular spread of 'Shanzhai']. *Xiuci Xuexi [Contemporary Rhetoric]* (1), 82-89.

Mills, A. J. (2012). Virality in social media: The SPIN Framework. *Journal of Public Affairs 12*(2), 162-169.

Møller, J. S. & Jørgensen, J. N. (2009). From language to languaging: Changing relations between humans and linguistic features. *Acta Linguistica Hafniensia 41*(1), 143-166.

Murphy, E. & Dingwall, R. (2007). The ethics of ethnography. In P. Atkinson, S. Delamont, A. Coffey, J. Lofland & L. Lofland (Eds.), *Handbook of Ethnography* (pp. 339-351). London: SAGE.

Nagaike, K. (2012). *Fantasies of Cross-Dressing: Japanese Women Write Male-Male Erotica*. Leiden/Boston: Brill.

Nanda, S. (2014). *Gender Diversity: Crosscultural Variations* (2nd ed.). Long Grove, IL: Waveland Press.

Navas, E. (2012). *Remix Theory: The Aesthetics of Sampling*. Vienna: Springer.

Nishimura, Y. (2015). Style, creativity and play. In A. Georgakopoulou & T. Spilioti (Eds.), *The Routledge Handbook of Language and Digital Communication* (pp. 103-117). Abingdon: Routledge.

NLPIR. (2015). ICTCLAS [Computer software]. Retrieved from http://ictclas.nlpir.org/downloads

Noh, S. (2004). The gendered comics market in Korea: An overview of Korean girls' comics, Soonjung Manhwa. *International Journal of Comic Art* 6(1), 281-298.

Nuckolls, J. B. (1996). *Sounds Like Life: Sound-Symbolic Grammar, Performance, and Cognition in Pastaza Quechua*. New York: Oxford University Press.

Papacharissi, Z. (2015). *Affective Publics: Sentiment, Technology, and Politics*. New York/Oxford: Oxford University Press.

Papadopoulos, S., Kompatsiaris, Y., Vakali, A. & Spyridonos, P. (2012). Community detection in social media. *Data Mining and Knowledge Discovery* 24(3), 515-554.

Quinn, C. J., Quinn, M. J., Olinsky, A. D. & Quinn, J. T. (2016). How information spreads in online social networks. In K. D. Lawrence & R. K. Klimberg (Eds.), *Advances in Business and Management Forecasting* (pp. 209-235). Bingley, UK: Emerald Publishing.

Rahman, J. (2012). The N word: Its history and use in the African American community. *Journal of English Linguistics* 40(2), 137-171.

Rampton, B. (1998). Language crossing and the redefinition of reality. In P. Auer (Ed.), *Code-switching in Conversation: Language, Interaction and Identity* (pp. 290-317). London: Routledge.

Sanderson, T. & Angouri, J. (2014). 'I'm an expert in me and I know what I can cope with': Patient expertise in rheumatoid arthritis. *Communication & Medicine* 10(3), 249-261.

Sandler, R. (2013). Real ethical issues in virtual world research. In C. Mallinson, B. Childs & G. V. Herk (Eds.), *Data Collection in Sociolinguistics: Methods and Applications* (pp. 58-62). London: Routledge.

Sankoff, G. (2006). Age: Apparent time and real time. In K. Brown (Ed.), *Encyclopedia of Language & Linguistics* (2nd ed., pp. 110-116). Oxford: Elsevier.

Schachter, P. & Shopen, T. (2007). Parts-of-speech systems. In T. Shopen (Ed.), *Language Typology and Syntactic Description* (2nd ed., Vol. 1, pp. 1-60). Cambridge: Cambridge University Press.

Scollon, R. (2008). Discourse itineraries: Nine processes of resemiotization. In V. K. Bhatia, J. Flowerdew & R. H. Jones (Eds.), *Advances in Discourse Studies* (pp. 233-244). London/New York: Routledge.

Shakarian, P., Bhatnagar, A., Aleali, A., Shaabani, E. & Guo, R. (2015). *Diffusion in Social Networks* (1st ed.). Berlin: Springer.

Shan, Z. (2015). Taiju fengkuang, renyao yeyou ai [Crazy Thai TV series, passionate lady boys]. *Qilu Zhoukan [Qilu Weekly]* (28), 46-47.

Shifman, L. (2011). An anatomy of a YouTube meme. *New Media & Society 14*(2), 187-203.

Shifman, L. (2014). *Memes in Digital Culture*. Cambridge, Massachusetts: The MIT Press.

Silverstein, M. (1993). Metapragmatic discourse and metapragmatic function. In J. A. Lucy (Ed.), *Reflexive Language: Reported Speech and Metapragmatics* (pp. 33-58). Cambridge: Cambridge University Press.

Silverstein, M. (2003). Indexical order and the dialectics of sociolinguistic life. *Language & Communication 23*(3–4), 193-229.

Simmel, G. (1971). *On Individuality and Social Forms: Selected Writings*. Chicago: University of Chicago Press.

Squires, C. R. (2002). Rethinking the black public sphere: An alternative vocabulary for multiple public spheres. *Communication Theory* 12(4), 446-468.

Squires, L. (2014). From TV personality to fans and beyond: Indexical bleaching and the diffusion of a media innovation. *Journal of Linguistic Anthropology* 24(1), 42-62.

Szablewicz, M. (2014). The 'losers' of China's Internet: Memes as 'structures of feeling' for disillusioned young netizens. *China Information 28*(2), 259-275.

Sze, W. P., Liow, S. J. R. & Yap, M. J. (2014). The Chinese Lexicon Project: A repository of lexical decision behavioral responses for 2,500 Chinese characters. *Behavior Research Methods 46*(1), 263-273.

Tagg, C. & Seargeant, P. (2014). Audience design and language choice in the construction and maintenance of translocal communities on social network sites. In P. Seargeant & C. Tagg (Eds.), *The Language of Social Media: Identity and Community on the Internet* (pp. 161-185). Basingstoke: Palgrave Macmillan UK.

Tang, Z. (2010). *Riben zhong du [The poisoned Japan]*. Beijing: China Renmin University Press.

Totman, R. (2003). *The Third Sex: Kathoey: Thailand's Ladyboys*. London: Souvenir Press.

Traugott, E. C. (1989). On the rise of epistemic meanings in English: an example of subjectification in semantic change. *Language* 65(1), 31-55.

Traugott, E. C. (1995). Subjectification in grammaticalization. In D. Stein & S. Wright (Eds.), *Subjectivity and Subjectivisation* (pp. 31-54). Cambridge: Cambridge University Press.

Traugott, E. C. (2010). (Inter)subjectivity and (inter)subjectification: A reassessment. In K. Davidse & L. V. H. Cuyckens (Eds.), *Subjectification, Intersubjectification and Grammaticalization* (pp. 29-71). Berlin: Mouton de Gruyter.

Traugott, E. C. & Dasher, R. B. (2002). *Regularity in Semantic Change*. Cambridge/New York: Cambridge University Press.

Turner, G. (2010). *Ordinary People and the Media: The Demotic Turn*. London: SAGE.

Varis, P. (2016). Digital ethnography. In A. Georgakopoulou & T. Spilioti (Eds.), *The Routledge Handbook of Language and Digital Communication* (pp. 55-68). Abingdon: Routledge.

Varis, P. & Blommaert, J. (2015). Conviviality and collectives on social media: Virality, memes, and new social structures. *Multilingual Margins* 2(1), 31-45.

Wang, C. (2015). Hulianwang shidai de IP jingji [The Intelletual Property economy in the Internet Era]. *Hulianwang Jingji [The Internet Economy]* (12), 62-69.

Wang, D. (2011). 'Ni dongde': Zuowei huayu biaoji de liuxingyu ['You understand': Catchphrases as discourse markers]. *Dangdai Xiucixue [Contemporary Rhetoric]* (6), 40-49.

Wang, T., Chen, Y., Wang, Y., Wang, B., Wang, G., Li, X., . . . Zhao, B. Y. (2016). The power of comments: fostering social interactions in microblog networks. *Frontiers of Computer Science* 10(5), 889-907.

Wang, Y. (2008). 1998-2007 nian Zhongguo wangluo yuyan yanjiu [A survey of Chinese cyber language study during 1998-2007]. *Qingdao Keji Daxue Xuebao [Journal of Qingdao University of Science and Technology]* 24(2), 70-74.

Weng, L., Flammini, A., Vespignani, A. & Menczer, F. (2012). Competition among memes in a world with limited attention. *Scientific Reports* 2(335), 1-8.

Weng, L., Menczer, F. & Ahn, Y.-Y. (2013). Virality prediction and community structure in social networks. *Scientific Reports* 3(2522), 1-6.

Wenger, E. (1998). *Communities of Practice: Learning, Meaning, and Identity.* Cambridge/New York: Cambridge University Press.

White, R. W. (2016). *Interactions with Search Systems.* New York: Cambridge University Press.

Wu, F. (2011). *Hanyu zhuguanxing yu zhuguanhua yanjiu [Subjectivity and Subjectification in Chinese Language].* Beijing: Commercial Press.

Wu, L. (2003). Wangluo yuyan zhong de zimuci gouci tedian fenxi [The analysis of abbreviation in the internet language]. *Guangzhou Daxue Xuebao [Journal of Guangzhou University]* 2(1), 39-44.

Wu, L. (2009). Wangluo liuxingyu de goucheng fangshi ji xingcheng yuanyin [The ways of and reasons for the formation of popular network language]. *Ningbo Guangbo Dianshi Daxue Xuebao [Journal of Ningbo Radio & TV University]* 7(3), 43-44, 117.

Wu, M. (2016). China's crackdowns on 'Internet rumours' and 'illegal' Internet publicity activities. In L. Yang & W. Shan (Eds.), *Governing Society in Contemporary China* (pp. 41-56). Singapore: World Scientific Publishing.

Xin, Y. (2010). Liuxingyu de kuosan: cong fanhua dao kuangtian. [The diffusion of popular expressions: From generalization to frame-filling]. *Dangdai Xiucixue [Contemporary Rhetoric]* (2), 33-49.

Xing, F. (2000). *Wenhua yuyanxue [Cultural Linguistics].* Wuhan, China: Hubei Education Publishing House.

Yang, G. (2009). *The Power of the Internet in China: Citizen Activism Online.* New York: Columbia University Press.

Yang, P. (2016). The taste of Ice Kacang: Xiaoqingxin film as the possible prospect of Taiwan popular cinema. *The IAFOR Journal of Asian Studies* 2(1), 74-84.

Yang, P., Tang, L., & Wang, X. (2015). Diaosi as infrapolitics: Scatological tropes, identity-making and cultural intimacy on China's Internet. *Media, Culture & Society* 37(2), 197-214.

Yang, Y. (2016). Wangluo liuxingyu yansheng, chuanbo de liju he fangxiang [On motivation and directions of the network catchwords' derivation and propagation]. *Xueshujie [Academics]* (2), 99-108.

Yu, G. (2001). *Zhongguo wangluo yuyan cidian [A Dictionary of Chinese Internet Language].* Beijing: China Economic Publishing House.

Yu, P. (2014). *Study on the history of the transformation of internet slangs in the past twenty years in China.* (Unpublished dissertation) Shanghai Jiaotong University, Shanghai.

Yu, Y. & Qiu, L. (2009). Kuangtianshi liuxingyu heyi ruci liuxing? [Why are constructional catchphrases so popular?]. *Xiuci Xuexi [Contemporary Rhetoric]* (6), 71-80.

Yue, Y. (2011). Cong 'bushi wo shuo ni' lei huayu biaoji de xingcheng kan huihua zhong zhuguanxing fanchou yu yuyong yuanze de hudong [The formation of 'I'm not criticizing you' as a discourse marker: Interactions between subjectivity and pragmatic principles in conversations]. *Shijie Hanyu Jiaoxue [Chinese Teaching in the World]* (1), 69-77.

Zanghellini, A. (2009). 'Boys love' in anime and manga: Japanese subcultural production and its end users. *Continuum 23*(3), 279-294.

Zappavigna, M. (2012). *Discourse of Twitter and Social Media*. London/New York: Continuum International Pub.

Zappavigna, M. (2015). Searchable talk: The linguistic functions of hashtags. *Social Semiotics 25*(3), 274-291.

Zeng, J., Burgess, J. & Bruns, A. (2015). *The challenges of Weibo for data-driven digital media research*. Paper presented at the IR16: Phoenix 2015, Phoenix, AZ.

Zhang, H. & Zhao, X. (2008). Xiaoju Zhongshu shijiao xia de 'hen X hen XX' jiegou. [The 'hen X hen XX' structure from the perspective of Clausal Pivot]. *Xiandai Yuwen [Modern Chinese]* (11), 39-40.

Zhang, L., Zhao, J. & Xu, K. (2016). Who creates trends in online social media: The crowd or opinion leaders? *Journal of Computer-Mediated Communication 21*(1), 1-16.

Zhang, M. (2012). A Chinese beauty story: How college women in China negotiate beauty, body image, and mass media. *Chinese Journal of Communication 5*(4), 437-454.

Zhang, Q. & Yu, L. (2016). Taiju zai Zhongguo de chuanbo ji qianjing fenxi [Analysis of the prospective diffusion of Thai television series in China]. *Dangdai Dianshi [Contemporary TV]* (10), 41-42.

Zhang, T. & Wei, H. (2011). Hulianwang huanjing xia yuyan wenzi yuqing jiance yu shizheng yanjiu [The empirical study of the monitoring of the public sentiment about language on the internet]. *Yuyan Wenzi Yingyong [Applied Linguistics]* (2), 6-12.

Zhang, W. (2016). *The Internet and New Social Media Formation in China: Fandom Publics in the Making*. New York: Routledge.

Zhang, W. & Kramarae, C. (2012). Are Chinese women turning sharp-tongued? *Discourse & Society 23*(6), 749-770.

Zhang, Y. (2006). Xinkebiao xia chengyu huodongke de changshi [New attempts of idiom practice courses under the new curriculum]. *Yuedu yu Jianshang [Reading & Evaluation]* (3), 12-15.

Zhang, Y. (2007). Wangluo yuyan de cihui yufa tezheng [Lexical and syntactic features of Internet language]. *Zhongguo Yuwen [Studies of the Chinese Language]* (6), 531-535.

Zhang, Y. (2015). Cong 'Duang' de zouhong, kan xinmeiti huanjing xia de wenhua kua quanceng chuanbo [On the popularity of 'Duang': the cross-circle diffusion of culture in the new media environment]. *Xinwen Yanjiu Daokan [Journal of News Research]* (5), 82-83.

Zheng, X. (2016). *Borderless fandom and contemporary popular cultural scene in Chinese cyberspace.* (Unpublished dissertation) University of Washington, Seattle, WA.

Ziegele, M., Breiner, T. & Quiring, O. (2014). What creates interactivity in online news discussions? An exploratory analysis of discussion factors in user comments on news items. *Journal of Communication* 64(6), 1111-1138.

Appendices

Appendix I.
Gossary of all unexplained CIV items in the text

Original form	Pinyin	Translation	Explanation	Note (if needed)
做人不要太cnn	zuoren buyao tai cnn	Don't act like CNN.	Don't be discriminatory or biased, like CNN does.	The phrase was used when the Chinese netizens accused CNN, BBC and other western media for distorting the truth when reporting on the riot in Tibet in 2008.
打酱油	dajiangyou	Buying soy sauce	Merely passing by, just an on-looker of something	
叉腰肌	chayaoji	Hands-on-waist muscle	A ridiculous 'make-believe' muscle quoted from Xie Yalong	Mr. Xie, a then official in charge of administering national football matters made a lay-man's remark about how to train athletes.
猪坚强	Zhujianqiang	Pig Strong	A pig that survived the 2008 Sichuan Earthquake	
三个俯卧撑	sange fuwocheng	three push-ups	A ridiculous and innocent way of being involved in a life-or-death situation.	A man in custody from Guizhou died after doing three push-ups, according to the local police report.
山寨	shanzhai	Mountain cottage (goods)	counterfeit goods; to copycat; to forge	
正龙拍虎	Zhenglong pai hu	Zhenglong photographs the tiger	To describe something as a total travesty	Zhou Zhenglong, a peasant from Shaanxi conniving with the local bureaucrats, reported that he sighted and photographed a live tiger in the wild, which turned out to be fake.
70码	70 ma	70 km/h	To mock something as unfair, deceitful, or involving malpractice	In 2009, a young man in Hangzhou was hit and killed by a racing car when crossing the road. In the police report, the driver was said to be driving at around 70 km/h, which most of the netizens didn't believe.

Original form	Pinyin	Translation	Explanation	Note (if needed)
图样图森破	tu yang tu senpo	too young, too simple	This phrase was the intentional phonetic approximation of the English phrase, which is partly taken from a comment made by the former Chinese president Jiang Zemin when he scolded a reporter from Hong Kong. It is used in such similar ways as the SN phrase that many would usually confuse the two.	
也是醉了	yeshi zui le	intoxicated as well	With its full form as 'I'm intoxicated as well', this phrase is usually used express at something that makes one annoyed, frustrated, awkward, flabbergasted, or simply speechless.	
没谁了	mei shei le	without anyone	With its possible fuller form of 'without anyone (to compete with, to compare to, to comment, etc.)', this phrase is colloquially used to predicate and describe something as too much in any ways.	
不要不要的	buyao buyao de	need-not, need-not	This phrase can possibly be considered as a largely grammaticalized item from the original verbal phrase 'need not' (possibly from 'need not say, need not compete, etc.') into an adverbial intensifier.	

Appendix II.
Netease Comments-tower

This illustrative comments-tower follows the news article Shaolin Temple responds to the 'forced donation' accusation: no such things after investigation, fake news, published on the Netease News on April 8, 2015. Interestingly, Netease picked out this comments-tower as the 'daily highlights'.[125]

少林寺回应"劝捐"事件:查无此事、新闻不实(图)	News article Shaolin Temple responds to the 'forced donation' accusation: no such things after investigation, fake news (image)	
网易吉林省长春市网友(*.*.*.*)的原贴 日本也不承认侵略	Netease user from Jilin Changchun (ip add.) Japan also doesn't admit to the invasions.	1
网易广东省手机网友(****)的原贴 苍老师也说过自己还是处女	Mobile Netease user [ID] from Guangdong Sensei Sola Aoi [a Japanese porn actress] once said she was still a virgin	2
网易北京市手机网友(****)的原贴 公交司机说后边车马上就来	Mobile Netease user [ID] from Beijing Bus drivers say more busses are coming soon	3
网易广州市手机网友(****)的原贴 亲戚说大过年的来就来嘛，带什么礼物!	Mobile Netease user from Guangzhou [ID] Relatives ask why you bring gifts to them instead of simply coming to their house for festivals	4
网易北京市手机网友(****)的原贴 男友也说就摸摸啥都不干	Mobile Netease user from Beijing [ID] My boyfriend says he would only touch and do nothing else	5
网易广东省梅州市手机网友(*.*.*.*)的原贴 医生说我们不收红包	Netease user from Guangdong Meizhou (ip add.) Doctors say they don't want any bribes	6
网易日本手机网友(*.*.*.*)的原贴 共同富裕	Netease user from Japan (ip add.) 'Common prosperity' (note: an official political slogan)	7
……	... [more floors omitted]	
网易湖南省手机网友(****)的原贴 办张会员卡，从明天开始锻炼身体	Mobile Netease user [ID] from Hunan Having subscribed to the gym, I'll start working out tomorrow	40
网易用户(****)的原贴 和妈妈说，我出去买衣服	Netease user [ID] Talking to my mom, I'm going out for buying clothes	41
网易上海市手机网友(****)的原贴 棒子说，银河系都是我们的!	Mobile Netease user [ID] from Shanghai Koreans say, even the Galaxy is ours!	42
网易广东省手机网友(*.*.*.*)的原贴 中石化说，年年亏本	Mobile Netease user from Guangdong (ip add.) Sinopec says, we're losing money every year	43
……	... [more floors omitted]	

125. Accessed from http://tie.163.com/gt/15/0409/08/AMOC7T1100304IRI.html on Jan. 10, 2016.

The above comment-tower is composed of at least 60 floors (and still counting by the time of collection), each one building onto the previous comments, which makes the whole tower as a meaningful whole. The whole tower is constructed as the users' collective mocking and disbelief as to the public statement made by the Shaolin Temple. Specifically, each floor contributes one piece of well-known (and funny) hypocritical excuse or disclaimer, and by implication highlights the very statement in the news as dishonest and untrue. Note that floor numbers are indicated on the side, by which users address each other and interact.

Appendix III.
Meaning/function categories

a. Number of the occurrences of 'duang' during Feb. 20-Mar. 8
Note: there may be multiple instances of 'duang' in a single message.

	1	2	3	4	5	6	7	8	9	10	11	12	13	14	15	16	17
1a	1	5	16	3	11		2										
1b		5	19	7	14		2										2
2a			3	5	13	4	11	4				1					
2b			5	2	13	1	3	1									
2d			2	3	10		6	16	7	2	2	5	2	1	5		
3					2	29	13	9	13	21	13	19	12	9	10	9	14
5			1	1	3	3	3	1	5	4			1	9	2	5	2
6			3	1	10	23	29	24	31	20	34	37	36	40	39	36	38
7a			1	1	3	10	10	14	7	23	15	11	8	3	7	7	8
7b					1	3	2	2	4	7		4	5	5	3	5	2
7c				3	7	16	16	11	6	15	8	8	2	8	6	12	3
7d			1	1	4	4	12	9	18	14	16	7	14	15	19	10	13
7e			1		4	15	5	14	20	16	17	24	16	11	11	13	22
8a		2	2		8	13	2		3		3	3	2	4		6	2
8b				2	3	11	6	3	10	7	6	8	7	7	6	7	11
9a					1			1	1	2				1			
9b				1	2	4		2	3		7	2	4	6	1	4	2
9c						3	4	5	2	2	3	3	5	3	8	7	4
10a					1	1						1	2	3	4	1	
10b								1			1	1	2			1	
11			1	1	3	5	3	4		1	2	3	2	2	1	2	3
total	1	12	55	31	113	145	129	121	130	134	127	137	120	127	122	125	125

c. Trends of the distributions of all major categories during February 30-March 8

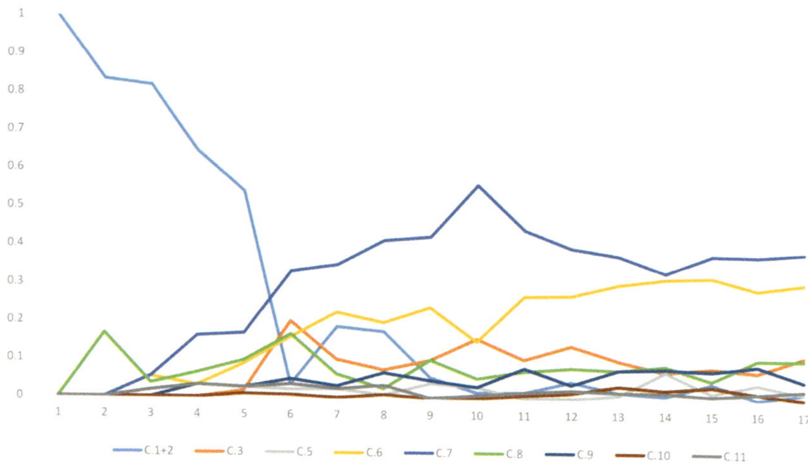

b. Ratios of major meaning/function categories during February 20-March 8

Note: All subcategories are subsumed in the major category. Categories 1 and 2 are combined, as explained in Section 4.1.2.

	2.20	2.21	2.22	2.23	2.24	2.25	2.26	2.27	2.28	
1-2	1	0.8333	0.8182	0.6451	0.5398	0.0345	0.18605	0.1736	0.0538	
3	0	0	0	0	0.0177	0.2	0.1008	0.0744	0.1	
5	0	0	0.0182	0.0323	0.0265	0.0207	0.0233	0.0083	0.0385	
6	0	0	0.0545	0.0323	0.0885	0.1586	0.2248	0.1983	0.2385	
7	0	0	0	0.0545	0.1613	0.1681	0.3310	0.3488	0.4132	
8	0	0.1667	0.0364	0.0645	0.0973	0.1655	0.0620	0.0248	0.1	
9	0	0	0	0.0323	0.0265	0.0483	0.0310	0.0661	0.0462	
10	0	0	0	0	0.0089	0.0069	0	0.0083	0	
11	0	0	0.0182	0.0323	0.0265	0.0345	0.0233	0.0331	0	

	3.1	3.2	3.3	3.4	3.5	3.6	3.7	3.8	
	0.0149	0.0157	0.0438	0.0167	0.0079	0.0410	0	0.0160	1-2
	0.1567	0.1024	0.1387	0.1000	0.0709	0.0820	0.0720	0.1120	3
	0.0299	0.0000	0	0.0083	0.0709	0.0164	0.0400	0.0160	5
	0.1493	0.2677	0.2701	0.3000	0.3150	0.3197	0.2880	0.3040	6
	0.5597	0.4409	0.3942	0.3750	0.3307	0.3770	0.3760	0.3840	7
	0.0522	0.0709	0.0803	0.0750	0.0866	0.0492	0.1040	0.1040	8
	0.0299	0.0787	0.0365	0.0750	0.0787	0.0738	0.0880	0.0480	9
	0	0.0079	0.0146	0.0333	0.0236	0.0328	0.0160	0.0000	10
	0.0075	0.0157	0.0219	0.0167	0.0157	0.0082	0.0160	0.0240	11

Appendix IV. Keywords in CIV evaluation

a. The attached picture of all the officially selected list of vulgar words[126]

Rank	CIV words in Chinese	Translation (explanation)	Occurrence in Chinese newspapers (titles)	Occurrences in Weibo posts
1	尼玛	Nima (sound approximation of "your mother")	3	249,646,340
2	屌丝	Diaosi (losers)	818	181,216,808
3	逗比	Doubi (sound approximation of "silly cunt")	276	150,043,492
4	砖家/叫兽	Zhuanjia/jiaoshou (wordplay on "expert"/"professor")	92/452	8,714,012/1 01,776,196
5	艹	Homophone of "fuck"	0	70,602,880
6	你妹	Nimei (your sister)	5	50,778,812
7	装逼	Zhuangbi (smart ass, or pretentious)	22	45,632,060
8	草泥马	Caonima (sound approximation of "fuck your mother")	81	41,516,308
9	我靠/我擦/我中艸茻艸	Wokao/woca/wocao cao hui mang (wordplays on the sound approximation of "I fuck")	3/4	39,103,768/ 32,847,660/ 932
10	妈蛋	Madan (sound approximation of "damn")	0	36,934,544
11	逼格	Bige (pretension)	65	30,109,324
12	他妈的/特么的	Tamade/temede (sound approximation of "damned")	4	29,362,880/ 10,083,180
13	撕逼	Sibi (bitch-fight)	7	20,356,064
14	滚粗	Guncu (fuck off)	12	19,131,236
15	蛋疼	Danteng (balls-hurt, butt-hurt)	38	18, 652,852
16	小婊砸	Xiaobiaoza (little bitch)	0	10,788,384
17	傻X	Sha X (stupid ass)	11	7,691,260
18	跪舔	Guitian (kneel and lick, suck up to)	4	6,301,472
19	绿茶婊/心机婊	Lvchabiao (green tea bitch, bitch who plays innocent)/ Xinjibiao (scheming bitch)	66	5,695,244

126. Retrieved from the Weibo post http://www.weibo.com/1642088277/CkJeJyYZE on June 18, 2015.

c. The 'deficient' case

Keywords excluding words and expressions from the original post

Rank	Keywords	Weight
4	语言贫乏症 language deficiency symptoms	19.81/30
5	张口闭口 to say something excessively	16.07/12
8	传统文化 traditional culture	15.40/56
10	装逼 zhuanbi (pretentious)	14.34/33
11	语言贫乏 language deficiency	14.08/94
13	矫情 melodramatic, hypocritical	13.01/26
14	热词 hot words	12.32/28
15	一堆 a bunch of	11.89/15
16	词穷 short of words	11.88/34
18	脑残 brain-damaged	11.15/13
19	中华文化 Chinese culture	10.92/14
20	满口 mouth full of	10.72/12